CULTURAL POLITICS
OF EVERYDAY LIFE

CULTURAL POLITICS OF EVERYDAY LIFE

Social Constructionism, Rhetoric and Knowing of the Third Kind

JOHN SHOTTER

University of Toronto Press

TORONTO AND BUFFALO

First published in North America in 1993 by
University of Toronto Press Incorporated
Toronto and Buffalo

ISBN 0–8020–0560–8 (cloth)
ISBN 0–8020–6982–7 (paper)

Canadian Cataloguing in Publication Data
Shotter, John
Cultural politics of everyday life: social
constructionisms, rhetoric and knowing of the
third kind

Includes index.
ISBN 0–8020–0560–8 (bound)   ISBN 0–8020–6982–7 (pbk.)

1. Thought and thinking.   2. Social interaction.
3. Discourse analysis — Psychological aspects.
I. Title.

BF441.S56   1993   153   C93–093662–0

Printed and bound in Great Britain

Contents

Foreword

There is no doubt that every one of us has some understanding of other people. In part this is because we have a mastery of that most subtle and sophisticated instrument, our ordinary language. In part this is because we have to a greater or lesser degree a mastery of the practical skills with which we conduct our everyday affairs. How could this understanding, this mastery and these skills be made available for contemplation and perhaps thereby enhanced? There are various possible models for such a project. In our time a huge effort has been expended on constructing a cluster of human sciences with which it is hoped both the intellectual and the moral aims of the project of the understanding of human life might be achieved. For many of us it has come to seem as if much of the effort has been wasted, lavished on projects whose metaphysical underpinnings have been confused and whose methodological procedures have been hopelessly inadequate to the subject matter.

But don't we already know how to manage people including ourselves, how to comfort them, to upbraid them, to train them and so on? Don't we already have representations of our history and the structure of our society upon which we can draw? And yet much that people do both individually and collectively can outrage and disconcert us. In a certain sense we are struck by the poverty of our knowledge of ourselves.

John Shotter's work, since I first became acquainted with it, has been a record of an unrelenting struggle to come to terms with the mysterious yet mundane character of everyday life. This book brings together two basic insights. The world of human existence does not exist independently of human activity, but is a product of that activity. In particular that world is constructed discursively. It is in the joint 'conversational' activity of multitudes of people that even the thoughts and feelings and projects of individuals come to be. This view is shared by an increasing number of contemporary students of human affairs. It is the position both of social constructionists and of the advocates of a thoroughgoing discursively oriented human science.

The second insight is very much Shotter's own. It is the insight that not only is there practical knowledge, displayed in what we know how to do; not only is there theoretical knowledge, displayed in our discourses about and representations of a necessarily distanced subject matter, there is also participatory knowledge, the knowledge we have of the products of our own constructive activity. The ultimate project of a human science could be none other than the making explicit of knowledge of the third kind, knowledge that grows with our participation in the acts of living.

In this important book John Shotter shows how the scientific project and the emancipatory project of the long tradition of the reflexive studies of our own lives by those who live them have begun to come together. Perhaps here, at last, we will find the sketch of a recipe for how the synthesis between science and political morality may finally be forged.

Rom Harré

Acknowledgments

The essays making up this volume were written between 1987 and 1992, at three very different institutions: the Rijksuniversiteit Utrecht, Swarthmore College (where I was the Cornell Distinguished Visiting Professor for the year 1990–91) and the University of New Hampshire. In each location, I was faced by new and stimulating challenges, and was (and am now) blessed with friendly, convivial, and committed colleagues of high quality. My move from a monodisciplinary department of Psychology (in Britain) to the General Social Sciences (ASW) Programme in Utrecht was especially challenging. I was very lucky in meeting there Bryan S. Turner and Hans Adriaansens, the two other ASW professors appointed to head up the new interdisciplinary study group, and our devising of the Citizenship and Development (Burgerschap en Ontwikkeling) Programme was fortunate indeed – it opened up for me the whole issue of the relation between academic knowledge and the public sphere that has continued to be of central importance. One of the original concerns of the programme was with European Unity and 1992, and whether there would ever be a common European identity – a question that was overtaken by the events in Eastern Europe in 1989, and which now seems naive in the extreme. Then, I did not realize what a child of the Enlightenment I was. At this point I must mention the many other people at Utrecht who contributed to making my stay there so pleasant and productive. First, I must mention all the members of the ASW section, Communicatie, Identiteit en Cultuur, I helped found: Robert Maier (who understood the possibility of forming such a group from the start), Ed Elbers, Kathy Davis, Chris Sinha, Vincent Duinden, Sylvia Nossent, Frits van Wel, Florike Egmond, Ine Gremen, Myra Kaiser and Mariette Hoogsteder. David Ingleby was a good friend and mentor, and Arie de Ruijter in the Research Institute always provided much appreciated support at just the right moments.

The Cornell Professorship at Swarthmore provided me with a much needed respite from the hectic concerns involved in organizing a new study programme. Ken and Mary Gergen have been good and caring friends, and important academic colleagues, to me for some long time, so it was especially pleasant to be in Swarthmore for that year. I would like to say an especial thanks to Joanne Bramley and Julia

Welborn for their hospitality, also to Jean Maracek, Barry Schwartz, Hugh Lacey, Richie Schuldenfrei, Richard Eldridge and Hans Oberdijk for some very good conversations. I am especially happy to acknowledge the congenial ambience provided by my new colleagues in New Hampshire: Sheila McNamee, Jack Lannamann, Larry Prelli, Mari Boor Tonn, Jim Farrell, Pat Daley and Josh Meyrowitz. A number of other people deserve special mention. Rom Harré has been a mentor and role model of mine for some time, and I must thank him for demonstrating what can be done if one has the energy to do it, as well as for writing the foreword to this book. Barnett Pearce and Vern Cronen in the Communication Department at the University of Massachusetts have been good friends too. Finally, Mick Billig has been a special friend and provided much encouragement.

A number of the chapters have been published before, but all have been in varying degrees elaborated for inclusion here. Chapter 1 " 'Getting in touch': the metamethodology of a postmodern science of mental life," was first published in *The Humanistic Psychologist*, 18, 7–22, 1990. Chapter 3 "Vico and the poetics of practical sociality," was first published under the title of "A poetics of relational forms: the sociality of everyday social life," in a special issue on "Evolutionary models in the social sciences," edited by T. Ingold, in *Cultural Dynamics*, 4, 379–396, 1991. Chapter 4 "Wittgenstein and psychology: on our 'hook up' to reality," was first published in A. Phillips-Griffiths (ed.), *The Wittgenstein Centenary Lectures*. Cambridge: Cambridge University Press, 1991. Chapter 5 "Rom Harré: realism and the turn to social constructionism," was first published in R. Bhaskar (ed.), *Harré and His Critics: Essays in Honour of Rom Harré with His Commentary on Them*. Oxford: Blackwell, 1990. Chapter 8 "Rhetoric and the social construction of cognitivism," was first published in *Theory and Psychology*, 1, 495–513, 1991. While Chapter 9 "What is a 'personal relationship'?: a rhetorical-responsive account of unfinished business," was first published in J.H. Harvey, T.L. Orbuch and A.L. Weber (eds) *Attributions, Accounts, and Close Relationships*. New York: Springer-Verlag, 1992. I want to acknowledge my gratitude to the editors and publishers for permission to publish revised versions of these essays here.

Preface

This book is about ways of knowing in terms of feeling and feelings. When I first left school, I went to work as an engineering apprentice in an aircraft factory. Two memories of that time are relevant to its contents. One is to do with filing different metals in the appentice's workshop. I remember now the oily slipperiness of brass, the way soft aluminium tore and clogged the file, the hard crumbliness of cast iron, the utterly intransigent nature of stainless steel, but the yielding friendliness of mild steel such that file and material seemed to have been made for each other. It was as if, with the file, I could 'feel into' the very crystalline structure of the metals themselves. Hammering was different, and revealed different properties in the materials. Other tools worked to reveal yet further characteristics. The other memory is to do with the fact that we thousand or so workers trooped in at 7.30 a.m., through a single little door at the back of the factory, jostling and pushing each other to make sure we clocked in on time, as every minute late cost us 15 minutes' pay. The 'staff' (management, drawing office, administrative, and other such personnel) and the Royal Air Force officer customers, came in ('strolled in' we thought) through big double doors at the front, up imposing steps, at 9.00 a.m. But more than that, 'they' had their lunch on a mezzanine floor raised five feet above 'us' in the lunch room; 'they' had waitress service and white tableclothes, 'we' buttered sliced bread straight from the paper packet on the formica top of the table; and so on. 'They' didn't just look down on 'us', 'they' treated 'us' like about-to-be-naughty children. Such incidents as these were paradigmatic of the thousand other small daily "hidden injuries of class" (Sennett and Cobb, 1972), or "degradation ceremonies" (Garfinkel, 1956) that then – in the 1950s (and for the next decade) – were an integral part of the British industrial scene, marked, as it was, by a large number of strikes, and a general level of anger, resentment and widespread bloody-mindedness expressed by all.

Looking back upon these little degradations, I was intrigued to realize that, while 'we' on the workshop floor had 'gone on' about these and other little incidents almost continually, the staff had seemed impervious to the fact that our anger was occasioned by their behaviour, their 'perks' (why should they care, they deserved them, didn't they?). As I came to realize, that is a part of the phenomenology of power: those who have it are least aware of it, for the world 'offers no resistances' to them and their desires. Only those without such power are aware of its workings 'in' the resistances they meet in trying to realize their desires. But I was also intrigued by the fact that, when workers had returned to the floor, seething, after a brush with management, and everyone had said "Oh, you've just got to complain about that," no one ever did. In the end, it seemed too trivial, and one knew it would be useless. To complain, for instance, about the windows in the men's toilets – put there so that the foreman could see that what was being done there was being done properly, and not wasting time – to complain just by saying "Well, I don't like being watched at those times," seemed both inadequate to the anger and unlikely to be effective. But what else could one say? Our rage was impotent rage; we didn't even know where our anger came from, so to speak. There seemed to be no adequate language within which express *why* we had become so angry, to explain why these little degradations mattered so much to us. And this, I suspect, made us even more angry, for we also became angry at ourselves, for trivializing ourselves at being so bothered by such trivial things.

It was hard to realize – and to sustain one's excitement at the fact – that the factory was in the business of building some of the most amazing engineering triumphs of the day. I have great admiration for engineers, and I still have; some of their feats are truly heroic (as well as some of their 'mistakes') – no doubt about it – but I left after one year, to return to school to become a mathematician, so that I could become 'staff', too. I was sixteen at the time. Then, I never thought that I would be writing a book like this, a book that in fact connects these two memories in two different ways. One way is to do with how (a) the 'feeling into' the hidden inner structure of materials *through* the use of a tool like a file, connects with (b) *sensing* the (also supposedly hidden) inner structure of the social world *through* the use of words-as-prosthetic-devices. But that, indeed, is one thing that this book is about. The other is to do with how (a) our lack of words to express how and why these 'trivial' things matter so much to us, connects with (b) how we still do not quite understand how to articulate the way these small things work to influence us in our feelings as to 'who' we are, that is, to influence us 'in' our identities. We still do not know how what one might call the self–other dimension of interaction works to 'construct' another dimension of interaction, seemingly independent of it – that between oneself as an individual person, and 'one's own world' – such that, if one feels oneself reduced as a person, one feels oneself as living in a reduced world.

But why do we still find it so difficult to appreciate the way in which these (horizontal, if you like) self–other interactions work to 'construct' for each of us, that (vertical) person–world dimension of interaction in terms of which, as individuals, we make sense of our own unique circumstances? With apologies for the 'sexist' (and 'Enlightenment') terminology within which the issue was then framed, I set the scene for this project in an earlier 1975 book as follows:

Men have created and are still creating the characteristics of their own humanity. It has been produced, not as a result of evolutionary processes –

processes that produce changes of a biological kind – for men seem to have stayed biologically constant for some time. Its development must be considered to be a historical, cultural one, a matter not of natural processes but of human imagination, choice and effort. And in 'inheriting' this manmade nature, this 'second nature', men's children do not inherit it genetically like blue eyes, but like the houses and cities, the tools and other more material artifacts they have fashioned, and besides teaching them skills at using these they teach them skills at fashioning more. Children 'inherit' their humanity, then, in a process of communication which takes place after birth . . . What has been overlooked in modern psychology, especially in its more extreme mechanistic-behaviouristic manifestations as a natural science of behaviour, is that man is not simply a being immersed directly in nature but is a being *in a culture* in nature. Thus people must not be treated like organisms that respond directly in relation to their position in the world, but as rather special organic forms which deal with nature in terms of their knowledge of the 'position' in a culture; that is, in terms of a knowledge of the part their actions play in relation to the part played by other people's actions in maintaining (or progressing) the culture.

(Shotter, 1975: 13–14)

It is precisely the attempt to understand what it is to act from within a 'position' in a culture, that entails focusing upon the nature of the third kind of knowing I want to discuss. It is not a seemingly decontextualized knowing 'that,' or knowing 'how,' but a knowing 'from within' a situation or circumstance. That is, instead of being concerned with how, as *already* an individual of a certain kind, one gains theoretical or practical knowledge relevant to acting within the situation one finds oneself in, it is concerned with the kind of knowledge involved in one *being* a person of this or that kind – and the kind of situation one finds oneself in as a result.

How might knowledge of this 'ontological' kind best be characterized? I argue (in Part II) that it has a 'developmental' quality to it: that it begins with a certain kind of 'feeling' – not to be confused with an emotion, which is to do with an evaluation of or an orientation towards one's own state of being, expressed in terms of feelings of sadness or anger, etc. – related to one's *socio-cultural* surroundings, just as if, rather than visually observing them, one were 'in touch with' them in some way; and that it involves a two-way process of *formulation* in which such feelings are 'given' or 'lent' a form 'from within' an occasion or situation that arises within the flow of activity constituting a discourse or speech genre (Bakhtin – see Chapter 6). This has a number of implications. First, it is important to notice that such 'feelings' are of an *ethical* nature: they not only indicate what the others around us might or might not 'allow' us to do – we can give our 'feelings' expression in a morally negotiated way, in a way 'approved' in a step-by-step manner in interaction with those around us – but also what it is about our own 'position' for which we alone can be 'answerable' (to use a term of Bakhtin's). Such 'feelings', I suggest (Chapter 3), are what Vico (1968) calls the 'sensory topics' which provide the 'roots' of a 'civil society'; they constitute the shared sense (*sensus communis*) which arises among a social group who already share a set of circumstances – and it is against the background of such feelings as these that any conceptualization of what we take our human nature to be can be judged for its adequacy.

But second, it is the 'developmental' nature of 'knowing from' which opens it up to an enormous range of different influences, and thus to different forms of investigation – centrally, its 'developmental' nature opens it up to a process of testing and checking, of justifying and warranting, of accrediting and legitimating, which bear upon its 'hook-up', so to speak, to the realities within which it is used (Chapter 4). As Austin (1970: 179) puts it, the question it opens up is that of "what is the detail of the complicated internal machinery we use in 'acting' – the receipt of intelligence, the appreciation of the situation, the invocation of principles, the planning, the control of execution and the rest?" For even the simplest, smoothest, most thoughtless social act – if it is to be appropriate to its circumstances – is a 'skilled' performance which must involve what I have called (see Chapter 5) a form of 'ethical logistics', that is, a process of 'managing' who is responsible for what in transacting the negotiation of a meaning. To investigate its details, Austin recommends the study of 'breakdowns' in the process, and in particular those in which *excuses* are offered, for as is so often the case,

> the abnormal will throw light on the normal, will help us to penetrate the blinding veil of ease and obviousness that hides the mechanism of the natural successful act. It rapidly becomes plain that the breakdowns signalized by the various excuses are of radically different kinds, affecting different parts or stages of the machinery, which the excuses consequently pick out and sort out for us.
>
> (Austin, 1970: 179)

What this means, I think, is that the claim (in mainstream psychology) that our cognitive abilities operate mechanically and systematically, requires serious reconsideration. Instead, if the comments above are true, they should be treated as reflecting in their functioning the same essentially rhetorical and ethical considerations as those influencing the transactions between people out in the world (see Chapter 6). From this changed point of view, it interesting to consider again how Austin (1970: 193) justifies his study of mere words, and what is going on in 'doing things' with them: for, by studying why some words are used rather than others, one can

> pick out the internal machinery of doing actions, or the departments into which the doing of actions is organized. There is for example the stage at which we actually *carry out* some action upon which we embark – perhaps we have to make certain bodily movements or to make a speech. In the course of actually *doing* these things (getting weaving [for instance]) we have to pay (some) attention to what we are doing and to take (some) care to guard against (likely) dangers: we may need to use judgement or tact: we must exercise sufficient control over our bodily parts: and so on. Inattention, carelessness,

errors of judgement, tactlessness, clumsiness, all these and others are ills (with attendant excuses) which affect one specific stage in the machinery of action, the *executive* stage, the stage where we *muff* it. But there are many other departments in the business too, each of which is to be traced and mapped through its cluster of verbs and adverbs. Obviously there are departments of intelligence and planning, of decision and resolve, and so on . . .

And if we interpret all this now, not in the instrumental, logically neutral fashion in which Austin clearly intended, but as all going on within an ethically and politically sensitive environment, in which the dangers and other ills to which we must attend are not ones of a merely technical kind, then we can see how it gives us a method useful to us. It is 'in' words-in-their-speaking that we can find the political and ethical influences of interest to us at work.

To take this approach to 'mind' then – that it is not a mysterious inner mechanism of a mechanical and general kind, operating according to its own universal *lingua mentis*, but that it is a cultural production, reflecting in its make-up different ethically and politically structured modes of operation in different circumstances – is to honour, it seems to me, Vico's claim quoted in the epigraph in the Introduction to this book: "the world of civil society has certainly been made by men, and that its principles are therefore to be found within the modifications of our human mind." Where the founding context, so to speak, of all our other modes of thought, is to be found within that third kind of knowing I have called 'knowing from.'

Traditions of argumentation and knowing of the third kind

In the night of thick darkness enveloping earliest antiquity, so remote from ourselves, there shines the eternal and never failing light of a truth beyond all question: that the world of civil society has certainly been made by men, and that its principles are therefore to be found within the modifications of our human mind. Whoever reflects on this cannot but marvel that the philosophers should have bent all their energies to the study of the world of nature, which since God made it He alone knows; and that they should have neglected the study of the world of nations, or civil world, which, since men made it, men could come to know.

(Vico, 1968: para. 331)

This book explores both our academic and our everyday ways of knowing. It is especially concerned with the nature of the 'background' upon which we draw in formulating not only our claims in everyday conversation, but also the disciplinary discourses within we discuss our claims to academic knowledge. The themes explored go against the grain of much in the tradition of thought embodied in the modern social sciences. In particular, the central theme of the book – that our disciplined ways of knowing are founded or 'rooted' in, and relevant to, rhetorically organized, two-sided, everyday traditions of argumentation – will seem to many to be especially shocking, not least because it assigns only an ephemeral nature to such disciplines. And their astonishment will be intensified when I add that, indeed, when seen in this light, the 'human sciences' now appear to be increasingly irrelevant to our times, to the pressing social issues of the day. For they are quintessentially products of a moment in the history of the West, the Modern age (Foucault, 1970), that is now passing, if not already over.[1] But to speak against science, and for tradition and for rhetoric, in this way is especially startling, for both the latter have been particularly disdained in modern times.

Respect for tradition has been seen as tantamount to a respect for prejudice, while rhetoric has been seen as "mere rhetoric," as having to do only with the adornment of speech in an effort to make it unreasonably persuasive. But, as Gadamer (1975: 240) says, "the prejudice against prejudice itself . . . deprives tradition of its power," while, as Billig (1987) has pointed out, the prejudice against rhetoric has also deprived it of its power, for it has led us to ignore its two-sided, argumentative nature, that is, the fact that those subjected to the claims of others can, if given the opportunity, justify answering back with equal and opposite claims. The 'prejudices' of modernity have made it difficult for us rationally to 'see' the role of such two-sided, argumentative (rhetorical) traditions in our daily social lives, and the way we justify our more professional academic activities in their terms.

The 'human sciences' were formed from within a social world which, at the time of their formation (see the section on the Enlightenment below), had a certain orderly and unitary 'style' to it, a widespread 'sameness' that no longer seems to be the case in the more disorderly, pluralistic, postmodern world we now inhabit. Thus, just as those in the natural sciences crucially assumed the uniformity of nature as a prerequisite to their investigations, so the originators of the 'human sciences' also assumed the 'background' of their social lives together to be uniform. The idea that we might live in a differentiated social world, a world containing regions and moments so different from each other as to allow the formulation of equal and opposite claims as to their nature – in line with Billig's (1987) claims about the two-sided nature of everyday, common-sense knowledge above – was unthinkable to them. For them, the world of the rich man and poor woman, the happy woman and the sad man, was everywhere the same. Thus, how could this uniform 'background' be of importance? If it exerted no differential effects upon their behaviour (and thought), how could its effects be detected?

However, times are changing. And if we apply the central theme already mentioned above, we can perhaps see that, as our ways of relating ourselves to each other start to change, so must our ways of knowing begin to change, too. Thus, as we begin to confront the *others* in the world around us as genuine 'others' who possess an otherness worthy of our interest and respect (unlike the 'indistinguishable atoms' in a natural science), so our ways of knowing must begin (and have begun[2]) to diversify also. Now, we do need to know about the nature of the 'backgrounds', the different forms of life from which our different ways of knowing emerge. Can our 'human sciences' help us in this task? Theoretically, yes. For the aim of a science *is* to describe the unity and coherence of its subject matter. Yet this is just what the modern 'human sciences' have notably failed to do. They have provided us with an ever increasing wealth of fragmentary data, but as yet no overall grasp either of our own mental functioning or of the nature of our everyday social lives. But this is not to do with the fact that we have not yet found the correct theory – as if with yet more research effort (and funds) we shall one day get it right. It is to do with the fact that we have failed to grasp not only what it is that we must 'theorize' here, but also what the task of 'theory' in this sphere is like. Indeed, as Taylor (1987: 477) remarks: "We cannot turn the background from which we think into an object for us. The task of reason has to be conceived quite differently." It must now be seen "as including – alongside the familiar forms of the Enlightenment – a new department, whose excellence consists in our being able to articulate the background of our lives perspicuously" (Taylor, 1987: 480–1).

"Joint action" and "knowing from within"

It is at this point that we can make contact with 'knowing of the third kind'. It reflects the claim made by Vico above: that we have neglected in our philosophies the study of a special kind of knowledge, quite different from that provided us in our sciences of the natural world. The natural sciences are concerned with us (as individuals) discovering the nature of already existing states of affairs. The knowledge of which Vico speaks (as we shall see in more detail below) is not to do with our discovering actualities individually, but with our realizing the possibilities we make available to ourselves, between ourselves socially – where either others, or we ourselves, have made the relevant *provisions* or *resources* required for their realization already available in their, or our, previous social activities together. In this sense, the two-sided traditions constituting such a civil society are both lived and living traditions. As MacIntyre (1981: 207) says, a tradition is a "living" tradition in the sense that it "is an historically extended, socially embodied argument, and an argument precisely in part about the goods which constitute that tradition," and thus to an extent, it is developed and developing tradition. On the other hand, such traditions are also "lived," in the sense that the resources required for maintaining them in existence, as socio-historically ongoing arguments, are continuously renewed and sustained in their own very conduct.

Thus the knowledge they embody is a strange kind of knowledge that can never be completely present in the head of any one of the individuals involved in its use. It only makes its appearance in the 'background' of our social activities. It is this kind of knowledge – of the provisions and resources we make available to ourselves for the realization of our different possible next forms of social behaviour – that is the special kind of knowledge embodied in the world of a civil society. And it is this that we must try to understand: both the nature of these socio-historical resources, and the nature of the social activities in which they are produced.

For me, the project of attempting to characterize the nature of this special kind of knowledge began in 1969, under the influence of Vygotsky (1962, 1986) and Mead (1934), before I was aware of Vico's existence. Then, I formulated its aim in ethical terms as being simply that of trying to understand what it is to be a responsible, autonomous human being, of trying to understand our own human making of our own human nature (Shotter, 1970, 1974a and b, 1975, 1980, 1984; Gauld and Shotter, 1977). Influenced now, both by Vico's concern with "civil society," and more explicitly by the issues of "otherness" mentioned above (exhibited politically now in so many places, both local and global, around the world), I have become more concerned with political issues, and what it is to be a citizen and to have a sense of *belonging* in a community, rather than merely being a legal part of it (see especially Chapter 9).

From 1980 onwards, central to my project has been the concept of "joint action"

(Shotter, 1980; but see also Chapters 3 and 7 of this book). It designates a third category of activities (or events?) lying in a zone of uncertainty somewhere in between the other two spheres of interest that have occupied our attention in the past. It lies neither wholly in the category of human *actions* (what 'I' as an individual agent do, explained by my giving my reasons) nor in that of natural *events* (what merely 'happens' to, in, or around me, outside my agency as an individual to control, explained by their causes), but shares (as we shall see) features of both. It is its very lack of specificity, its lack of any predetermined final form, and thus its openness to being specified or determined by those involved in it, that is the central defining feature of joint action. Without going into the concept in detail here, it is worth pointing out that the need for such a concept arises when human action is viewed not as the deliberate execution of a well-defined sequence of component actions – as in the monologic following of a script or plan – but when we act spontaneously, say, on the basis of what we 'vaguely felt' was 'required by the situation' we were in at the time.[3] Although we do not find it easy in such cases to give a well-articulated account of why we acted as we did, we would still claim to be acting sensibly, in a way appropriate to our circumstances.

The most obvious circumstance in which such joint action occurs is in dialogue with others, when one must respond by formulating appropriate utterances in reply to *their* utterances. What they have already said constitutes the 'situation on hand', so to speak, into which one must direct one's own reply. It is thus clear why, in such circumstances, we as individuals do not quite know why it is that we act as we do: rather than speaking 'out of' an inner plan (or mental representation), we speak 'into' a context not of our own making, that is, not under our own immediate control. Thus the formative influences shaping our actions are not there wholly within us, prior to our actions, available to be brought out ahead of time. Thus here, our interest is not in the structure of "already spoken words" (in *sentences*, as in linguistics), but in "words in their speaking" (in *utterances*, as I shall explain below). For, the actions of others are just as determinative of our conduct as anything within ourselves. Indeed, the outcome of joint action (within our current individualistic/ scientistic ideology) is seen as coming 'out of nowhere' – indeed, people's experiences on a 'Ouija' board are typical of the outcomes of joint action. And in that sense, in being unattributable to an individual agent and open (as mentioned above) to being specified or determined by those involved in it, it can seem to be either a *creative* event; an accidental, *unintended consequence* of the interaction; or, a just-happening, impersonal event attributable to an 'external' cause or agency, according to the circumstances of its occurrence.

Indeed, in this respect, even when all alone, writing down our 'thoughts' on paper, the situation is not dissimilar to us interacting with an 'other'. Here, too, each sentence works to specify a certain aspect of a situation-as-the-author-understands-it; and each word, too, seems required by what, of that situation, the author has already succeeded in specifying, in the sense that only certain forms of words will correctly express that aspect (though sometimes the author may judge it incorrectly). Thus, in this view, the act of writing or speaking involves a process like a process of 'growth' or 'development' in time, a passage from something less to more well specified or articulated. In this view, one's words are not fashioned to 'correspond' to one's already existing, well-formed thoughts, one does not put an 'inner' intention or thought accurately into an 'outer' linguistic expression; the process involved is one of a very different kind. Indeed, as Vygotsky (1986), Volosinov (1973), Billig (1987), and Vico (1968) all see it, the very possibility of a person's 'thinking', as such, is constituted in language, as a certain form of "inner speech" (see Chapter 7).

> What sort of reality pertains to the subjective psyche? *The reality of the inner psyche is the same reality as that of the sign.* Outside the material of signs there is no psyche; there are physiological processes, processes in the nervous system, but no subjective psyche as a special existential quality fundamentally distinct from both the physiological processes occurring within the organism and the reality encompassing the organism from outside, to which the psyche reacts and which one way or another it reflects. By its very existential nature, the subjective psyche is to be localized somewhere between the organism and the outside world, on the *borderline* separating these two spheres of reality . . . Psychic experience is the semiotic expression of the contact between the organism and the outside environment. That is why *the inner psyche is not analyzable as a thing but can only be understood and interpreted as a sign.*
>
> (Volosinov, 1973: 26)

It is because of this that one's "mind" is not just a general-purpose organ of general go-anywhere-anytime intelligence, but is 'at home' only in one's own times; one thinks both 'out of' and 'into' a certain cultural 'background'.

The special character of joint action is that it creates a 'developed and developing situation' from within which those who are involved in it can make sense of their activities. For, unintended though the results of joint action may be, as human activity, it nevertheless possesses *intentionality*, that is, it possesses a 'content', it 'points beyond itself', it has an 'intrinsic connectedness' of itself to its context. Or, to put it another way, as Gauld and Shotter (1977: 127) suggest, all mental activity has a specificatory function or aspect, in the sense that it is to do with making (in action) or noticing (in perception) differences. Thus such action 'points to' or 'specifies' a realm of other possible next actions, a 'world of meaning or reference' that seems to make its appearance even as the action occurs, and can thus function as the context from within which the sense of the action is understood and a reply to it formulated – where the reply makes a difference by specifying the already specified context further, and so on, such that the common joint product of the exchange formed is such, that the responsibility of all the parties to its construction is impossible to trace.

On a larger scale, Vico (1968: para. 1108) has described the nature of the genuinely social, individually unintended processes involved as follows:

> It is true that men themselves made this world of nations (and we took this as the first incontestable principle of our Science, since we despaired of finding it

from philosophers and philologists), but this world has without doubt issued from a mind often as diverse, at times quite contrary, and always superior to the particular ends that men have proposed to themselves; which narrow ends, made means to serve wider ends, it has always employed to preserve the human race upon this earth. Men mean to gratify their bestial lust and abandon their offspring, and they inaugurate the chastity of marriage from which the families arise. The fathers mean to exercise without restraint their paternal power over their clients, and they subject them to the civil powers from which the cities arise . . . That which did all this was mind, for men did it with intelligence; it was not fate, for they did it by choice; not chance, for the results of their so acting are perpetually the same.

The historical processes of human self-transformation involved can neither be understood in terms of the unfolding of a predetermined set of lawful possibilities; nor as a completely random process; nor as a voluntaristic process conducted according to plans of our own. The process involved is just as Marx described it: we do indeed make our own history, but not under conditions of our own choosing. However, we should not think of our unchosen conditions solely in terms of enablements and constraints (Giddens, 1984), but also as providing us with resources and other forms of "psychological tools or instruments" (Vygotsky, 1978, 1986) that constitute the make-up of our minds. Indeed, in Vico's view, as we 'grow' and 'develop' historically, resources of an entirely new (but not always morally better) kind can become available to us.

Thus, as he puts it, our historical development can be understood as a process of a *providential* kind: past human activities provide "organized settings" (Bartlett's term: see Chapter 4) which contain the *resources* necessary for the sensible continuation of these past activities; or, to put it another way, previous social activity works to create an "order of possibilities" (Wittgenstein's term: Chapter 4) from which we must choose in deciding upon our next actions – if, that is, they are to be actions 'appropriate to' or 'fitting to' their circumstances. The future cannot be made to occur by the sheer force of one's conviction as to its possibility; one must relate one's actions to what at any one moment is a *real* possibility within it. Thus, if we are to act in such a way, we must not act solely 'out of' our own inner 'scripts', 'plans', or 'ideas', but must be sensitive in some way to the opportunities and barriers, the enablements and constraints, 'afforded' to us by our circumstances, in order to act 'into' them. This grasp, this sensitivity of what is 'afforded' us by our circumstances, is what I mean by a knowing of the third kind.

Why I call it this can be made clear by the following rather long quote from Isaiah Berlin (1976: 107–8). He says of Vico that he:

virtually invented the concept of the understanding – of what Dilthey and others call '*verstehen*'. Others before him, philologists or historians or jurists, may have had an inkling of it; Vico brings it to light. No one after reading him will suppose that the sense in which we are said to understand a feeling, a gesture, a work of art, a man's character; an entire civilization or a single joke; the sense in which a man can be said to know what it is to be poor, to be jealous, to be a lover, a convert, a traitor, a banker, a revolutionary, an exile, is (to say the least) the same sense as that in which we know that one tree is taller than an other, or that Hitler wrote *Mein Kampf*, or how one text differs from another, or what neutrons are; nor is it like knowing the differential calculus, or how to spell, or play the violin, or get to Mars, or what an imaginary number is, or what prevents us moving faster than light. It is much more like the kind of awareness that is fed and developed by varied experience and activities of how things look in different situations, how the world appears, through concepts and categories, to individuals or groups in different social or emotional conditions. It is this kind of knowledge that is spoken of as plausible or absurd, realistic or idealistic, perceptive or blind; that makes it intelligent to describe the works of historians and social theorists, artists and men of action, not merely as well-informed, or skilful, or lucid, or misled, or ignorant, but also as wise or stupid, interesting or dull, shallow or profound – concepts which cannot be applied to knowledge in either of the other two senses discussed in our time by Gilbert Ryle [1949]: of 'knowing that' and 'knowing how.'

Such a form of knowledge cannot be formulated in terms of facts or theoretical principles ('knowing that'), for it is a form of practical knowledge, relevant only in particular concrete situations. But it is not practical knowledge in the technical sense of a craft or a skill ('knowing how'), for it is knowledge which only has its being in our relations to others. It is a separate, special kind of knowledge, *sui generis*, which is prior to both, and, in being linked to people's social and personal identities, determines the available forms of these other two kinds of knowledge. Indeed, unlike the other two kinds of knowledge, it is knowledge of a *moral* kind, for it depends upon the judgments of *others* as to whether its expression or its use is ethically proper or not[4] – one cannot just have it or express it on one's own, or wholly within one's self. It is the kind of knowledge one has *only from within a social situation*, a group, or an institution, and which thus takes into account (and is accountable to) the *others* in the social situation within which it is known. If it does appear that I can summon up such knowledge wholly from within myself – as a writer, say (Bakhtin, 1984) – then that will only be because, to repeat Volosinov's claim above, "the reality of the inner psyche is the same reality as that of the sign." Thus, it is from within a process of "inner speech," from within an inner conversation, that such knowledge emerges, and is made available to me – not from within my own "mind," but from within the words I use.

A shorthand term for such a form of knowledge, as its content is primarily derived 'from' one's circumstances – for it is do with a proper grasp of what they will 'afford', 'permit' or 'allow' (a terminology suggested by Gibson's (1979) so-called *ecological* approach to perception) – is 'knowing from within', to contrast it both with 'knowing that' and 'knowing how'. It is worth adding here, that in his discussion of these issues, Bernstein (1983) has linked his discussion of them to

Aristotle's notion of *phronesis* and described this kind of knowledge as knowledge of a *practical-moral* kind, and in many of the chapters that follow I have used this term, too.

The Enlightenment tradition

Enlightening is, Man's quitting the nonage occasioned by himself. Nonage or minority is the inability of making use of one's own understanding without the guidance of another.

(Kant, 1965)

As I mentioned at the outset of this introduction, many of the themes I shall pursue (although not all – see the quote from Kant above[5]) will go against the grain of much in the tradition of modern, social scientific thought in the 'human sciences'. This is because, it seems to me, many of these themes have become irrelevant to our times. How might we identify them? In line with my claim above, that our disciplined ways of knowing are founded or 'rooted' in, and relevant to, rhetorically organized, two-sided, everyday traditions of augumentation, I would now like to add a comment of Billig's (1987: 91):

to understand the meaning of a sentence or whole discourse in an argumentative context, one should not examine merely the words within that discourse or the images in the speaker's mind at the moment of utterance. One should also consider the positions being criticized, or against which a justification is being mounted. Without knowing these counter-positions, the argumentative meaning will be lost.

Thus, if we want to understand what is argumentatively 'done' by formulating one's claims in certain terms rather than others – thought in terms, say, of mental representations rather than, say, "inner speech," as I am proposing here – we must examine the argumentative context within which such formulations were (or are) fashioned. As many of the themes emphasized in the structure of the current 'human sciences' had their origins in Enlightenment thought and argumentation, it will be useful to trace the origins of those formulations relevant to our purposes here, back to the character of the social and political world within which that argumentation was conducted.

In particular, there are five features of Enlightenment thought that, for my purposes here, it will be useful to highlight: (a) its concern with analysis and (b) mental representations, and (c) with the formulation of such representations as systems; (d) its determination to break away from the authority of traditional, religious systems of thought and to find a new form of authority in ahistorical experience; and (e) its attempts to overcome the idea of original sin, the doctrine used to motivate people's participation in the rituals of organized religion, and its emphasis upon individuals' being able to find all the resources they require to be autonomous, psychologically, within themselves. It is all these features that, it seems to me, must not so much be replaced as be displaced to a degree, so as to allow their contemporary 'others' (the other side in a two-sided scheme of things) a 'voice' in the current arguments.

In the Middle Ages, the character of intellectual life was securely in control of a priestly class (Manuel, 1965). Only in the course of the seventeenth and eighteenth centuries did an independent class of popular philosophers begin to attain a degree of ascendancy over it. Unlike today, when most philosophers are professional philosophers, with appointments in State-approved institutions of higher education, those who fashioned Enlightenment thought were a loosely affiliated set of lay persons (seemingly all men), intent upon wresting the control of thought (and talk) from the priests. What united them was the conviction that, by comparison with all previous ages, especially the Middle Ages, theirs was the dawning of a new age, an age of illumination, of enlightenment; their aim was to shine the light of reason into those regions of human life that other ages had kept in the dark. Thus, they ventured to raise a whole lot of new questions, to do with the nature of man,[6] of society, and of the relations between the two. But in raising such questions – about the nature of human nature, about man's 'soul', about the origins and character of religion, about the state and its sources of authority, about the origins of law, and so on – they were treading upon far more dangerous ground than the physical scientists of the previous age – there were still heavy punishments for heresy at the time. Indeed, the questions they raised, and the terms in which they raised them, struck at the very foundations (the legitimacy) of organized religion and organized government.

While England had been a major source of novelty in thought, France was its great continental transmitter: Newton, Locke, and Descartes were among the Enlightenment's important precursors, while the major popularizers and developers of their views were the *philosophes*, among them d'Alembert, Diderot, Rousseau, and Voltaire, the self-pronounced originators of the Enlightenment. The seventeenth century – the Age of Reason – had seen the task of philosophy as the construction of a philosophical or metaphysical "system." Then, truly philosophical knowledge, as Descartes had envisioned it, could be achieved by beginning with clear and distinct (and indubitable) ideas, and proceeding by way of 'geometrical' chains of reasoning, thus to link all of knowledge together – by the method of proof and rigorous inference – into a great system of certainty.

I turn now to the importance of analysis. According to Cassirer (1951: 7), what characterizes the style of Enlightenment philosophizing in the eighteenth century is the "recourse to Newton's 'Rules of Philosophizing' rather than to Descartes' *Discourse on Method*, with the result that philosophy takes an entirely new direction." Although Descartes' conception of reason was retained, his starting point in clear and distinct ideas – in 'hypotheses', as Newton and his followers saw it – was rejected. A science must find its starting point, not in a theoretical abstraction, for such abstractions can be invented and modified as desired, but in observations, in experience. Thus, instead of proceeding by deduction from certain, that is to say, indubitable, axioms, Enlightenment philosophy aims at an *analysis* of experience into its basic facts. Thus, the analytic method involves not merely untutored observation

– that only describes mere appearances – but a special form of analytical observation: the grasping of an 'underlying', hidden reality behind appearances. This involves the splitting of apparently simple events into certain basic elements in such a way that, by reconstructing them according to certain laws or principles, they can be *represented* as events within a rational *system* . . . and thus explained![7] It is this emphasis both upon analysis, and upon its resultant in a systematic representation, that I want to stress, and to note that they still characterize much of our thinking in the 'human sciences' today (Foucault, 1970).

The Enlightenment begins, then, with a loss of faith in the older form of philosophical knowledge, the metaphysical system. It is still concerned, however, with explanations. "But in renouncing, and even in directly opposing, the 'spirit of systems' (*esprit de système*), the philosophy of the Enlightenment by no means gives up the 'systematic spirit' (*esprit systématique*); it aims to further this spirit in another more effective manner" (Cassirer, 1951: vii). Thus, although the turn from the deductive to the analytic method in the eighteenth century marks a shift of focus, from reason to experience, from a starting point in axioms to one in observations, certain continuities remain. The overall urge to be systematic in one's explanatory activities is retained:

> The value of system, the *'esprit systématique,'* is neither underestimated or neglected; but it is sharply distinguished from the love of system for its own sake, the *'esprit de système.'* The whole theory of knowledge strives to confirm this distinction.
>
> (Cassirer, 1951: 8)

For, without a system, without a rational framework within which to interlink contingent facts into a system of logically necessary entailments or dependencies, no soundly based, explanatory knowledge is possible in any field. We can only, seemingly, revert to the contingencies and likelihoods, the persuasions of rhetoric – the influences, once again, of mere opinion. The *systematic*, explanatory nature of the analytic process, is the third feature of Enlightenment thought I want to emphasize.

A fourth feature that is retained, is the methodical doubt, raised by Descartes, of any authority derived from intellectual traditions of the past. Discussing this move in his *Meditations* of 1640, he said that "although the usefulness of such extensive doubt is not apparent at first sight, its greatest benefit lies in freeing us from all our preconceived opinions, and providing the greatest route by which the mind may be led away from the senses" (Descartes, 1986: 9) – the senses which, he thought, could so easily deceive us. In other words, he seeks to establish the rules of properly conducting one's reasoning and of seeking truth in the sciences,[8] by first setting aside the influences of previous traditions of thought. "I realized," as he put it in the 'First Meditation', "that it was necessary, once in the course of my life, to demolish everything completely and start again from the right foundations if I wanted to establish anything at all in the sciences that was stable and likely to last" (Descartes, 1986: 12). It is thus that he instituted the idea that, if one is prepared to undertake the hard analytic work involved, one can throw over the intellectual commitments entailed in one's previous traditional involvements. And one can found a new intellectual system, not in a tradition, not in a way of life or in a way of being in the world, but in a set of theoretical principles, a set of foundational statements.

The fifth feature I want to mention is to do with the source of our own nature as human beings. Although Descartes claimed that the seemingly qualitatively diverse flux of our everyday ways of thinking could be analysed into clear and distinct elementary ideas of an *innate* kind, Locke's 1690 *Essay Concerning Human Understanding* suggested different origins. He suggested that all our complex ideas could be seen as having their origins in a complex of simple sensations, in the simple impressions written on the *tabula rasa* of the mind by the 'outside' world. And this was crucial to another aspect of Enlightenment thought. For if the thought of the *philosophes* was going to function as a *Weltanschauung*, a sufficiently comprehensive intellectual system to contest the traditional medieval Catholic as well as the Protestant world-views, it had to meet certain requirements: it not only had to provide a programme of action for social reform, and a utopian vision of the future of mankind on earth, instead of in heaven, it also had to provide a plausible story about man's past to replace the religious story of man's original sin. Locke's views made it possible to argue that the supposed evil of ordinary people was not an innate, natural evil, but an evil that had been generated externally, and had been imposed upon man by society, by his environment.

Till this time, the belief that man, after the Fall (as in Genesis), was naturally corrupt, and that from the time of Adam this corruption had been passed down through every successive generation, had been vital in all traditional Christian theology. This doctrine explained the existence of evil in the world and justified people's suffering. Thus, although Christians might disagree about the precise rituals required for one's salvation in heaven, none disagreed that such ritual observances and obeisances were required here on earth – for there could be no cure for man's naturally occurring evil nature in this life. And since the natural evil in man has to be curbed, to be kept in check by an external force established by God, kingship by divine right was eminently acceptable. Thus, in combating the idea of original sin with the idea of the basic goodness (or at least not evil nature) of "the natural man," the *philosophes* were contesting the very idea that the current historical institutions of State and society, of Church and religion, were the legitimate institutions to minister unto the needs of man.

But if man was not naturally evil, if there was no innate viciousness to be curbed, if man's natural abilities to change the world were greater than had been imagined, then perhaps a more optimistic, brighter prospect for the future of man might be possible. Thus, as Manuel (1965: 6) says, "fortified by this great myth of natural goodness, the age of the Enlightenment came to express a buoyant optimism . . . natural man was the symbol leading the age out of medieval darkness." Indeed, as Kant expresses it above, what was (and still is) at issue is the question of whether (and in what sense) people themselves can be self-determining; must they always (in some sense) be under the yoke of others? It is this latter, emancipatory concern of the Enlightenment that I do not want to give up. So the question I want to explore is this: by finally giving up, in social affairs, the urge for a unified system of dependencies and the urge for an explanation of everything; by giving up (partially) the 'systematic spirit'; by giving up (partially) the desire for 'ahistorical' decontextualized knowledge; by accepting (partially) people's dependency upon each other; by recognizing that we conduct our academic affairs from within two-sided traditions of argumentation, is it possible to further the spirit of this emancipatory concern in another more effective manner? Is it possible to fashion a new discursive 'space' or 'situation', a new discursive 'activity' or 'movement'[9] (not a framework, nor a system, nor a model – the metaphors chosen here are of outstanding importance), from within which to discuss and debate these concerns?

Social constructionism: a rhetorical-responsive version

As I see it, that movement is already developing (Harré, 1983; Shotter, 1984; Gergen, 1985). Common to all the versions of it known to me is the central assumption that – instead of the study of the inner dynamics of the individual psyche (romanticism and subjectivism), or the already determined characteristics of the external world (modernism and objectivism), the two polarities in terms of which we have thought about ourselves in recent times[10] (Taylor, 1989; Gergen, 1991) – it is the contingent flow of continuous communicative interaction between human beings which becomes the central focus of concern: a self–other dimension of interaction. But until recently, as I have made clear above, this flow of diffuse (feelingful or sensuous[11]) activity has remained in the background as the unordered hurly-burly or bustle of everyday social life. Under the influence of the Enlightenment tendencies or cravings embodied in our social sciences, it has awaited (unsuccessfully) systematic representation in terms of supposed principles either of mind or of world.

What in particular social constructionists want to explore, is how speakers and listeners seem to be able to create and maintain between themselves, in certain of their 'basic' communicative activities, an extensive background context of living and lived (sensuously structured) relations, within which they are sustained as the kind of human beings they are (Shotter, 1984). In other words, social constructionists are concerned with how, without a conscious grasp of the processes involved in doing so, in living out different, particular forms of *self–other relationships*, we unknowingly construct different, particular forms of what we might call *person–world relations*: the special ways in which, as scientists, say, we interact with the different worlds of only theoretically identified entities; the routine ways in which as ordinary persons we function in the different 'realities' we occupy in our everyday social lives; as well as the extraordinary ways in which we act, say, when in 'love' (see Chapter 9). In this sense, a number of person–world dimensions of interaction can be seen as produced *within* the self–other dimension of interaction in a society, as in Figure 1. Where person–world dimension of interaction is, to an extent, orthogonal

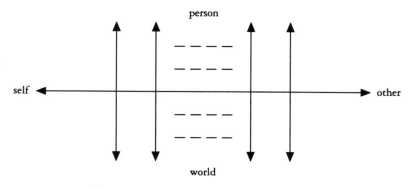

Figure 1 Self–other, and person–world dimensions of interaction.

to the self–other dimension; it is not orthogonal to the extent that it is *not independent* of the interests, etc., of particular persons or groups in that dimension (see Chapter 5).

In this scheme of things, then, the ways of 'being ordinary' available to us in our society, are just as much socio-historical constructions as our ways of being a scientist, or a lover. In other words, not only do we constitute (make) and reconstitute (remake) our own social worlds, but we are also ourselves made and remade by them in the process. It is the dialectical emphasis upon *both* the contingency *and* the creativity of human interaction – on our making of, and being made by, our social realities – that is, I think, common to social constructionism in all its versions. What is distinctive in the rhetorical-responsive version that I want to offer, is (I claim) a way of seeing how, as a result of biases in the self–other dimension of relation, we unknowingly construct biases in our person–world relations.

Turning then to my rhetorical-responsive version of social constructionism, I have chosen to give it a distinctive title because, as I see it, social constructionism currently contains at least two distinct strands. In one of them, what we might call its representational-referential strand, there is a focus upon "already spoken words." This latter strand is influenced primarily by the writings of Saussure (1960), Derrida (1976), Lyotard (1984), and Rorty (1980, 1989), who talk of language as working in terms of already existing, decontexualized systems of conventionalized meanings or usages, characterized either by systems of differences, or in terms of rule-governed language games. This strand is currently in political trouble (Eagleton, 1986, 1989; Lazarus, 1991; Norris, 1990, 1992; Parker, 1992) for its apparent slide into 'absolute' relativism, occasioned by an "uncritical adherence to a theory of language and representation whose extreme anti-realist or sceptical bias in the end gives rise to an outlook of thoroughgoing nihilism" (Norris, 1992: 191). I do have some objections to this strand myself (see Chapter 2), but I am not in agreement with Norris.[12] As might be expected, I feel its difficulties have a different origin: in its commitments still to the Enlightenment themes I have described above.

The strand I want to pursue, as I have already made clear, takes a more two-sided stance towards these commitments, attempting to open up a new discursive space. For, if we want to study the phenomenon of "words in their speaking," to study the 'formative' or 'shaping' function of speech as distinct from its referential function, we must divest ourselves to an extent of certain Enlightenment 'cravings' embodied in our current discourses. In wanting to distinguish my approach from the representational-referential approach I want to incorporate the work of three (already mentioned) people: the turn to rhetoric in the recent work in social psychology by Michael Billig (1987, 1991; Billig *et al.*, 1988), and also the 'dialogical' work of Mikhail Bakhtin (1981, 1984, 1986) and Volosinov (1973),[13] and the responsive theory of understanding they propose (to contrast with the representational-referential account currently hegemonic in linguistic studies) – hence, the characterization of my stance as a 'rhetorical-responsive' one.

A number of points are of immediate relevance to us here, if we are to characterize this version of social constructionism further. Firstly, as I have already mentioned, we must note that all our behaviour, even our own thought about ourselves, is conducted in an ongoing argumentative context of criticism and justification, where every argumentative 'move' is formulated as a response to previous moves. This accords, secondly, with a familiar aspect of rhetoric, to do with its *persuasive* function, its ability to materially affect people's behaviour, to 'move' them to action, or 'affect' their perceptions in some way. Thirdly, we must also note that, in accordance with MacIntyre's views quoted above, what we have in common with each other in our society's traditions is not a set of agreements about meanings, beliefs or values, but a set of intrinsically two-sided 'topics' [Greek *topoi* = 'places'] or dilemmatic themes or 'commonplaces' for use by us as *resources*, from which we can draw the two or more sides of an argument. Finally, we must note another, more unfamiliar aspect of rhetoric, related to those aspects of language to do with 'giving' or 'lending' a *first form* to what otherwise are in fact only vaguely or partially ordered feelings and activities, to do with the study of how common understandings are established *before* one turns to their criticism. It is this fact – that we 'see' just as much 'through' our words as through our eyes (Vygotsky, 1978: 32) – that is, for us here, rhetoric's most important characteristic. For even in the face of the vague, indescribable, open, fluid, and ever changing nature, appropriate forms of talk can work 'to make it appear as if' our everyday lives are well ordered and structured.

I mention these points here, because what makes the version of social constructionism I want to pursue distinctive is its recognition, on the one hand, of the *reality*[14] of the two-sided, commonplace resources mentioned above, but also, on the other, its recognition, among the many other problems to do with representations and their contested nature, that a "means of representation [can] produce something imaginary" (Wittgenstein, 1981: no. 446) – thus, an acceptable characterization of their nature is not that easy to come by.[15] Without attempting to argue the issue further here (but see Chapter 8), in attempting to characterize the nature of the resources our culture makes available, along with both Billig (1991) and Bakhtin (1984), I shall not attempt to impose a *monologic*, theoretical resolution upon the essentially *dialogical* activity to which they give rise. Not only would that be to attempt to merge people's unique and distinct consciousnesses and points of view all into one, but it would be to ignore the contested nature of these resources. Thus, I shall suggest that – if our task now is to render rationally visible the communicative resources our 'background' makes differentially available,[16] thus to make them more available, practically, to all – then instead of attempting to represent the nature of communicative activity in a unified, systematic theory, we must display its dilemmatic character in other than an analytic way. We must both investigate its nature in use, *and* display it in a usable form.

And we can achieve both these aims *through* the use of the image of the utterance (see Chapter 1 on images as prosthetics and Chapter 4 on Wittgenstein's notion of 'grammatical' investigations). For we can both discover and display the nature of the resources people use, by studying how they 'shape' the everyday communicative activities in which they are involved *in practice*, that is, people 'see' and 'act' through their use of words, just as much as through their use of their eyes and limbs. Their influence is, thus, revealed in the 'grammar' of our perceptions and actions. Hence Wittgenstein's (1953: no. 373) claim that: "Grammar tells us what kind of object anything is." And we can attempt, rhetorically, to display the nature of these resources in the same way: by the use of images and metaphors (see Chapter 6) through which to 'see' (at least an aspect of) their nature. This is not to claim that what one is 'representing' in such an 'image' is an accurate characterization that corresponds to the reality of the resource, it is merely to claim that one has managed to characterize an aspect of what its reality 'allows' or 'permits' – a claim that, even though it may be contested, can, if taken seriously, alter the terms of current debate, and thus alter the structure of current social relations.

The stance taken above – the renunciation of systematic theory in favour of "practical-theory" (Shotter, 1984), or the equipping of an image 'tool-kit' – respects the unfinalizable nature of dialogue, and the fact that dialogic forms of talk occur within a "plurality of unmerged consciousnesses" (Bakhtin, 1984: 9). For although we all may draw upon resources (to an extent) held in common, every voice, every way of speaking, embodies a different evaluative stance, a different way of being or position in the world, with a differential access to such resources. It is this that keeps everyone in permanent dialogue with everyone else, and gives all the processes of interest to us their intrinsic dynamic. And by studying the different ways in which different people, at different times in different contexts, resolve the dilemmas they face *in practice*, we can both characterize the resources available to them in those contexts at those times, and 'plot', so to speak, their political economy, that is, the fact that they are very much more scarce in some regions and moments of our social ecology than in others (Shotter, 1984).

What this book is about: identity and belonging

I mentioned above the overall project, of which the characterization of 'knowing from' is just a component part. Let me now say a few more words about that project.

As I mentioned above, I was originally concerned with what it was to grow up in a society as a self-determining, autonomous person with one's own identity in that society (Shotter, 1975). Then, I thought that to be a person and to qualify for certain rights as a free, autonomous individual, one must also be able to show in one's actions certain social competencies, that is, to fulfil certain duties and to be *accountable* to others in the sense of being able to justify one's actions to them, when challenged, in relation to the 'social reality' of the society of which one is a member (Shotter, 1984). To be someone in this sense is clearly a rhetorical achievement.

But due to the increasing appearance of issues to do with 'otherness', both in fact and theory, it became increasingly clear that, politically, the possession of certain social competencies was still not enough to provide one with a 'sense of belonging', with a sense of 'being at home' in the reality which one's actions help to reproduce. To live within a community which one senses as being one's own, as 'mine' as well as 'yours', as 'ours' rather than 'theirs', a community for which one feels able to be answerable, one must be more than just a routine reproducer of it; one must in a real sense also play a part in its creative reproduction and sustenance as a 'living' tradition of argumentation. And the questions the essays in this book attempt to address are: What is involved in doing this? And what part might academic 'tool or image-makers' play in promoting its greater possibility?

PART I

FROM SYSTEMS TO TRADITIONS OF ARGUMENTATION

ONE

'Getting in touch': The metamethodology of postmodern sciences of mental life

As I have already mentioned in the introduction, there is currently a movement away from *modern* 'sciences' of the social world toward *postmodern* alternatives (Toulmin, 1982; Lyotard, 1984). Here, I want to explore in more detail the character and meaning of the changes involved, especially the factors preventing us from grasping all that we might. Among the many changes entailed is a shift in the character of not only standpoint and investigatory activity, but also its focus and mode of expression: There is a movement, first, from the standpoint of the detached, theory-testing onlooker, to the interested, interpretative, procedure-testing participant-observer; second, from a one-way style of investigation to a two-way interactive mode; third, with a focus upon a wholly new set of research topics to do with what does or can go on between people; and fourth, giving rise to a non-cognitive, non-systematic, rhetorical, critical social constructionist approach to psychology. Here I want both to critique from a postmodernist perspective the methodology of modern science implicit in modern psychology, and to outline the nature of a research programme for a postmodern science of mental life. My critique will have a number of strands to it, but central among them will be, again, an examination of how our commitment to thinking within a system, from within an orderly or coherent mental representation – the urge in reflection to *command a clear view* (Wittgenstein, 1953: no. 122) – in fact *prevents* us from achieving a proper grasp of the pluralistic, non-orderly nature of our circumstances.

Knowledge 'by looking' and 'by being in touch'

Central to the different perspective I want to formulate, is this claim by Rorty (1980: 12): "It is pictures rather than propositions, metaphors rather than statements, which determine most of our philosophical convictions." Thus, instead of the image (a) of the mind as a (passive) mirror of Nature; (b) of knowledge as accuracy of representation; and thus (c) of the scientist as an external observer, I want to substitute another set of images: The image (a) of the scientist being as if one of a community of 'blind' persons exploring their surroundings by the use of sticks or through other such instruments; (b) of the knowledge important to them as being to do with them 'knowing their way around' in ways communicable between them; and (c) of the mind as actively 'making sense' of the *relatively invariant* (Bohm, 1965; Gibson, 1979) features they discover in their instrument-assisted explorations of their surroundings – a shift from a way of knowing by 'looking at' to a way of knowing by being 'in contact, or in touch with'. Indeed, I want to argue that it is only in terms of activities like these that the kinds of knowledge we possess and make use of in conducting our everyday affairs are possible.

The change in conducting one's investigations from an onlooker standpoint to a position of instrumentally mediated (or prosthetically aided – see below) involvement is central to a postmodern alternative to the 'human sciences' I want to discuss. But it is not the only change taking place, for this change implies many others. For instance, associated with the adoption of an involved rather than an external, uninvolved *standpoint*, are the different attitudes, values, aims, as well as the guidelines, apparatuses, and devices that can be used in relation to such standpoints; there are also changes in *starting-points* (whether one starts one's investigations when a 'breakdown' occurs, or during the flow of successful activity, in types of *investigative procedure*, in attitudes to language, and especially in modes of *legitimation* (Lyotard, 1984). In detail, there is a shift, first, from a concern with *theories* to *practices*, from theorizing to the provision of practical, instructive *accounts*; second, from an interest in *things* to an interest in *activities* and the *uses* to which we can put the 'mental tools' or 'psychological instruments' (Shotter, 1989a; Vygotsky, 1966) of our own devising; third, away from what goes on in the heads of individuals to an interest in the (largely social) nature of their surroundings, and what these can (or will) 'allow', 'permit' or 'afford'; fourth, from procedures conducted on one's own, to their 'negotiation' with others; fifth, from starting-points in reflection (when the flow of interaction has ceased) to local starting-points embedded in the historical flow of social activity in daily life; sixth, from language being primarily for the representation of reality, to it being primarily for the coordination of diverse social action, with its representational function working *from within* a set of linguistically constituted social relations; seventh, from a reliance upon our experiences as a basis for understanding our world, to a questioning of the social processes of their 'construction' (Gergen, 1985); and eighth, and perhaps most importantly of all, a shift away from investigations *based* in foundations already accepted as authoritative – which thus claim an acceptability for their results ahead of time – towards modes of investigation which allow for error-correction 'on the spot', so to speak (Barnes, 1982; Bernstein, 1983; Rorty, 1980), which find their 'warrants' in locally constituted situations or circumstances.

The shift from third-person observation to second-person 'prosthetics': from metatheory to metamethodology

In the past, in assuming our procedures of inquiry to be secure, and our problems to be located (mainly) in the nature of our subject matter, we have indulged in a great deal of *metatheoretical* and *epistemological* discussion (see, for example, Gergen and Morowski, 1980) — we discussed *theories* because we felt accurate theories were the goal of our investigations. In the approach being canvassed here, our supposed objects of study are of less concern to us than the general nature of our investigatory devices and practices. In other words, instead of metatheory, we become concerned with *metamethodology*: primarily, from our new position as 'blind' investigators, we become interested both in the procedures and devices we use in 'socially construct-ing' the subject matter of our investigations in concert with our fellow investigators, and in how we establish and maintain a contact with it. For the 'hook-up', so to speak, between such devices and our surroundings, determines the nature of the data we can gather *through* their use. Thus, we must move away from the stance of individual, third-person, external, contemplative observers, away from collecting *fragmented* data from a position socially 'outside' of the activity observed, and bridging the 'gaps' between the fragments by the imaginative invention of theoretical en-tities, towards a more interpretative approach concerned with making 'sense' of our circumstances. We must move away from the use of *inference* — the *assertion* (on some basis, of course) that essentially unobservable, subjective entities, supposedly 'inside' individuals, none the less exist, towards a concern with modes of *hermeneutical* inquiry. We must move away from theoretical interests towards interests of a much more practical kind, to do with the aids and devices we might possibly use in mediating the different kinds of contact that we might make with our surround-ings. But while we move away from such concerns, we do not — as will be made clear below — turn away from them entirely.

To see the consequences of such a shift, let us examine just one major point of difference between knowledge 'by looking' and 'by being in touch'. The devices through which we must conduct our more sensuous investigations, unlike the visual devices providing us with 'pointer readings' which reside 'on the side of' the world, so to speak, reside 'on our side', that is, they function as prostheses, as extensions of our selves.

Prosthetic devices, we might say, reside 'on the side of the agent'; we may come to "dwell in" them (Polanyi, 1958), and learn how to *embody* them as an instru-mental means *through* which to achieve our ends. As such, they are 'transparent' — blind people do not feel their sticks vibrating in the palms of their hands, they experience the terrain ahead of them directly as rough, as a result of their stick-assisted 'way' of investigating it in their movement through it; just as the carpenter 'feels' the hardness of the wood, and adjusts the blows of the hammer accordingly as she or he hammers a nail home. Two distinct processes of 'sense making' seem to be at work in such mediated investigations or activities as these: Firstly, following

Bohm (1965: 223–4), we can note that in actively probing or acting upon one's surroundings through an instrument, there is always a response to one's testing and acting, and "it is the relationship of variations in this response to the known variations in the state of the instruments that constitutes the relevant information in what is observed (just as happens directly with the sense organs)," as he says. It is in the relation between the outflow of activity for which one is oneself respons- ible, and the inflow for which one is not, that one makes available information about 'the other' to oneself – with each sweep of the stick, each blow of the hammer, each test, more information is revealed. Here, we must turn to the second stage of the process: As Polanyi (1958: 55–7) describes it, we attend in such activities *from* an ongoing and changing "subsidiary awareness" of the information(s) provided us by the instruments we use, *to* a "focal awareness" of their organized result – for example, *from* the vibrations occasioned by our movements of a stick *to* the rough- ness or smoothness of the surfaces over which it is moved; *from* the felt movement of the nail in hammer blows *to* the hardness of the wood; *from* the disparate two- dimensional views given by the movements of our *two* eyes over a visual scene *to* a unified three-dimensional view; and so on.

Consider now, the others around us, prosthetically reaching out to us through similar such devices. For us, they are not prostheses but indicators. In these circum- stances, rather than on our side, we might say that these devices reside 'on the side of the world'. Now we must confront them, not as a means, but as having a *meaning* which we must interpret (like a 'text') – as blind people sense a 'spatial array of objects' from out of the cacophony of sounds around them.[1] In this mode, such devices do have a content: they indicate a content given them by those using them, a state of the world. Here, too, we may say that a 'from–to' structure of sense-making is involved, but now we must attend *from* all the fragments of data provided *to* an overall organized resultant. But as it is not now open to us further to investigate the world *by their use*, to fill in any gaps – for indicators are not prostheses – *imaginative completion* is required if we are to achieve coherency. While prostheses, to the extent that we come to embody them, may be accounted as a part of ourselves, our relation to indicators is different; they remain 'other than' or 'outside' of us. Rather than as a means for our use, our relationship to them is a *hermeneutical* one; if we can interpret the information they provide – by placing all its parts suitably within a larger whole – then they present us with a meaning, a state of affairs to which we might need or want to react.

At least, this would be the case if all our dealings with the others around us were of a one-pass nature, so to speak. But they are not, they are dialogic. The detection of 'gaps' in the content of another's speech, instead of motivating their hermeneutical 'filling in', can motivate us, of course, to yet further prosthetically guided investigation of what they might mean.

Up until now, in our vocabulary of knowledge 'by looking', it is the hermeneutical relation to our language that has been most salient to us. That *is* how, when we stop to reflect upon the matter, it seems to us that we *must* make sense of our circum- stances. We know that the eye flicks about over the world, seemingly gathering bits and pieces of data from here and there. Thus, perception *must* work by the organizing of the fragments into an order, and the imaginative filling in of supposedly missing elements which must, originally, have been there, mustn't it? But what occurs in reflection is what occurs in making sense of data from indicators, which, as I said above, involves the imaginative filling in of gaps. Whereas, in one's practical, prosthetic grasp of the meaning of one's circumstances, few such gaps exist; in practice, they are filled in. Thus, what fragmentary data take on in one's reflections upon them, is not so much meaning as *intelligibility*, that is, they become capable of being grasped reflectively and intellectually, by being placed within an order, or system – or, as we shall see in a moment, by being placed within a coherent, narrative form. As Wittgenstein (1953) points out, that order is not in our reality, but has been constructed by drawing upon a syntax, upon a 'grammar' implicit in our language. The *true* meanings of events in the living of our lives cannot be properly understood within the confines of an order; they are only to be found in the not wholly orderly, practical living of our lives.

The prominence of the hermeneutical stance, however, has hidden from us the equally important prosthetic relation: for mostly, we 'see through' the language we use and are unaware of its prosthetic functioning. Only when the flow of activity between ourselves and our interlocutors breaks down, do we find ourselves confronted, so to speak, by just our utterances. To restart the flow, to clarify their meaning, they then seem to require interpretation – hence the apparent primacy of a hermeneutical account of language. But interpretation in that sense is *not* required as long as the flow is maintained. One's words are a transparent means through which one can achieve a sensible contact with those around one. Only if we switch our metaphors, only if we begin to talk of knowledge 'by being in touch' do we begin to raise the kinds of question that make contact with the issues here: to do with the rhetorical 'shaping' and 'moving' functions of language.

With prostheses, we are in an *embodiment* relation to them, we "dwell" in them (Polanyi, 1958); while with indicators, our relationship to them is a *hermeneutical* one. Clearly, words may serve in either capacity, and, as I indicated above and have emphasized in the introduction, it would be wrong to argue *in favour* of either side. As I see it, language possesses what one might call a 'tool/text' ambiguity. Indeed, even in one's own speech, as each utterance is used prosthetically in its *saying* to 'move' another person and thus to reveal in those movements something of their character, so what one has *said* remains on hand, so to speak, as a text, constituting an aspect of the situation between oneself and one's interlocutor. Thus, if we now put the matter in terms of which is better, the knowledge 'by being in touch' metaphor, which has revealed to us a form of knowledge which was otherwise invisible (*sic*) to us, or the knowledge 'by looking' metaphor, which is seemingly necessary to our being able to say anything at all, we are unable to decide between the alternatives. Our ways of knowing seem to be at least two-sided.

'Making' and 'finding'

Indeed, if the claims above are accepted, the process involved in the development of our knowledge is quite unlike any so far discussed in the empirical tradition: it is not induction (for it does not depend upon the discovery of regularities), nor is it inference (for the *unique* and *particular* nature of circumstances cannot be understood by assimilating their details to any already established theoretical categories and premises). As each investigatory 'move' generates a result, a 'fact', a mental 'whole' has to be fashioned to accommodate it. Mentally, we have to 'construct' a context (a world) into which such a result can fit and play its part – where each new fact 'points to' or 'indicates' a 'world' in which they all have their place or function. Prosthetically, in an outflow of activity through one device or another, we can make 'sense' of our contact with the 'otherness' of our surroundings, in terms of the relation between that outflowing activity and the incoming result (Bohm, 1965) – again we might take first the example of the blind person's stick, but next we must imagine the activity of speaking to another and 'moving' them to a response with our words. And the hermeneutical process continues as each new result of each 'movement' is added into the whole constructed so far – where that whole must be progressively transformed and articulated, metamorphosed in fact, in a back-and-forth process, in such a way as to afford all the parts of the whole an undistorted accommodation.

In this view, the utterances of dialogic speech constitute a two-way, psychological 'flow' or 'movement' in which a prosthetic outflow of activity for one speaker constitutes the resulting, inflowing, responsive activity for the other, and the speakers, in their utterances, in the 'movement' between their sense of what they want to achieve in their utterance and their use of particular words, attempt successively to develop suitable expressions. But how is this possible? How can an expression be 'developmentally' formulated in a more or less routine way, word by word, and checked in the course of its 'construction' for its appropriateness? Because, argues Bakhtin (1986: 88):

> Neutral dictionary definitions of the words of a language ensure their common features and guarantee that all speakers of a given language will understand one another, but the use of words in live speech communication is always individual and contextual in nature. Therefore, one can say that any word exists for the speaker in three aspects: as a neutral word of a language, belonging to nobody; as an *other's* word, which belongs to another person and is filled with echoes of the other's utterance; and finally, as *my* word, for, since I am dealing with it in a particular situation, with a particular speech plan, it is already imbued with my expression. In both the latter aspects, the word is expressive, but, we repeat, this expression does not inhere in the word itself. It originates at the point of contact between the word and actual reality, under the conditions of that real situation articulated by the individual utterance. In this case the word appears as an expression of some evaluative position of an individual person . . .

It is in a speaker's particular use of a particular word at a particular point in time – as with the carpenter's particular use of a chisel stroke to slice off a wood sliver at a particular point in a piece of joinery – that the speaker can sense what its use achieves in the construction desired. To repeat Bakhtin's comments above, a word's meaning does not inhere in the word itself, but originates *at the point of contact* between the word used and the 'movements' it achieves in the conditions of its use.

In this prosthetic/hermeneutical account of knowing, then, a process of 'making' or construction is at work. Indeed, even the seeing of objects involves an active psychological process of construction involving socially derived knowledge – doesn't it? Yet currently, we feel that the opposite is the case: that in our 'experience', outer 'objective' events cause inner 'subjective' effects. And we make use of this in our theories about the nature of knowledge and modes of inquiry. We feel some claims to truth are *certain*, not because of the arguments given for them, but because in some way they are *caused* in us or imposed upon us by the outer, objective nature of the world. These truths can be used as 'foundations' upon which to base our further inquiries. Deconstructive analyses such as Rorty's (1980), however, have shown such beliefs to be an illusion. To build knowledge upon foundations constructed upon an analogy between perceiving and knowing, is to see *certainty* as a matter of the world 'outside' our human world imposing something upon us, rather than as something we achieve both in interaction with it and in conversation between ourselves, isn't it?

Well, yes (to a degree) and no (to a degree); and in fact, in my view, both are true – they are both moments in the two-way, interactive mode of investigation I mentioned above. What such a deconstructive analysis means, I think, is that we must finally face up to the lack of any pre-established orders in the world: first, that instead of thinking of our task as that of finding such an order, ready-made, we must consider activities which begin with vague, but not wholly unspecified, 'tendencies' which are then open to or which permit a degree of actual further specification; and second, instead of thinking it possible for special individuals trained in special methods simply to make 'discoveries', any further specifications of states of affairs, if they are to be considered *intelligible and legitimate* to those around us, must be negotiated in a back-and-forth process with them. In other words, we must now think in terms of processes of investigation involving both 'finding' *and* 'making'.

I have tried to include the main aspects of this two-way process in Figure 2. To adapt the useful 'direction of fit' terminology introduced by Searle (1983), what this shows (bottom limb) is that in the world-to-agent direction of fit, as in classical empiricist approaches, we *could say* (that is, the facts will 'afford' us saying) that our ways of talking depend upon the world; they are 'rooted' or 'grounded' in its nature: to that extent our talk is about what we 'find' to be there. But on the other hand (top limb), in line with *hermeneutical* or interpretative views, in the agent-to-world direction of fit, it is equally true to say that what we take the nature of the world to be depends upon our ways of talking about it: to the extent that they 'give' or 'lend' its otherwise open nature a determinate (and legitimate) structure and significance, its significance for us 'is' as we 'make' it to be.

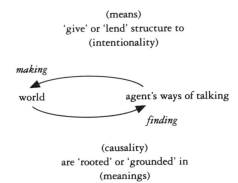

(means)
'give' or 'lend' structure to
(intentionality)

making

world   agent's ways of talking

finding

(causality)
are 'rooted' or 'grounded' in
(meanings)

Figure 2 Two-way, interactive mode of investigation.

Thus the fact is, not only *can* one make both of these claims, but one *must* assert that both are true. Indeed, as Derrida (1976) would point out, they owe their distinct existences to their *interdependency*; one claim is an *absent-presence* in 'lending' intelligibility to the other. Thus although one should say only what the facts will permit, the nature of the facts here is such that, although they draw upon different *systematic discourses* for their representation, two equal and opposite truths can, and must, be asserted. And this, of course, is precisely what Billig (1987) is now arguing in relation to the importance of rhetoric and the two-sidedness of human thinking generally.

Currently, however, we find such two-way or two-sided accounts very difficult to accept. For all kinds of reasons, not just in the history of philosophy (see, for example, Cassirer, 1951), but also because of our socialization into the official communicative practices of academic life, we are still committed to an Enlightenment image of knowledge as being both *systematic* and *unitary*, that is, a hierarchical structure of one-way dependencies. What other form could it have? Institutionally, only certain forms of investigation and argumentation can (morally) 'make sense'. We *must* talk in terms of such systems of one-way dependencies, in terms of relations of dominance. We cannot build two-sided truths into an atemporal system. Of the two equal and opposite claims — about which is or should be the *dominant* dependency relation — we feel that it is impossible for *both* to be true. Failing to give any place to time, or to 'moments' in a process in our current ways of thinking, we claim such two-sided truths to be unthinkable.

Grammatical illusions, the *ex post facto* facts fallacy, and entrapment

Why is it so difficult for us to recognize the nature of our own involvement in such temporally constituted, constructive processes? Why are we continually *tempted* to espouse what are essentially philosophical 'assumptions' (and are initially presented as such) as undeniable 'givens' in our investigations?

As I said above, our major 'prosthetic device' – through which we can gain a grasp of the nature of the 'others' around us – is *language*; and it is the nature of the social conditions required for its proper, communicative usage that is of interest to us in our metamethodological inquiries. But if, instead of thinking of language as being used in this way – to 'make contact' with those around us – we still insist upon thinking of our sentences as *pictures*, where we can *see* in the structure of the sentence the 'things' it represents, then we can mislead ourselves in fundamental ways. Committed to a 'picture' theory of linguistic function, as Wittgenstein (1953: no. 114) says (still using a visual idiom, but now ironically): "One thinks that one is tracing the outline of the thing's nature over and over again, and one is merely tracing round the frame through which we look at it." In other words, as he (Wittgenstein) also says elsewhere, a way of speaking is what prevents us from seeing the facts (that is our practices and procedures of usage) without prejudice. And it is overcoming our own misconceptions about our own use of language (and the temptations to misinterpret its nature that it itself offers us) which is one of our main aims in our metamethodological investigations.

But we mislead ourselves in other more complex ways than simply by such 'grammatical illusions'; there are other kinds of ways in which we can 'entrap' ourselves within linguistic worlds of our own making. Stolzenberg (1978: 224) describes such traps as:

> a closed system of attitudes, beliefs, and habits of thought for which one can give an objective demonstration that certain of the beliefs are incorrect and that certain of the attitudes and habits of thought prevent this from being recognized.

This gives rise, Stolzenberg (1978: 224) says, to "methodological errors" which are "those failures to take into account considerations of standpoint that have the effect of *maintaining* the system." These, whatever the nature of the system in question, function to undermine the proper processes of rational argumentation and debate, and to bias its outcome always in favour of the status quo. They are errors *in method* because, of course, the fundamental nature of all scientific methods of investigation *ought* to be such that they are always open to the correction of error; this, however, is not the case when one is 'entrapped'; objections to the system of thought are either rendered unintelligible or assimilated to it in some way. One only has to call to mind one's own attempts to argue with Piagetians, Freudians, Skinnerians, or cognitivists, to understand what Stolzenberg means by such 'closed' systems of thought.

The 'fall' into such a trap comes about as follows:

1 A statement is formulated as a description of a state of affairs which, although we may not realize it at the time, is open to a number of possible interpretations.
2 We are then tempted to accept the statement as true.

3　By its very nature the statement then 'affords' or 'permits' the making of further statements, now of a better-articulated and more *systematic* nature.

4　The initial interpretation (already accepted as true) is now perceived *retrospectively* as owing its now quite definite character to its place 'within' the now well-specified context produced by the later statements – it has been 'given' or 'lent' a determinate character in their terms which it did not, in its original *openness*, actually have.[2]

This is how it comes about that something which was at first merely an *assumption* takes on the appearance of a *definition*; and what had a social *history* of its production appears as an atemporal, ahistorical system of natural necessities.

Fleck (1979) has studied its nature in relation to scientific developments. He comments upon the general nature of the process as follows:

> once a statement is published it constitutes part of the social forces which form concepts and create habits of thought. Together with all other statements it determines 'what cannot be thought of in any other way'. Even if a particular statement is contested, we grow up with its uncertainty which, circulating in society, reinforces its social effect. It becomes a self-evident reality which, in turn, conditions our further acts of cognition. There emerges a closed, harmonious system within which the logical origin of individual elements can no longer be traced.
>
> (Fleck, 1979: 37)

In attempting retrospectively to understand the origins and development (and the current movement) of our thought, we describe their nature within our to an extent now finished and systematic schematisms. But the trouble is, once 'inside' such systems, it is extremely difficult to escape from them.

What Stolzenberg and Fleck show, then, is how a system of thought and expression can work to disconnect itself from its own social and historical origins, and also (seemingly) from its rooting or grounding in the social practices which maintain its appearance of autonomy, and creates the illusion of it being about "a world of things" existing independently of it and external to it. Indeed, the process Stolzenberg describes is entirely general. Ossorio (1981) calls it the "*ex post facto* facts paradox."

The difference between a genuinely scientific approach and an approach within an entrapping system of belief, lies in their respective methodologies: in genuine science, one can *ironicize* one's experience (Pollner, 1975), whereas in a *system* of belief, all acts of observation, judgement, etc., are performed solely from within the particular standpoint of the system itself.

> Specifically, the ironicizing of experience occurs when one experience, tacitly claiming to have comprehended the world objectively, is examined from the point of view of another experience which is honoured as the definitive version of the world intended by the first.
>
> (Pollner, 1975: 412)

The irony resides in the subsequent appreciation that the initial experience no longer possesses the objective nature it was originally felt to have – if, that is, it is possible for the recipient of a supposed ironic claim to interpret it non-systematically, that is, as in fact ironic. But the use of irony is not always successful. Entrapping systems possess a methodology which prevents the ironicizing of experience in Pollner's sense; this means that intended ironic statements are often not seen as such. For, by their very nature, such systems rule out of court forms of criticism, that is argumentative 'moves', not intelligible within the terms decreed by their own methodology – there are many such approaches with such a character within the human and the psychological sciences.

As Feyerabend (1978) suggests, they promote a kind of professionalized incompetence, an incapacity to read accurately, that is, in a way that hermeneutically constructs a whole to accommodate precisely what an author has written; and also, an incapacity to appreciate what is going on in an argument, if what a writer is doing is other than arguing from within a system, that is, using argument in ways other than to justify factual statements. To repeat Stolzenberg's point above, one's entrapment within a system gives rise to a failure "to take into account considerations of standpoint that have the effect of *maintaining* the system." As an example, Feyerabend (1978) discusses how his attempts, in his *Against Method* (Feyerabend, 1975), to be ironic or to use mockery were systematically misinterpreted. As an example of a failure in reading, he discusses the following case (useful to us for how it exemplifies the two-sidedness of things claimed by Billig) in which he made what he thought was a claim of one particular kind, only to have it read as a claim of quite another kind by a critic, K:

> In AM Chapter 2 I write: 'My intention is not to replace one set of general rules by another such set: my intention is, rather, to convince the reader that *all methodologies even the most obvious ones, have their limits*. The best way to show this is to demonstrate the limits and even the irrationality of some rules which she or he is likely to regard as basic. In the case of induction . . . this means demonstrating how well the counter inductive procedure can be supported by argument': counter induction . . . [is] not introduced as [a] new method to *replace* induction or falsification . . . Yet K says that I have a methodology and that 'anything goes' is its 'central thesis' . . .
>
> (Feyerabend, 1978: 185–6)

In other words, his attempt, like Billig's, to show how arguments can reasonably be made out for *both* sides of a case, thus to show up the *limits* of method, that what one must deal with is *beyond* all methodology, is misinterpreted as him proposing yet *another* methodology! It is as if one can no more extract oneself from the 'tradition' within which one is embedded, which one has 'embodied', than one can jump out of one's skin.[3] But why is this? Why is it that, even in 'reflection', we seem unable easily to ironicize our standpoints? What is the source of the 'urges' or 'cravings' we feel to implement one, rather than another, way of knowing?

Narrative entrapments

The answer can be found, I feel, in an examination of the forms of "inner speech," or what Lyotard (1984) calls the *metadiscourses*, currently available to us in our 'thinking' (see Part II). Put this way, as Lyotard sees it, the term *modern* "designates any science that legitimates itself with reference to a metadiscourse . . . making an explicit appeal to some grand [meta]narrative" (1984: xxiii), while the term *postmodern* signifies an "incredulity toward metanarratives" (1984: xxiv). We have already examined in some detail the nature of the entrapments engendered by theoretical systems; here we must examine those created by narrative structures. I want to suggest that we should be not only incredulous towards grand narratives, but also suspicious of all stories, even little ones, for all are concerned with the 'urge' already mentioned above: the production of intelligibility, that is, the production of an *order*, capable of being grasped reflectively and intellectually (Mink, 1978).

As Kuhn (1962: 4–5) points out, organized, professionalized inquiry can only proceed when it has been decided what the fundamental entities are under investigation; how they interact with each other and with the senses; and what questions may be legitimately asked about them and what techniques employed in seeking solutions. And, just as in a court of law, where a witness's 'story' can, if told appropriately, work to specify quite precisely the evidence required to corroborate or refute it, so in the sciences, narratives function to construct the requirements in terms of which the reality they specify can be checked out. In other words, the narrative form not only 'lends' itself to but also can 'provide a unifying context for' a great variety of language games, and thus legitimate rational inquiry.

This, as Lyotard (1984) has pointed out, is just what in the past has happened: scientific activities have been justified by appeal to one or another "grand narrative," to the great narrative of the emancipation of humanity, or to the theoretical unity of all knowledge (underpinned by a philosophical system). But it is not just in science that narratives are important, they also have a number of important parts to play in everyday life; in particular, they provide the resources in terms of which the relation of knowledge production to the State is routinely formulated (such that it needs no justification, for it is shown to conform to 'who we are', to fit in with a nation's identity). For, a "narrative tradition" is, says Lyotard (1984: 21),

> the tradition of the criteria defining a three-fold competence – "know-how," "knowing-how-to-speak," and "knowing-how-to-hear" – through which the community's relation to itself is played out. What is transmitted through these narratives is the set of pragmatic rules that constitutes the social bond.

Where, as Lyotard (1984: 11) says elsewhere,

> Simplifying to the extreme, it is fair to say that in principle there have been, at least over the last half-century, two basic representational models for society: either society forms a functional whole, or it is divided in two.

Here, then, is our dilemma. We cannot, as Lyotard realizes, intellectually grasp the nature of the relation between our ways of knowing and the State in an orderly manner, in a way that allows explanations and predictions, unless we plump for one, or the other, of these two schemes. It is, as he says, "tempting to avoid the decision altogether by distinguishing two kinds of knowledge . . . [But] I find this solution unacceptable . . . [the] solution itself is still caught up within a type of oppositional thinking that is out of step with the most vital modes of postmodern knowledge" (1984: 14). As he sees it, what characterizes the pluralism of the postmodern condition is not so much oppositions, as a kind of non-oppositional diversity, represented by a lot of little functional wholes. Where these can all be characterized in terms of the concept of "language games," that is, as rule-governed systems. And this, too, as we shall see in the next chapter, is the solution also offered by Rorty (1989) and Bauman (1987). I want to say little more about it here, except to make three remarks. The first is that, as Wittgenstein points out (see Chapter 4), the choice Lyotard makes is a 'theoretical' choice, motivated by an urge *to explain* current circumstances. But in indulging that urge, he runs the risk of failing properly *to describe* what our current circumstances *are*.

Secondly, the theoretical choice he makes is *his* choice, not necessarily ours. In choosing ahead of time in favour of *orderly* systems, he precludes, once again, the possibility of these issues being debated in disorderly, more public forms of argumentation. Finally, he finds the two-sided, descriptive solution unacceptable, because, in interpreting our current circumstances only from within the either-or logic of systematic thinking, he finds it leads to the 'unbridgeable' divisions of "oppositional thinking that is out of step with the most vital forms of postmodern knowledge." The both-and logic of dialogue, of conversation as distinct from rule-governed discourse, however, as we shall see (Chapter 7), is to do precisely with the bridging of such gaps.

A research programme for a postmodern science of mind

In the light of all these concerns, how might we now proceed in a postmodern science of mental life? On the one hand, the switch from a detached, theoretical, individualistic standpoint to a practical, socially involved (interactionist and constructionist) stance for the conduct of socio-psychological inquiries opens up a whole new set of two-sided topics for investigation and questions about them. It suggests not only new forms of professional disciplinary inquiry and the means for validating their results, but also a new vocabulary for new conversations and debates about the nature of our ways of knowing, and their place within our everyday social lives. On the other hand, as I mentioned above, to participate in a conversation is not necessarily to participate in a disciplinary discourse, for, as Rorty (1980) points out, saying things is not always saying how things are. Often, conversational speech is simply responsive, not representational; in not "expressing a view about a subject" (1980: 371), a speaker can be expressing an evaluation, an attitude, an expression of how one is placed in relation to the point of view being expressed by another speaker.

In what follows, I shall not pursue this issue further. It is one thing to outline the context and the nature of disciplined inquiries within a postmodern scheme of things, and quite another to outline the character of the activity appropriate to their criticism (it will be there in abundance in subsequent chapters). In turning to the traditional psychological topics of investigation, although we may be suspicious of such 'origins', we must now see them all as structured or informed (if not in a grand narrative) at least by one or another *local* narrative: where, to repeat Lyotard's claim above, such narratives supply the set of pragmatic rules that constitute the social bond, and thus provide a framework for showing the relevance of the knowledge 'discovered' by such disciplines to our *social identities*, that is, its relevance to how we are 'placed' in relation to those around us. For clearly, a form of knowledge relevant to those at the centre of things, is seen by those at the margins as not only quite irrelevant, but also often as completely unintelligible. Postmodern 'scientific' knowledge thus requires contextualization: those to whom it is addressed require a grasp of 'where it is coming from'. It must be relevant to how people are placed in their world. For our *position*, our *situation*, has to do with the rights and duties, the privileges and obligations, the invitations and barriers to practical action 'afforded' us by our surroundings. Thus, in the context of practical, postmodern, daily social life, all our traditional topics of research in psychology must be seen in this new, contextualized, narrative light. Where the new narrative context legitimating our studies (formulated in one or another local versions) is the 'story' I have so far provided above, of our ways of knowing as being of a two-sided, rhetorically-responsive, socially constructed kind. In this light:

1 *Thinking* becomes, not a matter of computational processes, but *argumentative*: the image of thinking provided by information-processing and rule-following models "curiously demeans the nature of thought itself, for it describes processes which are principally thoughtless . . . Rules do not exist only to be followed: they also have to be created, interpreted and challenged" (Billig, 1986: 11; 1987). The whole new *rhetoric of inquiry* movement is explicitly a postmodernist enterprise (McCloskey, 1983; Nelson and Megill, 1986).

2 Talk of *motives* becomes talk of reasons for action, that is, justifications offered to others (and perhaps to oneself) in rendering one's actions reasonable or appropriate in their context of occurrence (Mills, 1940; Peters, 1958; Edwards and Potter, 1992) – while the study of practical action in a context becomes a *prospective* enterprise (see below).

3 Studies of *emotion*, too, become more concerned with 'movements' in one's position in relation to those around one: they can be viewed as "transitory social roles" (Averill, 1980), and accounted for in terms of one's (moral) relations to others (Harré, 1986e).

4 Studies of *memory* cease to be about the nature of 'storage' and 'retrieval' (of a present record of past events) and become (as Bartlett, 1932, originally formulated the problem) studies of collective remembering (Middleton and Edwards, 1990), or of socially constructed memories (Bransford *et al.*, 1977; Meacham, 1977),

and indeed, of socially constructed amnesias also (Jacoby, 1975); remembering in a social group clearly raises matters of authority, and the right to formulate what is to count as the group's memory, as well as what should be taken as the relevant materials for the formulation.

5 *Learning* ceases to be the sole process for the gaining of knowledge; and knowledge ceases to be solely an epistemological matter: it becomes an ontological one also. For only those who are already constituted as *socially* competent within a particular setting can go out and gather 'information' about the nature of that setting in a wholly individualistic way; but they cannot gain their social competence in that setting in the same way. That involves a different kind of 'learning' altogether; it involves 'instruction' by another person, an interactive process – indeed, it involves acquiring the knowledge of how to collaborate effectively in institutions of learning (Shotter, 1984; Vygotsky, 1986; Wertsch, 1991).

6 To be instructed in how "to be" in different particular settings is to be instructed in the accepted ways (procedures) of making sense of the "affordances" (to use a Gibsonian term) available to one in that setting. *Perception* thus takes on a noncognitive, ontological aspect; and studies of perception become concerned with (a) what there is available to be perceived in one's surroundings; (b) the strategies or procedures required to 'pick up' the information available; and (c) the nature of the social conditions required for their development – much of this work is now being pursued by those taking an 'ecological' approach to perception (Gibson, 1979).

7 Finally, *language* is no longer seen as serving solely a representative function, but as also being *formative*; that is, rather than being of use merely to refer to circumstances within a situation, it functions to formulate the situations in which we are involved *as* situations, *as* states of affairs, to formulate them as common 'places' in terms of which we can relate ourselves to one another, to 'lend' them a form which they 'afford' or 'permit' but which they would not, in themselves, otherwise have (Harris, 1981; Mills, 1940; Wittgenstein, 1953). Indeed, rather than our mental processes, our 'thoughts' being the source of our talk, what our 'thoughts' *are* is also constituted or formulated in our talk (Edwards and Potter, 1992).

These reorientations in attitude towards the major topics of psychological investigation outlined above are merely general; rather than settling their nature, they all become, in Gallie's (1962: 169) terms, "essentially contested" concepts, that is, concepts "the proper use of which involves endless disputes about their proper usage on the part of their users." But what is clear is that their effective investigation will not be a matter of 'proving a theory true' but of exploring the scope and limits of a *practical procedure* informed by an image or paradigm (the intersubjective 'feelings' against which the adequacy of a theory's formulation is judged) shared among the members of a research community (McGuire, 1973; Smedslund, 1980). The empirical content of a science can then be judged, not in terms of its possession of true theories, but in terms of the number of interpretative standpoints which have won a place within it (Toulmin, 1982), that is, the degree of systematic (or disciplined) pluralism it affords.

In such circumstances, the "essentially contested" nature of concepts becomes the norm. This does not mean that such concepts are therefore unusable; it simply means that their usage becomes itself a research topic – the science must possess the resources to ironicize its own claims. It also means that the very hurly-burly of social life, as an ecology of interdependent, local, *heterogeneous*, regions and moments of self-reproducing orderliness, suspended in a more chaotic (but 'nutrient') medium, requires study (Prigogine and Stengers, 1984) – not now as if from a position on another planet, but from within the finitude of our own situation, from how we find ourselves historically placed, our current 'placement' being itself a contested topic of research.

Concluding comments

What is utterly strange to us at the moment – because, whenever we attempt to engage in rational discussion of its nature, we mystify ourselves by routinely adopting a decontextualized, theoretical stance – is our ordinary world of everyday social life. A postmodernist approach to its understanding requires us, first and foremost, to abandon the "grand narrative" of a theoretical unity of knowledge, and to be content with more local and practical aims. This means abandoning one of the deepest assumptions (and hopes) of Enlightenment thought: that what is 'really' available for perception 'out there' is an orderly and systematic world (potentially) the same for all of us – such that, if we really persist in our investigations and arguments we will ultimately secure universal agreement about its nature. But we also should note that although no such unity as yet exists, and experts continue to argue as to what might lead to its discovery, everyday social life still continues in spite of its disorderliness. Our failure to understand how this is possible is an important failure: we continue to treat what is probably a unity of *heterogeneity* (that is, a system of differences) as if it is a unity of *homogeneity* (a system of similarities).

In other words, our failure stems not just from the atomistic individualism implicit in modernism – which has it that people can be treated for the purposes of science as the indistinguishable atoms of physics – but also from us committing what Bhaskar (1989) calls "the epistemic fallacy": our reformulation of (ontological) questions of *being* in terms of our *knowledge* of being. Although I disagree with Bhaskar about the precise character of the ontological dimension he proposes (Shotter, 1990a; 1992), and about the separation of ontological from epistemological questions,[4] I am in total agreement with him about the necessity for social theorists to concern themselves with ontological matters. Indeed, my arguments above have mostly been 'conditions of possibility' arguments in the ontological sphere, that is to say (metaphorical) accounts of what something must *be* like for it to be able to produce what we already know of and take to be a real part of our existence. This also, I might add, is what gives a social constructionist approach a *critical* dimension,[5] for the formulation of ontological forms of talk not derived from prior epistemological forms provides us with a means for confronting claims to knowledge with the question: 'Could it be otherwise?' Thus, as Bhaskar (1989: 23–24) points out about his own *transcendental realism*:

> It entails the acceptance of (i) the principle of *epistemic relativity*, which states that all beliefs are socially produced, so that all knowledge is transient, and neither truth-values nor criteria of rationality exist outside historical time. But it entails the rejection of (ii) the doctrine of *judgemental* [or moral] *relativity*, which maintains that all beliefs are equally valid, in the sense that there can be no rational grounds for preferring one to another.

And I also would like to make the same claim, except to add that the rational grounds of which Bhaskar speaks cannot be grasped by the forms of explanatory social science he envisages. As I see it, justifying one's claims to knowledge comes to an end, not by their being linked to supposedly scientifically proved propositions, but by their 'placement' within a way of being and acting, a tradition of argumentation, or, in Wittgenstein's (1953) terms, particular *forms of life*, and good reasons being offered for them from within that tradition. In other words, a complex relation between people's identities and their 'hook-up' to their surroundings is involved (Chapter 4; Shotter, 1990b), a relation which a postmodern psychology must explore.

Without exploring it any further here, we can still draw the following conclusions. Although the postmodern *self* may be something of a mosaic, no self is completely an island. In postmodern everyday life, as well as in postmodern science, one occupies a multiplicity of standpoints, each within at least a local community; and within such communities there are standards, ways of judging, to which one must conform if one is be accounted a member. This does not mean, however, that it is only the standards within one's own 'clan' which count. For along with one's own ways of judging, one can ask: 'Could they be otherwise?', 'What other ways of judging might be possible?' And it would be intellectually irresponsible (as well as being rude, unjust, illegal, libelous, partisan, discriminatory, etc.) to ignore those who judge their lives in other ways, and not to treat their claims seriously too. As Toulmin (1982) points out, from the postmodern standpoint questions of *justice* take an equal place in the forum of scientific judgement with those of *truth*. Indeed, we may find that on different occasions, for different purposes, we have *good reasons* for switching from one standpoint to another, for taking up a position within a different community of inquiry. But none (of our reasons) will have the absolute 'knockdown' certainty we crave, because there are no universally accepted systems of knowledge to which to appeal. So, although we can find reasons for preferring some ways of life to others, no single way of life is obviously best – and that is, perhaps, just as well!

TWO

Power on the margins:
A new place for
intellectuals to be

Living as we did — on the edge — we developed a particular way of seeing reality. We looked both from the outside in and from the inside out. We focussed our attention upon the centre as well on the margin. We understood both. This mode of seeing reminded us of the existence of a whole universe, a main body made up of both margin and centre. Our survival depended upon an ongoing public awareness of the separation between margin and centre and an ongoing private acknowledgment that we were a necessary, vital part of that whole.

(Hooks, 1984: ix)

In the view of knowledge discussed so far, it is difficult to separate our idea of what knowledge is from our talk about it. As I have already suggested, the focus of our studies has shifted. We no longer want to locate an already determined, *real* world beyond the social and historical, and to attempt to discover this world in the depths of either people's organic or psychic nature, or, perhaps, in abstract principles or systems. Then, it was the task of language accurately to represent the reality of these (hidden) worlds. But now, many take seriously Foucault's (1972: 49) claim that our task "consists of not — of no longer — treating discourses as groups of signs (signifying elements referring to contents or representations) but as practices that systematically form the objects of which they speak."

In other words, when we talk about such entities as 'society', 'social relations', 'history', 'the individual', 'the self', 'persons', 'language', 'communication' — as well as 'ideology' — we can no longer assume that we all know perfectly well what the 'it' is that is represented by the concept of the entity we are talking about. It is not just that these concepts are "essentially contested" concepts and involve "endless disputes about their proper use on the part of their users," as Gallie (1962: 123) claims. It is that the entities they are supposed to represent are not 'already there' in existence in a wholly determinate form, prior to our talk 'about' them. Thus the disputes involved are deeper than just with matters of the proper use of language, for they are not about what already exists. They are, so some of us claim, to do with attempting to make new forms of human being *possible* – for "to imagine a language is to imagine a form of life" (Wittgenstein, 1953: no. 19). Thus, in the social constructionist approach I want to explore, new ways of talking do not always merely redescribe (Rorty, 1989) what already exists. In revealing new possibilities for human beings and in instituting new forms of human relationship, they can involve genuine political struggles to do with bringing new forms of social life into existence.

Given such a claim, the subversion of older, systematic, objective realist ways of talking by social constructionist versions, does not just involve the substitution of one 'view' of things by another. The fact that we now seem to lack secure, agreed, principled foundations upon which to base our claims about already existing cir-cumstances is an indication of a change in our practical-social ways of doing things. In fact, what I want to claim in this chapter is that, in one of its versions, the shift can be seen not only as a change in the general 'shape' of our society, but in particular as a change in the position, role and skills of professional academics. Thus, in attempting to say something about these changes, my concern in this chapter is to try to rethink the nature of social life, not in terms of how it appears to us academics from within the orderly 'disciplines' we occupy in our more pro-fessional moments – as consisting in either a system or a plurality of systems – but to explore instead what it might look like from a position located more in the zones, the boundaries, the margins, the everyday public spaces, between the more systematic institutions we occupy in those, for us, extraordinary, that is to say, rationally invisible,[1] moments, the moments when we exist as ordinary people. We need to imagine what it might be like to live, not only in a genuinely pluralistic world, only fragmentarily known and only partially shared, but also in a differentiated world, in which its marginal regions are of very different character to its central ones.

If we are to do this, we must rethink not only the nature of our social lives but also the nature of language and thought as possessing, within these (for us) extra-ordinary regions and moments, a non-systematic, formative or creative character – for it must (as we shall see) have the ability to 'bridge' what are otherwise not obviously connected aspects of people's lives. And this will be to privilege the role of rhetoric in these marginal regions over that of logic. Furthermore, we must rethink the workings of ideology and power in the same way, that is, as not exerted by individual agents in the control of cause and effect processes at the centre, but as formative, to do with the shaping – in communication with genuinely different other people – of a collective, sharable form of life, so that all come to live in a 'world' of their own making. Indeed, to repeat a theme which I shall reiterate throughout this chapter, it is precisely at these moments of indeterminacy, undecidability and ambivalence, in which different people meet each other in the socially constructive encounters in everyday life, that political struggles are their most intense, and where ideology can be detected at work.

Ideology critique: versions of realism and
social constructionism

Turning to the question of ideology critique in these present circumstances, we can note that in recent times, the concept of ideology has been in trouble (Eagleton, 1991; Billig, 1991; Simons and Billig, in press). The 'realist' framework, within which discussion of 'already existing' social conditions was theorized and criticized, has seemingly been undermined. "Realism as trust in language is no longer readily available" (Baumgarten, 1982: 117). Indeed, as one aspect of its current problematic nature, Eagleton lists sixteen distinct and often mutually incompatible definitions of ideology. Clearly, it *is* the case that we no longer know what the 'it' is that we are talking about when we try to talk about ideology.

This, at least to those of us on the left who worry about such things as social justice and feel that it is one of the tasks of intellectuals to understand the nature and conditions of human emancipation, is cause for concern. For politically, the point in discussing the functioning of a supposed *ideology* (or ideologies) within a society – as distinct, say, from the overall character of its social life (its ethos) – was to focus upon the question of why, in the struggles and contests that still arise in people's different attempts to express themselves within that society in peaceful, rational ways, it is almost always the case that certain groups of people seem (unfairly?) to prevail over others. Ideology critique has been concerned, then, to study just those aspects of human knowledge and communication which seem to prevent human emancipation rather than to promote it, which seem to establish social injustices rather than alleviate them. Thus politically, the concept of ideology functioned as an intellectual instrument in terms of which to criticize a society's functioning from within. Is there any way in which we can recover it? Eagleton (1991: 221) concludes that "the rationalist view of ideologies as conscious, well-articulated systems of belief is clearly inadequate." We must now explore the idea that ideological issues are fought out in the actual, practical circumstances of communicative activities and practices in everyday life. As Eagleton (1991: 223) puts it, ideology becomes "a matter of 'discourse' rather than 'language' – of certain concrete discursive effects, rather than of signification as such. It represents the points where power impacts upon certain utterances and inscribes itself tacitly within them."

To an extent in line with Eagleton's suggestions above, the stance I shall argue for in this chapter is a social constructionist one – in which all the topics of interest to us are located in the communicative processes between people – but it is a stance in which realist and social constructionist claims (although always contestable) are not in fact incompatible: for claims about the social constructions people *could* produce remain purely theoretical or idealist unless also accompanied by some kind of claims about the actual or real possibilities (and resources required) for such constructions to be available to them in their circumstances. It is just that claims about the possibilities and resources in fact available to them must, like claims about the constructions they might produce, also be warranted in some way from within the contingent flow of continuous communicative interaction between the human beings involved. We might call the kind of realism involved a non-systematic, situated realism.[2]

This focus upon the actual 'formative' or 'form-giving' moment in speech communication, as distinct from that which takes a retrospective view of linguistic systems of meaning as its central concern, is, as I see it, an issue that separates different strands in the social constructionist movement. Very roughly, this strand can be characterized in terms of its focus upon "words in their speaking," while other strands focus upon the characteristics of "already spoken words." This latter strand – which later, I shall claim, is still in thrall of the "systematic spirit" of the Enlightenment (Cassirer, 1951) – is influenced primarily by the writings of Derrida and Rorty, and emphasizes already existing, decontextualized systems of conventionalized meanings or usages; while the first – in its dialogical, not its monological, individualistic, romanticist form – is primarily influenced by Wittgenstein (1953), Vygotsky (1987), Bakhtin (1986) and Billig (1987), and emphasizes the unique, social, relational (and intrapersonal) functions of situated language use. And it is from within this dialogical strand of the movement that I want to attempt my recovery of the concept of ideology. For if it is only at the actual point of contact between people, in the course of a communicative exchange between them, that the asymmetries in power between them become apparent, that their differential access to resources is exhibited, then there is no prior, external, Archimedean point from which critique can be conducted. Critics must also locate themselves at points, positions, places and moments such as these.

Hence the point of this chapter's title: for it is by definition those on or in the margins of social life, not in the centre of things, who lack power. Indeed, it is in the very nature of the phenomenology of power that those at the centre who have it experience its workings the least. In their world, opportunities open themselves up before them; to have power is to find no resistance to the realization of one's desires. The kind of power of interest to us is not power at the centre, but that at work *between* centre and margins. It is those without power who find at every turn resistances to the realization of their desires. Indeed, they find that it is precisely in the 'formative' or 'form-giving' function of speech they lack the power to participate. They find that certain ways of talking, with their associated forms of life, are already in operation such that, whatever their own experience, whatever their particular projects, they must be formulated, that is, given intelligible and legitimate form, within a certain "vocabulary of motives" (Mills, 1940) not of their own making. They must be seen as intelligibly related to what are taken, by certain other groups, to be ultimates in justificatory conversation. Indeed, at any one moment, these 'basic' ways of talking can seem to be so pervasive (and persuasive) that although there are clearly many other important spheres of human activity, they *dominate* a people's form of life in the following (judgemental) sense: given that the people in a society mutually judge and correct each other as to the 'fittingness' of their actions to what they take *their* (whose?) ultimate reality to be – if, that is, they are to sustain those intralinguistic realities in existence by continually remaking them in their everyday, social activities — it is in this 'basic' kind of talk that all such ultimate judging and evaluating, that is to say, final accounting, must take place. Indeed, as Wittgenstein (1953: no. 242) insists, "if language is to be a means of communication there must be agreement not only in definitions but also (queer as this may sound) in judgments."

But whose intralinguistic reality is it?

But the question is, within *whose* intralinguistic realities is all this judging and correcting to be done? This, I think, is the ideological question. For ideological influences are at work in our very attempts to formulate our utterances and to have them taken seriously by our listeners. Indeed, as Bakhtin (1986: 121–2) says:

> A word (or in general any sign) is interindividual. Everything that is said, expressed, is located outside the 'soul' of the speaker and does not belong only to him. The word cannot be assigned to a single speaker. The author (speaker) has his own inalienable right to the word, but the listener has his rights, and those whose voices are heard in the word before the author comes upon it also have their rights (after all, there are no words that belong to no one).

Indeed, as he adds later (1986: 293–4), a word becomes 'one's own':

> only when the speaker populates it with his own intentions, his own accent, when he appropriates the word, adapting it to his own semantic and expressive intention. Prior to this moment of appropriation, the word does not exist in a neutral and impersonal language (it is not, after all, out of a dictionary that the speaker gets his words!), but rather it exists in other people's mouths, in other people's contexts, serving other people's intentions: it is from there that one must take the word, and make it one's own.

And, as he could also have added, it also only becomes one's own when the others addressed by one's utterances are prepared to listen to them, and to hear in them one's own accent or tone, one's own semantic and expressive intentions, the 'shaping' one gives to it that is expressive of one's own very being. It is here, at these moments, when meanings are being 'negotiated' (to put it mildly) or 'fought over' (to put it more strongly), that politics is at its most acute.

If we turn now to the other social constructionist strand exemplified in some of Rorty's (1982, 1989) writings, we can perhaps now see why it is not without a certain degree of irritation and disdain that they are viewed on the left. For in dropping the idea of language as being 'about' the world, as working to represent one or another reality, Rorty seems to have retained the Enlightenment idea of the philosopher's task: that as professionals it is still their task, monologically and in detached contemplation, to find, and to specify ahead of time, the nature of that deeper, ahistorical order of things behind appearances; only now, he claims, that order of things is to be found solely within certain, systematic ways of talking, within particular "final vocabularies," or "language games." Yet, for the 'players' within them, the 'users' of them, these 'games' seemingly have no point of contact with a reality that is 'other than' the speaker's own; they speak seemingly into a resistance-free context. Indeed, as he says (Rorty, 1989: 21), "it is essential to my view that we have no prelinguistic consciousness to which language needs to be adequate, no deep sense of how things are which it is the duty of philosophers to spell out in language." Thus much of what those on the left still care about he finds ridiculous or ludicrous; as for the notion of ideology, as Eagleton (1991: ix) points out, Rorty finds it "useless" (Rorty, 1989: 59). As he sees it, "a liberal society is one which is content to call 'true' (or 'right' or 'just') whatever . . . view wins in free and open encounter" (67), where such encounters can only concern, not the description of any 'actual' or real' states of affairs, but only the different "final vocabularies" people use in justifying their beliefs, actions and lives to themselves and to the 'us' who share in the vocabulary.

So, although one may have felt at first attracted by the idea that discourses constitute the objects of which they speak, one's feelings of frustration and disempowerment increase when one discovers what seems to be entailed in Rorty's version of this claim. For, continuing with what he has to say about the nature of our "final vocabularies," we find that those who hold them (Rorty calls them "liberal ironists") both have "radical and continuing doubts about the final vocabulary [they] currently use," and realize that "argument phrased in [their] current vocabulary can neither underwrite nor dissolve these doubts" (Rorty, 1989: 73). Indeed, the only recourse available to us (if we are to follow the form of life his language game entails) seems to be that of trying to make our own views look good and our opponent's look bad, where the liberal ironist realizes "that anything can be made to look good or bad by being redescribed" (1989: 73). But why is this? Why is it a mere matter of what 'looks' good or bad, or, merely a matter of what can be 'talked of' as such? Why cannot people argue for their vocabularies, for a way of talking which, they claim, reveals actual aspects of their social lives hidden by other forms of talk? For Rorty (as for Lyotard), all these questions are answered by the crucial fact that, at least as he sees it, rational argumentation *can only occur within a language game*. For, he claims:

> When the notion of 'description of the world' is moved from the level of criterion-governed sentences within language games to language games as wholes, games which we do not choose between by reference to criteria, the idea that the world decides which descriptions are true can no longer be given a clear sense.
>
> (Rorty, 1989: 5)

This is the critical move. For, as he sees it, not all words are meaningful: "To have a meaning is to have a place in a language game. Metaphors, by definition do not" (1989: 18). Thus, for him, only certain words are meaningful. This is not because (as I have been assuming) utterances can have, in their very nature, a formative or shaping function – the ability to give form to feeling, to formulate linguistically our embodied 'sense' of our circumstances – but because their use is rule-governed.

Their meaning is a consequence of the existence of a prior order; a system of already established, conventionalized meanings.

It is this move, however, that I think is a major mistake: While the idea that "the world decides which descriptions are true" may not make much sense *theoretically* outside the context of a language game, it is not difficult to find a sense for it within everyday, *practical* contexts of communication. Indeed, when we move from a retrospective, decontextualized concern with the characteristics of "already spoken words," and turn to a focus upon the use of "words in their speaking" in a context, then I think it is perfectly possible to see how, in particular practical communicative contexts, it is always possible to argue that one's claims, if not exactly corresponding in every detail to 'the world', are such that they are at least permitted by, or afforded by, the circumstances prevailing in those contexts. In other words, our talk *can* bear in an important sense upon what is *real* in those contexts, even though others may contest what we say, and claim that other (and better!) accounts capture what our circumstances afford more adequately. But more than that – and here is another crucial feature missed in Rorty's individualistic, privatized approach to language and speech communication – the words we use to describe our circumstances, whether contested for their adequacy or not, may not just be chosen as we please. For again, as Bakhtin (1981: 293) puts it,

> there are no 'neutral' words and forms – words and forms that can belong to 'no one'; language has been completely taken over, shot through with intentions and accents. For any individual consciousness living in it, language is not an abstract system of normative forms but rather a concrete heteroglot conception of the world. All words have the 'taste' of a profession, a genre, a tendency, a party, a particular work, a particular person, a generation, an age group, the day and hour. Each word tastes of the context and contexts in which it has lived its socially charged life . . . The word in language is half someone else's. It becomes 'one's own' only when the speaker populates it with his own intention, his own accent . . .

But given the 'tastes' of past usages, language does not pass

> freely and easily into the private property of the speaker's intentions; it is populated – overpopulated – with the intentions of others. So, although the meaning of a word is to do with how it is used by the speaker at the point of contact between the speaker and those to whom the speaker's words are addressed, a word is not available to be used in just way the speaker pleases. Expropriating it, forcing it to submit to one's own intentions and accents, is a difficult and complicated process

(Bakhtin, 1981: 294)

Thus if we ask now, "Whose intralinguistic reality must we participate in constructing, if we are to read Rorty's text with understanding?" we find that it is not just Rorty's own idiosyncratic form of life, but that of a philosopher in the *analytic tradition* that is at issue.

The "systematic spirit"

To see this, we can ask a series of questions. Why is it that, in Rorty's version of social constructionism (and in the other 'postmodern' versions similar to it), issues such as those raised by Bakhtin are missed? How is it that we find in Rorty no discussion of the role of dialogue, or of the dialogic nature of language;[3] no provision for non-systematic argumentation, for the rhetorical discussion of the possible; no discussion of practical reasoning in practical contexts or of how initial misunderstandings might be resolved in social negotiations? How is that, although Rorty (1989: 189) says that what "I have been urging in this book is that we try *not* to want something that stands beyond history and institutions," the actual making of history or the emergence of genuine novelty seems to be impossible in his world — for, as Rorty (1989: 99) sees it, there are "only little mortal things to be rearranged before being redescribed"? Why is it, given that he sees the function of conversation as being to do with the generation of new descriptions and "as the ultimate context within which knowledge is to be understood" (Rorty, 1980: 389), that he provides no *rational* role for free and open conversation, claiming that all of rational importance can only go on within a language game, within *systematic*, rule-governed ways of talking? Thus, strong poets (and Madison Avenue executives?) rather than ordinary people are the heroes of his society, because in the "free and open encounters" he envisions, the poet's ways of talking is the talk that will win out.

And finally, why is it that, although he distinguishes between "normal," mainstream, systematic philosophers who are constructive and offer arguments, and "abnormal," peripheral, edifying philosophers who are reactive and offer satires, parodies and aphorisms (Rorty, 1980: 369) — and clearly casts himself in the latter role — he has such trouble with understanding "otherness," with trying "to extend our sense of 'we' to people whom we have previously thought of as 'they'" (Rorty, 1989: 192)? How does he envision his relation to 'us', his readers? Where does Rorty position himself in our current social scheme of things such that he still feels confident that he will be listened to and taken seriously, even though he casts himself into such a (supposedly) marginal role? What actually is Rorty's image of a living society?

As he himself says (as I noted earlier), "it is pictures rather than propositions, metaphors rather than statements, which determine most of our philosophical convictions" (Rorty, 1980: 12), thus, if we are to take him at his word, to answer the questions above, we must seek the 'pictures' and 'metaphors' that currently shape his philosophical activities. But where should we locate our search? Clearly in the history of his philosophical "final vocabulary".[4] What is the overall 'formative or organizational tendency' present in Rorty's writing that gives it its style? The tensions and tendencies in Rorty's ways of working, in his practices (rather than his claims), can be explained, I think, by the still unreconstructed Enlightenment concerns — the 'taste' of past usages — his vocabulary incorporates. In other words, he embodies precisely the "systematic spirit," along with the analytic method, described by Cassirer (1951) as characterizing the style of Enlightenment philosophizing.

Without a *framework* within which to interlink contingent facts into a system, no rational explanations of phenomena are possible. It is this that Rorty is unwilling to embrace; he is still writing within the tradition of analytic philosophy.[5] He is still concerned to explain phenomena by analysing them into their supposed observable elements and their orderly interconnections; to produce a monological, ahistorical, detached, theoretical account that can specify ahead of time the order of things behind appearances – thus, to show us, by comparison with supposedly more 'traditional' accounts, the extent of our current mistakes and misunderstandings. He claims, for instance, that morality lacks any 'deep' justifications to be found in anything we share in common form with all other human beings. For him, morality just is a social practice, and "'moral principles' . . . are reminders of, abbreviations for, such practices, not justifications for such practices . . . [such that] the core meaning of 'immoral action' is the sort of thing *we* don't do" (Rorty, 1989: 58–9). For him, there is either *one*, correct, theoretically well-grounded answer (which many are now agreed is unlikely) to a problem, or no answers at all can be well grounded. While he could treat "moral principles," not as reminders, but as versions, as people's formulations of certain, deeply sensed aspects of the human condition,[6] which others see as justified but contest on the grounds of their partiality, their favouring of some aspects of our condition over others.

But, as he sees it, if no theoretically well-grounded justification for the existence of such a sense of solidarity with others can be given, then, it is justified to claim its non-existence – because we do not have to listen to arguments not "from the interior of a language game" (Rorty, 1989: 47). This, I submit, is for Rorty a move to the centre, a move away from the marginal position of the edifying, responsive, ironic philosopher he first presented himself as being, towards once again the position of the professional analytic philosopher at the centre of things, whose task it is make things orderly, in order to explain, predict and control. Thus, consistent with analyses in terms of unitary, systematic language games, we find he assumes for societies also single, all-encompassing, monolithic forms of social life, forms of solidarity. Where "our sense of solidarity is strongest when those with whom solidarity is expressed are thought of as 'one of us', where 'us' means something smaller and more local than the human race" (Rorty, 1989: 191), where in fact, "'us' is, typically, contrastive in the sense that it contrasts with a 'they' which is also made up of human beings – the wrong sort of human beings" (1989: 190). This systematic, monolithic form of life, I submit, is not exactly the 'picture' of our societies we require if we are to make sense of what we now take our pluralistic, postmodern, social conditions to be. While Rorty may help us negatively, in understanding what might *prevent* us from properly grasping how language constitutes reality, it is difficult to see what *positively* he provides by way of alternative pictures and metaphors that might break the hold of the systematic spirit upon us. Where might we search for an alternative vision?

Before I suggest my own answer to this question, let me examine Bauman's (1987) answer, for not only has Bauman been particularly concerned with the relation between postmodernity and the function of the intellectual in society, but his views parallel those of many others, such as Habermas (1979, 1984). In his view, the movement from a state of modernity to postmodernity *is* a movement from a view of the world as a systematic totality to a pluralism of different orders or systems. "The typical post-modern view of the world is, in principle, one of an unlimited number of models of order, each one generated by a relatively auto-nomous set of practices" (Bauman, 1987: 4). Hence, like Rorty, he believes: "There are no criteria for evaluating local practices which are situated outside traditions, outside 'localities'. Systems of knowledge may only be evaluated from 'inside' their respective traditions." Thus, as he sees it, although intellectuals have now lost their modernist position as legitimators and legislators at the centre of an "orderly total-ity," they can become interpreters or translators, working from 'inside' various dif-ferent systems of knowledge. "What remains for intellectuals to do, is to interpret such meanings [as those in which a community is founded] for the benefit of those who are not of the community which stands behind the meanings; to mediate the communication between 'finite provinces' or 'communities of meaning'," he says (Bauman, 1987: 197). Thus, in this view, intellectuals still occupy a position inside *a system* of one kind or another (albeit not now one very big one), and they are still concerned to play the same language game that Enlightenment, analytical intellectuals have always tried to play, one way or another, that is to say, monologically, to represent its supposed hidden or underlying character accurately within a unified system of knowledge from the standpoint of a detached observer. In other words, Bauman's view of the intellectual as an interpreter clearly does not involve any very radical change in our roles or skills. We speak from a privileged centre still, albeit now one of a more local kind. What goes on in the boundary zones, in the margins between the orderly and systematic centres, is, it seems, none of our concern.

The move to the boundaries: joint action

However, if we no longer feel motivated to participate in these 'analytic' language games — producing representations of supposed realities behind appearances — and would like to engage more directly in current social and political issues (being prepared to risk having what we say challenged by ordinary people), how might we now best proceed? How might we move away from the Olympian, disembodied, individualistic and personally uninvolved standpoints which, as academics, we have adopted in the past, standpoints from which we have attempted to provide *theoretical* accounts of (assumed already) *systematic* states of affairs? Instead, what might it be like to be embodied, interested persons, living in the as yet unsystematized bound-ary zones between systematic centres, i.e., on the margins, facing the task of speci-fying or articulating the character of life within those zones practically and dialogically, in interaction with the others around one? What might help to break the hold of the Enlightenment, monologic, analytic, systematic spirit upon us?

As a first step, it is at this point, in attempting to characterize the nature of those dialogical moments, in which a second person spontaneously responds to the actions or utterances of a first, that I would like to return to the concept of "joint action"

I introduced earlier (Shotter, 1980). For us as intellectuals, this is a very unusual kind of activity; as intellectuals, we pay most attention to those kinds of activity in which we suppose people to know what they are doing, in which they put their plans into action, or theories into practice. But as I mentioned earlier, there are many other human activities in which – though we may be loath to admit it – we all remain deeply ignorant as to what we are doing, or why we are doing it. Not because the 'ideas' or whatever, supposedly in us somewhere informing our actions, are too deeply buried to bring out into the light of day, but because the formative influences shaping our conduct are not wholly there, in our individual heads, to be brought out. Activity of this kind occurs in response to what others have already done, and we act just as much 'into' the opportunities and invitations, or 'against' the barriers and restrictions they offer or afford us, as 'out of' any plans or desires of our own. Thus, the stony looks, the nods of agreement, the failures of interest, the asking of questions, these all go towards what it is one feels one can, or cannot, do or say in such situations. This is joint action; it is a spontaneous, unselfconscious, unknowing (although not unknowledgeable) kind of activity.

Let me repeat in slightly more detail its ideal characteristics. As I see it, joint action has two major features: It gives rise to *unintended consequences*, that is, outcomes which are not intended either by *you* or by *me*, but which in fact are *our* outcomes. However, as they cannot be traced back to the intentions of any particular individuals, it seems *as if* they have a 'given', 'natural', or 'externally caused' nature, that is to say, they are *real* in the sense of being independent of the desires or opinions of any of the particular individuals involved.[7] Also, as human activity, joint action still has *intentionality*, that is, at any one moment in time the outcomes people construct between them have a meaning or significance, such that only certain further activities will 'fit' and be appropriate, while others will be sensed as unfitting or inappropriate and will be ignored or even sanctioned. In other words, as an outcome of the joint action between them, people find themselves 'in' a seemingly 'given' situation, an 'organized' situation that has a 'horizon' to it and is 'open' to their actions. Indeed, its 'organization' is such that the constraints (and enablements) it makes available influence, that is to say, 'invite' or 'inhibit', people's next possible actions. Above, I called these features ideal for the following reason: in the terminology I introduced earlier, if it is in the self–other dimension of joint action that our person–world dimension of interaction is produced, then only if everyone is able freely to participate in that dimension can the person–world dimension of interaction be truly independent of any particular individuals or groups – otherwise, so to speak, these two dimensions are not orthogonal to each other, the person–world dimension is 'infected' by events in the self–world dimension.

It is in this way that joint activity is important, much more important, I would argue, than those actions in which people supposedly *do* know what they are doing. For it is in joint action with others, in sustaining between ourselves what Giddens (1979) and Bhaskar (1989)[8] have called the "unacknowledged (background) conditions" of our social actions, that we continually participate in recreating those circumstances in which, mysteriously, some feel much more at home than others.

They do so because the circumstances in question are *theirs* – they have had more to do with their construction than others. We may attempt, in such situations, to appropriate their words for our use, but (as Bakhtin noted) it is not that easy; a 'taste' of their past usage remains.

We, as academics, do of course often occupy such boundary or marginal regions – but not if we can help it. It is not in those situations that we experience ourselves as having our ordinary, everyday, professional being. Those situations are occupied by the 'others' who lack what 'we' prize: the rational 'power' (at least to seek) to put our own considered plans into action, or tested theories into practice. In those places, power is exerted on the spot, not so much thoughtlessly as planlessly, in a 'streetwise' way we academics do not understand, and disdain. Given a preference, those places are not among our preferred places to be; we prefer places upon the podia, in front of 'civilized' and 'disciplined' audiences. We, in our language games, still want to sustain our own forms of life.

And this is why – when claiming to represent the needs of others unlike ourselves, the poor and the oppressed, those 'outside' our language games – we fail to grasp why our representations of them are demeaning. We exclude their voices; they can play no part in those fleeting, extraordinary moments of indeterminacy, undecidability and ambivalence, when we determine each other's being, each other's identities. Our conversational politics excludes them. By our insistence upon the use of certain 'professional' textual practices, we do not allow ourselves to be influenced in our identities, as the academic professionals we are. Thus, no matter how benevolent we may be towards those we study – no matter how concerned with 'their' liberation, with 'their' betterment, with preventing 'their' victimization, etc. – the fact is that 'we' do not make sense of 'their' lives in 'their' terms. 'We' do not even make sense of 'their' lives 'with them', thus to arrive at a version upon a common 'ground' between 'us', that is, not 'us' here, but 'us' here and 'them' there as a new 'us'. While what they say is treated as 'data', they themselves are not treated seriously as being able to speak the truth about their own lives; their claims do not pass 'our' institutional tests. Thus, although our social scientific 'findings', as a relation of dependency between cause and effect, may institute a relation of domination between us and them, they are silenced. They must live lives described publicly in ways which makes sense only to those who 'rule' them. And we, in our preferred mode of being, sustain this dominant (and dominating) mode of talk, for we as yet still do not possess a way of representing these extraordinary, marginal moments institutionally.

Common-sense traditions of argumentation:
practical-moral action

Here, it will be useful to take another step in the attempt to break the hold of the systematic spirit upon us: reminding ourselves of Billig's work mentioned earlier, we can move from the idea of knowledge as only existing in already interconnected, unitary 'bodies' of knowledge, to the idea of it existing as a fragmentary, and even two-sided, *resource* – from which systematic bodies of knowledge might be fashioned – but which does not itself already exist as a system. Billig (1987: 41) traces the origins of the idea that such processes are two-sided, back to the origins of Rhetoric and to the claim of Diogenes Laertius that Protagoras was "the first person who asserted that in every question there were two sides to the argument exactly opposite to one another." Although there are many important implications of this view of knowledge – as fragmentary resource rather than as a system – the aspect of importance to us here is the opportunity it affords us of conceiving of the tradition, or culture, or ideology associated with a form of life as consisting in something other than a system. Instead, we can think of it as consisting in a continuously developing, historically and socially extended argument, embodying a continual, unresolvable movement between the two-sided nature of the 'topics' or 'commonplaces' constituting it, topics which not only give it both its *style* and *content*, but also its life!

And it is here that we can make contact with our worries about the state of ideology critique, and whether we can overcome them. In their important book (building on Billig, 1987), Billig *et al.* (1988) point out that the meaning of ideology itself is nothing if not itself two-sided, or (as they say) "dilemmatic": they distinguish between the idea of a "lived" and an "intellectual ideology." While an intellectual ideology is a *system* of political, religious, or philosophical thinking, that is very much a product of professionals, and exerts its influence in the making of self-consciously monitored decisions in institutional settings. Whether defined in terms of 'styles' or 'habits of thought', as *Weltanschauungen* or as 'distortions of reality', the effect is the achievement of a 'closure' of an otherwise 'open' (and thus to an extent chaotic) state of affairs in favour of a particular *social order* – often in the interests of a particular group or class. A "lived ideology" is quite different. It exhibits what Billig *et al.* claim are the *contrary or dilemmatic themes* that are intrinsically present in the "common sense" of a society. Indeed, as they see it, "the very existence of these opposing images, words, evaluations, maxims and so on is crucial, in that they permit the possibility not just of social dilemmas but of social thinking itself" (Billig *et al.*, 1988: 17) – they do not just constrain thought, but both motivate and enable it. They are "the *seeds*, not *flowers* of arguments," they say (1988: 16), quoting Bacon (1858: 492).

Thus, as a resource to draw upon, a lived ideology exerts its influence at just at those dilemmatic moments of uncertainty in everyday human affairs when routine forms of coordination break down, and people must construct between themselves a new way of going on. It will determine the positions they put forward and the justifications they offer. Thus, while an intellectual ideology may provide the basis for the resolution of a final dilemma, a lived ideology provides all the resources for the struggle producing it.

It is this emphasis upon the dilemmatic or two-sided nature of everyday human thought and action that is the crucial step, and which marks off the stance of Billig *et al.* from that of both Rorty and Lyotard, and of many other postmodern thinkers in fact. Indeed, in this respect it is interesting to note what Perelman and

Olbrechts-Tyteca (1969: 85) have remarked about this two-sidedness of human thought: They suggest that it is "possible to characterize societies not only by the particular values they prize most but by the intensity with which they adhere to one or the other of a pair of antithetical *loci* [values]." If this is so, then the pair of antithetical loci which, it seems to me, identifies the Western world as Western, and has done so for some long time, is, first, the dream of a harmonious, unified *system* of knowledge (fashioned for us by experts) which, one day, will give us a single true answer to each and every one of our questions, with all the answers being compatible with each other, thus to form a framework to help dissolve for us ahead of time all the struggles we now face between our conflicting values; versus, second, the fear that certain of our values simply may not be compatible, that there is no methodical, systematic way, discoverable by experts, to resolve our conflicts, and that chaos and disorder will therefore reign. This latter fear is the systematic spirit's "other." And it is this – not just, as Rorty claims, the radical contingencies of our being – that we must face: the dilemma raised by the realization that *both* sides of such loci play a part in our social lives together. In other words, what we as academics must face is the fact that our claims to disciplined and systematic forms of expert knowledge, have their basis in more public, everyday, common-sense forms of knowledge and argumentation – forms of knowledge that we as social scientific experts often claim, without a proper realization of their nature and function, must be replaced with better and more 'scientific' forms.[9]

Instead of attempting to replace common sense, however, how might we rethink both its nature as a resource (rather than as a system), and also the nature of language, as making use of it in the boundary regions of our interest? Well, in this respect, it will be interesting to turn to what a number of people have already said about its general nature. Common-sense knowledge in general is "unformulated and only vaguely conceived," says Heider (1958: 2). "It embraces the most heterogeneous kinds of knowledge in a very incoherent and confused state" (Schutz, 1964: 72); it is "immethodical" (Geertz, 1983: 90), that is, it caters both to the inconsistencies and diversity of life, it is "shamelessly and unapologetically ad hoc. It comes in epigrams, proverbs, *obiter dicta*, jokes, anecdotes, *contes morals* – a clatter of gnomic utterances – not in formalized doctrines, axiomatized theories, or architectonic dogmas," Geertz adds. Yet strangely, as he goes on to say, for all its disorder, such knowledge has "accessibleness" as another of its major qualities. Or, as Barthes (1983: 214) says, "the power of the Image-repertoire is immediate: I do not look for the image, it comes to me, all of a sudden," on occasion after occasion, called out by (internal or external) accidents of one's situation, at "the whim of trivial, aleatory circumstances" (Barthes, 1983: 33). In short, common sense already seems to function perfectly well, if not as an overall theory in terms of which to explain everything ahead of time, then as a practical resource in terms of which to make sense of things on the spot, as required in a way appropriate to one's own circumstances. So, although it is clearly a cultural formation, it in no sense consists in a system or a framework; that would seem to preclude its use as a practical resource.

Given the nature of common sense as a practical resource, how should we rethink language, that is, think of it in non-systematic, non-cognitive, more sensuous terms? Well, what might it be like if we were to reckon as if there had been no books in the world? It is the (for us) extraordinary nature of spoken forms of communication that we must understand. We must grasp the nature of a form of communication which does not consist in an orderly, sequential occurrence of events or things, or in a series of component meanings, but merely 'subsists' in the continuous flow of sensuous, 'moving' activity between people. Indeed, one of "the most basic defects of traditional approaches to the study of psychology," says Vygotsky (1987: 50), who has worried about this issue, "has been the isolation of the intellectual from the volitional and affective aspects of consciousness." We must attempt to recover a *sense* of, or quite literally, a *feeling* for, what the activity of speaking must have been like – before as children we learned to replace the sensory aspect of words with images of words – to treat the activity of speaking as "a unity of affective and intellectual processes" (1987: 50).

Here, we make contact with the idea of the prosthetic function of the speaking of words, outlined in the previous chapter. Rather than as already having mean*ings*, we must think of words as a *means*, as 'tools' for use in the making of meanings.[10] Not primarily as a means for the ultimate making of textual or go-anywhere, decontextualized *meanings*, but as primarily for use in communicative transactions, in the here and now, in the making of a *sense*, which works not so much to communicate ideas (out of my head and into yours), but to prompt in us an affective reaction, a 'sense' *through which* others can feel the movement of our minds, *to which* they feel they must respond in some way. Indeed, it is precisely this active, rhetorical-responsive form of understanding – as distinct from the passive, Saussurian referential-representational form – that Bakhtin (1986: 68) suggests we must adopt if we want to understand the function of living utterances in speech communication (rather than the structure of sentences in linguistics).

Conclusions

It is in these terms, I think, that we need to make the ontological gestalt switch required to understand how a lived ideology works. But all the changes discussed above mark a major rupture in current traditions of philosophical thought. Indeed, they are radically shocking and not easy to accept. For, as I have already said, our thought about thought and language – and the fundamental nature of the world, for that matter – is still influenced by images first fashioned during the Enlightenment, images which are currently embodied in the lived ideology in our academic disciplines. Thus currently – although we might intellectually accept that discourses, as practices, systematically form the objects of which they speak – we still *nevertheless* find it extremely difficult in practice to accept that often in our talk we are not talking 'about' anything which actually exists. Nor is it easy to accept that it is no longer appropriate to invent general, abstract entities and processes – such as 'social class', 'social institutions', 'social transformations', 'equilibration', 'reification', 'objectification', etc. – as the mysterious *agents* responsible for the changes taking place in social life. For it is just this move which works to hide all the actual, socio-political processes of importance – to hide those moments of indeterminacy, undecidability and ambivalence when real politics is at work.

In the same way, we find it difficult to accept the worth of unsystematic, dialogical, rhetorical-responsive thought, the kind of thought that goes on in joint action in ordinary conversation with others. We feel that, if thought is *not* ultimately con-tained within an already existing, commonly recognized system of some kind, then there can be no shared standards, no shared meanings. It is thought of as a some-what worthless kind. Indeed, if contradictory claims are tolerated, then, 'anything goes', doesn't it? No, not at all. Instead, what we have in common can be seen not as a set of agreements about meanings, beliefs or values, but as a set of – for us in the situation of our argument – *real* societal resources, that is, two-sided *themes* or *topics*, and a set of 'means', or 'tools', for giving shape to the topics relevant to our momentary circumstances. And, as long as we use them in ways which are intel-ligible and legitimate to those around us, then 'on the ground of human inter-action', so to speak, we are (or ought to be) free to use them as we please in giving form to our lives – their judgements are relevant to our uses. Thus we cannot – by the same token – just use them in *any* way we please. In this sense, such resources can be both enabling *and* constraining, or disabling.

Implicit in the version of social constructionism I have attempted to set out above, then, is a radical reappraisal of the nature of the embodied, common-sense, practical-moral, dialogical knowledge possessed by the members of a society. In this view, new knowledge neither grows out of a special method, nor the special mind of a 'genius', nor "new theoretical monologues" (Billig *et al.*, 1988: 149), but "the voices of ordinary people in conversation" (1988: 162). This is not to say that academic intellectuals cannot play an important role in this process – indeed, if it were not the case, there would be little point in the writing of this book. But note its form: it has been concerned not with supposed accurate representations of actual states of affairs, but with pictures and metaphors, with images – joint action, lived ideology, traditions of argumentation, etc. – which have allowed us (partially and at a cost), to 'see' influences at work that otherwise would have remained rationally invisible to us. But none of these metaphors should be allowed (as currently that of the language game bids fair to do) to become discursively hegemonic. For that, once again, would be to privilege systematic theory, and the theorist's form of life over that of practitioners. Thus, for us as academics, the move from the orderly centre to the disorderly margins marks a new task: that of identifying the real possibilities and resources present in those fleeting, extraordinary, non-professional moments of indeterminacy, undecidability and ambivalence in the boundary zones between the more orderly aspects of our institutional lives, in which we encounter those about whom we care.

Moving we confront the realities of choice and location. Within complex and ever shifting realms of power relations, do we position ourselves on the side of colonizing relations? Or do we continue to stand in political resistance with the oppressed, ready to offer our ways of seeing and theorizing, of making culture, towards that revolutionary effort which seeks to create space where there is unlimited access to pleasure and power of knowing, where transformation is possible? This choice is crucial. It shapes and determines our response to existing cultural practice and our capacity to envision new, alternative, oppositional aesthetic acts. It informs the way we speak about these issues, the language we choose. Language is also a place of struggle.

(Hooks, 1990: 145).

For, to repeat an earlier theme, a new way of talking institutes a new form of human interrelationship; thus a 'voice' from the margins can formulate the commonplace topics that give our culture its style from a new point of view.

PART II

FROM DISCOURSES
TO CONVERSATIONS

THREE

Vico and the poetics of practical sociality

It was Mead who saw that the linkage of dialogic communicative rationality and the institutionalization of democratic forms of life require a new understanding of the genesis and development of practical sociality.

(Bernstein, 1992: 49)

Here, I want to agree wholeheartedly with Bernstein's claim above, and to remark how much also I have been influenced in my own work by Mead (1934; Shotter, 1986a). However, it seems to me that there are a number of clear lacunae in Mead's writing: the lack of a sense of the *historical* nature of cultural development; the lack of a sense of the normative nature of social action, the requirement that an actor be not just intelligible, but accountable to others; as well as the assumption that communication is tantamount to cooperation, and thus his communities lack conflict (Mead, 1934: 348). Mead was influenced by Darwin and took an evolutionary approach to psychology. In particular he saw a continuity between biological activity and human reasoning. As he saw it, "the whole drift of modern psychology has been toward an undertaking to bring will and reason within the scope of evolution; and if this attempt is successful, rational conduct must grow out impulsive conduct. My own attempt will be to show that it is in the social behavior of the human animal that this evolution takes place" (Mead, 1934: 348). Indeed, very much in line with the responsive account of understanding I have already begun to develop following Bakhtin (1986), Mead (1934: 77–8) claimed that "the mechanism of meaning is present in the social act before the emergence of consciousness on awareness of meaning occurs. The act or adjustive response of the second organism gives to the gesture of the first organism the meaning it has."

Indeed, there is much to recommend in Mead, yet in spite of that, in this chapter I want to discuss someone else: Vico. For it seems to me, for reasons that will become apparent to us as we proceed, that it is his account, not Mead's, that provides us with the new understanding of the genesis and development of practical sociality that we need. For, as we shall see, given our interest in disciplinary discourses and in rhetoric, it is a part of Vico's method to be alive to the 'conceits' to which scholars can fall foul, as well as to 'see' the 'making' of civil society as an activity conducted neither by poets or philosophers, but, in the tradition of rhetoric, by ordinary people. Indeed, in his history, philosophers came last on the tree of knowledge: "First [were] the woods, then cultivated fields and huts, next little houses and villages, thence cities, finally academies and philosophers: this is the order of all progress from the first origins" (Vico, 1968: para. 22).

Academic discourses: their scope and their limits

In his discussion of what he calls the classic Enlightenment 'texts of evolution', Ingold (1990: 209) remarks, "there is a tension at the heart of western thought, one that has been with us for many centuries, between the thesis of humanity's separation from the world of nature, and the counter-thesis that humankind exists alongside other life-forms on an uninterrupted continuum or chain of being." He goes on to show how all the modern biological, evolutionary, and anthropological discourses have each been "constituted within this dialogue, bounded on one side by the opposition between humanity and nature, and on the other side by the opposition between living and non-living things" (1990: 209), each issuing from a different 'position' in the dialogue, and each trying to present a completely *systematic* account of life by privileging just one or the other side in the oppositions mentioned above. In his 'deconstruction' of these discourses, however, Ingold goes on to show that in their constitution – in terms only of differences and oppositions – they fail precisely in that in which they claim to have succeeded:[1] they fail to provide any 'in principle' explanation of life. And he locates the trouble in the fact that, in constituting themselves by focusing only upon one or another distinctive feature of the life process, none are able to account for the *unity* that links all the features together. Hence, "an impoverished biology that has lost touch with the reality of organisms meets an equally impoverished social science that leaves no space for people" (1990: 208).

Here, I would like to endorse (almost) wholeheartedly both Ingold's 'deconstruction' of these classic 'texts of evolution', and his claim that if the difficulties he has detected are to be overcome, an investigatory vocabulary of *relational* terms is required. It is indeed an important achievement to show that it is possible to give an account of *both* how human beings are constituted as unique individuals by the nexus of relations within which they are embedded, *and* how, as thinking, individual persons, they are able also to contribute to the transformation of those relations, all within the compass of a more general, biological theory of organisms. And at various points below, I shall make explicit use of some of them in my own account. But I wish to go further, not only to link Ingold's advances with other both classical and contemporary work, but also to be critical of his deconstructive analysis in an important respect: to contest his claim that it is a "*logic* of relationships" that we need. Here, I think, Ingold's deconstruction does not go far enough. He is still committed to a central feature in all the Enlightenment texts he deconstructs: For although he talks of "organisms and persons [being] . . . formed from *activities* which they create anew" (Ingold, 1990: 225, emphasis added), he still feels bound by the requirement that (properly academic accounts of the nature of) knowledge be formulated as *systems*. Instead of a logic, I shall argue that in attempting to set out a theory of sociality, what we need, at least at the beginning of our enterprise, is a poetics of relationships, a way of talking which leaves their precise nature open. It is to limitations in the nature of our academic discourses, and how talk of systems perpetuates them, that we must first turn.

My reasons for objecting to talk of systems here are, in short (but see further below), as follows. First, that such a form of talk induces in us a misleading *realism*, in the sense that it commits us ahead of time to a particular way of thinking about our topic. The narrative power of a well-crafted text makes us feel that we already have a clear concept of the kind of thing we seek, when in fact the opposite is the case. We find it difficult to accept that our as yet unknown 'objects' are not in some primordial sense *already there*; we fail to notice that our sense of their 'reality' has been 'developed', not by reality imposing itself upon us, but by our 'making sense' of them from within a discourse. This brings me to my second reason: talk of systems suggests also that everything of importance is already in existence (within the system) somewhere. This hides from us (or at least makes it difficult to recognize) the reality of growth, the irreversibility of time, and the possibility of genuine creativity; we fail to realize the still incomplete nature of what it is we seek.

But finally and most importantly, such talk fails to take the problematic (that is, alienated) nature of people's relations to their surroundings seriously. If we are not related to each other and our surroundings in certain already established ways, but we can and do make contact with each other, and with our surroundings, in a whole multitude of different, *self-constructed 'ways'* (according on some occasions to how we already believe we ought, morally, to be related), then the form of these contacts is essentially *unsystematizable*. This means that between people and their surroundings are 'gaps' or 'zones' of an uncertain kind. It is in these 'gaps' or 'zones' between people (organisms) and their surroundings, within these diffuse, only partially structured boundaries, or, to coin a term, 'thick interfaces', that I suggest (in line with Ingold) form is created. "Life cuts across the boundary between organism and environment," says Ingold (1990: 217).

These considerations suggest a new point of departure: that we should, perhaps, begin with vague, creative *activities* whose very character is open to change according to their own creative products. The trouble is, however, given the nature of our current academic practices (especially those of a scientific kind), this is not easy to do. For it is *de rigueur* to begin with clear, self-evidently true and acceptable, systematic definitions; to move in an *analysis* from the simple to the complex; while all the time testing and checking for accuracy and completeness. Thus all our claims to knowledge must be formulated as positions *within* well-established, systematic discourses which, if we follow Saussure's (1960) account of language,[2] consist only in systems of differences.

This, at least, is how we are supposed to proceed in the natural sciences. But in those social sciences to do with studying what a living human culture is, we face a problem of a very special kind. More than just finding a defensible position within a discourse, we face the task of understanding how any discourse as such is possible at all – a problem equivalent to that in biology of understanding the coming into existence of a form. In other words, our current academic practices themselves mislead us; they allow us to formulate 'positions' but not the character of the 'movement' or the 'formative activity' occurring between them related to their own development, maintenance, or change. Thus, as Ingold (1990: 224) sees it, "traditional cultural anthropology . . . has fallen into precisely the same error as modern genetics, in supposing that [developed and developing] forms are exhausted by their differences." Each produces a science only of decontextualized, wholly spatial (positioned or located), atomic things or events.

About the effects of such formulations in attempts to understand something as simple as the reflex arc, Dewey (1944: 356–7) long ago wrote that

> as a result, the reflex arc is not [seen as] a comprehensive or organic unity, but a patchwork of disjoined parts, a mechanical conjunction or unallied processes . . . [They] leave us nothing but a series of jerks, the origin of each jerk to be sought outside the process of experience itself, in either an external pressure of 'environment', or else in an unaccountable spontaneous variation from within the 'soul' or the 'organism'.

To capture that original sense both of unity and continuity and of autonomy and embeddedness, in a way which does justice to the perceptions which drove us to try to distinguish between living and non-living things in the first place, as I have already mentioned, Ingold suggests that what we require are *relational* formulations: formulations which not only take into account *both* differences *and* relations, but which also take *time* seriously. For everything living is not just constructed from pre-existing components, but *grows* within a bio-socio-historical context, and constitutes its own components parts from within the development of its own form (Bohm, 1980; Prigogine, 1980; Prigogine and Stengers, 1984).

Similar proposals, to do with the need for relational formulations, are on the agenda in the social constructionist movement in psychology, too (Gergen, 1990a, 1990b). While, of course, what I have had to say so far about the concept of *joint action* in this book has been directed towards these problems also. As Gergen (1990a: 584) says: "In [such an approach] the theorist shifts attention away from the single individual; the central units of understanding become social collaborations or relational forms."

But as already mentioned, the introduction of a vocabulary of relational forms is not an easy task, for, as we can perhaps already see, it is not a merely theoretical matter: a 'gestalt switch' is also required at a *practical* level, in not just our own common-sense, taken-for-granted forms of thought and perception, but in our actions and practices, too. For, as many writers have made clear (Geertz, 1975; Taylor, 1989; Sampson, 1985, 1988), the view of the living individual as always already existing as an isolated, bounded, unique, organized centre of awareness, action and motivation, set apart from other such unities, within an already existing social and natural environment with which it must deal, is a taken-for-granted aspect of the liberal-humanist ideology of our times. Its terms exist not only explicitly in our texts, but 'subsist' implicitly in our research and theoretical practices. Thus, if the tensions in our current forms of knowledge cannot be systematized away, and if understanding the 'movement' *between* our current socio-historical discourses is crucial to a grasp of what it is that makes them possible, another way of beginning our claims to knowledge than the mere establishing of a systematic position in an argumentative discourse is required.

Hence my claim: that our need is not for a logic of relationships, but for a poetics (and a rhetoric). In saying this, I am taking my cue from Vico who, in his discussion of the nature and formation of 'sensory topics' in his *New Science* of 1744 (Vico, 1968), has given us just the hint we need to begin our work. But before we can appreciate its character, we must prepare ourselves, Vico suggests, by 'undoing' some of the training we receive in the study methods of our times.

Vico and the 'conceits of knowledge'

In our attempts to explain language and mind, Vico warns us against taking it for granted, that how they *now* seem to be represents how they have always been. As a central methodological axiom in his *New Science*, he recommends that our "doctrines must take their beginnings from that of the matter of which they treat" (Vico, 1968: para. 314). In other words, in our attempts to understand the nature of human mentality, we should try to begin where human mentality begins. Ingold too, in his discussion of an anthropology of persons, suggests that we must begin from a theory of how persons are possible, from what he calls a theory of *sociality*. Where by "sociality," he says (Ingold, 1990: 221), "I refer to the generative properties of the relational field within which persons are situated." But what actually is involved in doing this? Where could we find the proper beginnings of such a field, and how should its "generative properties" be characterized? Upon what should we focus our attention? For, as we have seen above, we should guard against formulating our claims yet again as only an 'argumentative position' in a discourse. Such a move disconnects and separates the very features whose interrelations we want to explore. Indeed, it does more, for our current ways of making sense (while undeniably revealing in all kinds of ways), are also concealing. They hide from us not only the processes which went into their own production, but also (because of the demand for clarity) the proper character of their beginnings.

Aware of just these difficulties, Vico suggests that we must undertake some prior preparations of ourselves if we are to overcome them. To recognize the character of the kind of beginning points we need, we must change our attitudes in some way. To this end, Vico (1968: para. 330) discusses two conceits, or *borie*, to which we as scholars (inexperienced as we are in a knowledge of practical activities) can fall victim:

> On the one hand, the conceit of nations, each believing itself to have been the first in the world, leaves us no hope of getting the principles of our Science

from the philologians. And on the other hand the conceit of scholars, who
will have it that what they know must have been eminently understood from
the beginning of the world, makes us despair of getting them from philosophers.
So, for purposes of this inquiry, we must reckon as if there were no books in
the world.

We can bring these *borie* up to date. In the first, we can see Vico as warning us
against a form of entrapment which, as mentioned previously, Fleck (1979) can
currently be seen as having identified: that from within the closed, harmonious
systems of thought, to which theoretical knowledge gives rise, it is not only difficult
to trace its origins back to particular, unsystematic sources, but also, even were we
to try, impossible adequately to express the previously ill-defined character of such
sources within our now well-defined concepts. As a result, we tend to deny reality
to all that lies outside our familiar systems of interpretation. With this in mind, we
should see Vico in this *boria* (in the context of his whole approach in the *New Science*)
as implying a number of related claims. The first is that we cannot get our beginnings from 'within' a culture (nation); they lie 'outside' at least its *normal* forms of
reality. Within a culture, they will be thought to be *extraordinary*. Second, it is not
the case that human forms of life were invented by an original nation which then
passed on its inventions (its culture) to others. But third, cultures arise 'naturally',
so to speak, as a result of the 'providential' nature of (or of the provisions immanent
within) social relations – a process examined in more detail below in the section on
'joint action'. Hence, fourth, our claim that as trained scholars, we are in a good
position to study the problem of the origins of human society, is the opposite of the
case. We need to 'undo' a good deal of our training, to see the extraordinary as the
source of the ordinary.

This brings us directly to Vico's second *boria* and his claim that we must reckon
as if there were no books in the world, and the extraordinary stance it requires if
we are to take it seriously. For, as many writers, such as Goody (1977), Harris
(1980, 1981), Luria (1974), Ong (1978) and Vygotsky (1962), point out, literate
peoples, those like us who speak a language which also exists in a written form,
experience their knowledge of their language in a wholly different way from oral
peoples. But in what way differently? What does it mean to take Vico's maxim
seriously? As Harris (1980) points out, the literate peoples of the West have all
thought of themselves, and many still do think of themselves, as giving in their
speech 'outer' expression to pre-existing 'inner' ideas, images or thoughts, which
already exist in them as if preformed things. But:

> Suppose we strip away the superficial phonetic garb of the sentence, what lies
> underneath it? Something which must have all its words in place, their order
> determined, their grammatical relationships established and their meanings
> assigned – but which simply lacks phonetic embodiment; a string of words
> with the sound turned off. In short, a linguistic abstraction for which there
> is only one conceivable archetype so far in human history; the sentence of
> writing. What the contemporary . . . model of sentence generation provides,

albeit unintentionally, is a revealing anatomy of the difficulties inherent in an essentially literate society's attempt to conceptualize something it has already forgotten, and which cannot be recalled from its cultural past; what an essentially non-written form of language is like.

(Harris, 1980: 18)

I have quoted Harris here at length to bring out the force of Vico's corrective: if we do have to reckon as if there were no books in the world, it is the (for us) extraordinary nature of oral, preliterate (but nor prelinguistic), non-conceptual, non-logical, poetic, rhetorical forms of communication that we must understand. We must grasp the nature of a form of communicative activity which consists, not in a sequential occurrence of events or things, not in a series of products or of component meanings, but 'subsists' in the continuous flow of sensuous, 'moving' activity between people. And which is sustained in existence by being continuously reproduced in people's social activities; for as Vico (1968: para. 134) says, "things do not settle or endure out of their natural state" – their creation and maintenance are a human achievement.

Without the metaphor of written texts to help us, how might we imagine the nature of such activity? In what might we find the beginning not only languages but also of letters? It is this sensory or sensuous aspect of speech which is so difficult for us now, as literate people, to recognize and to describe; it is, however, this sensuous aspect of speech which will be our main concern below.

Vico and 'sensory topics'

In such an unbroken flow of responsivity, in which at first, as Vico (1968: para. 703) puts it, "each new sensation cancels the last one", how do people manage to create and establish within the flow of experience between them a 'place' (*topos*), an 'is', within the flux of sensation that can be 'found again'? How is a recognizably distinct but socially shared *feeling* about one's circumstances, to which all those involved can later return, formed? For without the possibility of referring to something recognizable as familiar, individuals would live, as Mead (1934: 351) puts it, "in an undifferentiated now," responsive like animals only to immediate and proximate influences. How, without the metaphor of written texts, and of meanings as static images (representations) to help us, how might we imagine the nature of people's first mental activity? While modern theories of knowledge begin with something present to the mind – for example, Descartes begins with self-evidently true, clear, and simple innate ideas – Vico begins by asking how it is that the mind comes to have anything present to it at all (Verene, 1981).

And it is precisely to this question that Vico claims to have an answer; indeed, it is the master key of his science. "We find," he says,

> that the principle of these origins both of languages and of letters lies in the
> fact that the early gentile people, by a demonstrated *necessity* of nature, were
> poets who spoke in poetic characters. This discovery, which is the master key

of this Science, has cost us the persistent research of almost all our literary life, because with our civilized natures we moderns cannot at all imagine and can understand only by great toil the poetic nature of these first men.

(Vico, 1968: para. 34; emphasis added)

But to understand what he means here by saying that the early people were, by necessity, poets (where the word "poet" is from the Greek *poietes* = one who makes, a maker, an artificer), we must divide the process of making involved into two parts: the first, to do with the forming of a *sensory topic*, and the second, with the forming of an *imaginary universal* which, from a 'rooting' in it, 'lends' the topic a determinate form. We shall find the resources we need in characterizing both in the following paradigm example.

In the *New Science*, Vico (1968: paras. 379–81) discusses what he calls the "civil history" of the ancient Roman saying that it was "From Jove that the muse began." Taking it seriously, he suggests that fear of thunder indeed functioned to give rise to both the first sensory topic and imaginative universal. For, as everyone runs to shelter from the thunder, all in a state of fear, an opportunity exists for them to realize that it is the *same thing* that they all fear; and a look or a gesture will communicate this. What we might call a 'moment of common reference' exists between them. What the 'inner mechanisms' might be which make such a realization possible is not Vico's concern here; his concern here is with the 'outer' social conditions. And here it is the fear shared in common which provides the first fixed reference point which people can 'find again' within themselves and know that others 'feel the same way'.

For this kind of fear, this fear of thunder, is not an ordinary fear of an immediately present dangerous event to which one can respond in an effective manner. There is no immediate practical response available to them in response to thunder. It is "not a fear awakened in men by other men, but fear awakened in men by themselves" (para. 382). Their fear is of a kind which seems to point *beyond* the thunder. When people hear it, they become confused and disorientated, they move furtively and with concern for each other – the thunder's presence is the *unspoken* explanation of their actions. And often, "when men are ignorant of the natural causes producing things, and cannot explain them by analogy," says Vico (1968: para. 180), "they attribute their own nature to them" (see epigraph quote). Thus at this point:

> The first theological poets created the first divine fable, the greatest they ever created: that of Jove, king and father of men and gods, in the act of hurling the lightening bolt; an image so popular, disturbing and instructive that its creators themselves believed in it, and feared, revered and worshipped it in frightful religions . . . They believed that Jove commanded by signs, that such signs were real words, and that nature was the language of Jove. The science of this language the gentiles believed to be divination . . .
>
> (Vico, 1968: para. 379)

And it was by learning to read the auspices (natural 'signs') that one could learn how, ahead of time, to conform oneself to Nature's (Jove's) requirements.

But the fable of Jove, the imaginary universal, 'lent' form to, and was 'rooted' in, the prior establishing of a *sensory topic*, a sensuous totality linking thunder, with the shared fears at the limits of one's being, and with recognizing the existence of similar feelings in others because of shared bodily activities. It is created, not out of a heterogeneous amalgam of events, but *within* a developed and developing totality of relations between people.

> The first founders of humanity applied themselves to a sensory topics, by which they brought together those properties or qualities or relations of individuals and species which were so to speak concrete, and from these created their poetic genera.
>
> (Vico, 1968: para. 495)

The sensory topic from which the image of Jove originated, is thus a 'topos', a 'place' in which it is possible to 'refeel' *everything* which is present at those times when 'Jove' is active. And, as such feelings are slowly transformed into more external symbolic forms, the inarticulate *feelings* remain as the 'standards' against which the more explicit forms may be judged as to whether they are adequate characterizations or not.

Sensory topics are the primordial places, the *loci*, constituting the background basis of the mentality of a people. They make up its common sense, its *sensus communis*. Without a common sense, there is no basis in which to 'root' the formation of any imaginative universals. Yet, such a common sense is in no way *systematic*. As we have seen earlier (Chapter 2), it is vague, heterogeneous, and unformulated, yet (as Geertz, 1983: 84–92) puts it, it has 'naturalness', 'practicalness', 'thinness' (that is, nothingbutness), 'immethodicalness' (Billig's two-sidedness), 'accessibleness'. Indeed, as Vico points out, it is first in *practical* activities that people must create (by ingenuity/ *ingengno*) the meaningful links between 'what' is demanded in a situation, and 'what' is available (by way of resources) – a meaning must be 'lent' to the sensing of one's surroundings.

What Vico outlines above then, is a poetic image in terms of which one might understand the *mute*, extraordinary, common-sense basis for an articulate language – where such a basis constitutes the unsystematized, primordial contents of the human mind, its basic paradigms or prototypes. And as Wittgenstein (1953: no. 50) says about the functioning of such a paradigm or prototype: "In the language-game it is not something that is represented, but it is a means of representation . . . something with which comparison is made." They are the feelings or intuitions against which the adequacy of our concepts may be judged.

Time and the 'generative potentials' in a relational field

So: within a sensory topic, within an identifiable 'place' in the flow of sensuous activity between people, are "brought together [all] those properties or qualities or relations of individuals and species which were so to speak concrete," upon which a poetic genus, an imaginative universal, may be based. Thus these first anchor points are to do not with 'seeing' in common, but with 'feeling' in common, with the 'giving' or 'lending' of a shared *significance* to shared *feelings* in an *already shared* circumstance.

How might we imagine the nature of such 'common places'? Could we call them structures? What does it mean to say that they 'contain' (are a locus of) 'generative potentials'?

We are helped here, I think, by Prigogine's (1980; Prigogine and Stengers, 1984) account of the dynamic stabilities (I shall call them *loci*) occurring in processes of flow. They are created and maintained (by being continually reproduced) within the continuous but turbulent, structurizing processes at the boundaries between two kinds of flowing activity, processes which seem to be closely related to living processes. They have some quite extraordinary characteristics, not least in the nature of their 'inner' complexity and their continual generation of novelty. Their extraordinary nature stems, Prigogine claims, from an emphasis upon what in the past has been ignored: namely, *time*. Upon reappraising the role of time we find that our "belief in the 'simplicity' of the microscopic [the 'building block'] level now belongs to the past" (Prigogine, 1980: xv). In the new time-space:

> The elementary particles that we know [which above I have called loci of activity] are complex objects that can be produced and decay. If there is simplicity somewhere in physics and chemistry [and in other fields of study], it is not in microscopic models. It lies more in idealized macroscopic representations.
>
> (1980: xiii)

It is the temporal nature of the component activities constituting such loci, and the fact that they are always on the way to becoming other than what they already are, which accounts for their continual novelty.

The growth of such loci (their emergence out of chaos and their sustaining within their chaotic surroundings) is an irreducible aspect of their temporal nature. It cannot be partialled out and 'added in' later when convenient. Thus it makes no sense to talk of such loci as being constructed piece by piece and then set in motion; they cannot be made up of 'parts' (if that is still an appropriate term) themselves devoid of temporality, that is, out of previously *unrelated* 'parts'. In their emergence, they grow from simple into richly structured loci in such a way that their 'parts' at any one moment in time owe not just their character, but their very existence both to each other *and* to their relation with their 'parts' at some earlier point in time. In other words, the 'history' of their relations is just as important as their 'logic' – if, that is, it still makes sense to talk in these terms, when both modes of description require representation within the coherent forms of order thought intelligible within a culture (cf. Vico's 'conceits').

Thus, no matter how remarkable the 'static' geometrical structure (the structure at an instant) of such flowing processes may appear to be, they cannot properly be called *structures* at all. For strictly, any genuinely spatial structure contemplated at a given moment is *complete*, that is to say, all its parts are given at once, simultaneously, whereas the temporally developing loci of which we are speaking are always *incomplete*. There is always more to come within such loci, they are intrinsically creative in the following sense: rather than static unities of homogeneity (made up of similar 'building blocks'), Prigogine calls the stabilities within a flow unities of heterogeneity, for they can only be seen as (dynamic) unities if their regions are at every moment *different*, in some sense, from what they were at a previous moment (else they would appear as 'frozen'). But in what sense? The difference cannot be a change in configuration, else the stability would not remain recognizable as the same stability (as having the same form) from one moment to the next. There must be an irreducible *qualitative* difference between its successive phases for it to be recognizable as a stability within a flow; each phase must be novel in some respect by contrast with the phase preceding it – a novelty which is expressed in its capacity to retain its unity in relation to a whole range of unpredictable changes in its surroundings.

Thus, in relational terms, what we have here is a unity in which its phases and aspects are related to each other not as *separable*, existentially identifiable component parts, but only as *sensibly* distinct and distinguishable[3] aspects of the same flowing totality. Each locus is a region of structurizing activity (an agency?), within which a diffuse, dynamic unity is continually, creatively sustained by the (disorderly) exchanges at its boundaries, exchanges between it and the other activities surrounding it . . . which depend in their turn upon dynamic exchanges at greater and lesser levels, and so on.

Thus, in the now *time-full* world introduced by Prigogine, the idea of building up a complex structure by constructing it out of simple parts ('building blocks', 'elementary particles', etc.) must be relinquished. If we are to talk of a 'sensory topic' as a 'human construction', then as a construction it cannot be similar to a building, or a mechanism, or to any structure put together out of previously unrelated parts. Whatever its 'elementary components' are, we can feel sure that they are in some sense relational, that is to say, they exist only as sensibly distinct, *novel* moments within an otherwise flowing totality. In other words, there is no point in thinking of relational fields and the nature of their 'generative potentials' as systematically ordered 'things', they are loci of activity. Although they have no specifiable *form*, they can be specified by their *formative* powers. Elsewhere (Shotter, 1980), I have characterized their nature as having an "already-specified further-specifiability," that is, they give rise to a particular *style* of continuous unforeseeable originality.

This aspect of loci of activity suggests to us another fundamental change we must make in our thinking. While in classical modes of explanation we focus upon the repetition of identical *forms*, in relational terms, every event occurs within a context of previous events to which they are related. Thus it is not in an event's repetition but, as Bakhtin and Volosinov might claim about the use of a word, in its *novelty* that its significance (its function) should be sought.

'Divine providence' and the self-specifying nature of practical-moral sociality

We return now to relate the above comments to the nature of 'sensory topics'. The point to draw out of the unsystematic, *poetic* account above – of the dynamic stabilities created at the boundaries between different kinds of flowing activity – is that it makes intelligible the idea of sensory topics as *originary sources*. It makes it intelligible to think of them as 'places' in which it is possible not only to find again *everything* that was sensed at the time of their formation, but also to find it again *but now as modified* by the current surroundings. Thus it is possible, as was said above, not only to 'refeel' in the sensory topic from which the image of Jove originated, everything that was present when 'Jove' was active, but also to relate such feelings to current circumstances (cf. Geertz's "accessibleness"). Furthermore, as such feelings become represented in external (symbolic) forms, the refeelings possible remain on hand, so to speak, as the 'standards' against which explicit forms may be judged as to their adequacy. In other words, Prigogine's account of dynamically self-reproducing loci, as I have called them, 'lends' intelligibility to Vico's claim that sensory topics are the originary *loci* constituting the background mentality of a people. They can be seen as providing their common sense, their *sensus communis*, the communal standards or ethos in terms of which they constitute a relational community rather than a collection of unrelated individuals.

The nature of such loci is, however, extraordinary; they stand 'outside' of everyday life. While they can be thought of neither as the causes nor as the reasons for people's actions, they can be thought of as the sources or resources people draw on in 'shaping' their actions. For in Vico's terms, in his doctrine of *divine providence*, there is a 'natural provision', so to speak, in the very character of our practical social activities, of the resources required for their own further development, their own further 'shaping'. Earlier, in the context of a discussion of "joint action," I suggested that such provisions occurred as the unintended consequences of such action. Vico's views are similar. As he sees it, his *New Science* must "be a demonstration, so to speak, of the historical fact of providence, for it must be a history of the forms of order which, without human discernment or intent, and often against the designs of men, providence has given to this great city of the human race" (Vico, 1968: para. 342). Thus, for Vico, what is at work in the making of civil society is clearly not rational choice, but neither is it a matter of chance or necessity; something else is at work, something *sui generis* which operates "without human discernment or counsel". In calling it "divine providence," however, he does not mean a supernatural agency, something external to the social activities of everyday life which imposes a form upon them.[4] He means that *within* practical social activity itself there is a natural *provision* of the resources required for its own further evolution or transformation (or dissolution) – for it cannot settle or endure unless sustained in the appropriate human activity.[5]

Such activity is, one might say, *self-specifying* in the following sense: that, as many workers today have suggested (among them Bartlett, 1932; Dewey, 1944; Mead,

1934), our past activities can be thought of as creating (as Bartlett put it) an "organized setting" for their own sensible continuation. Thus, rather than acting 'out of' an inner plan or schema, we can think of ourselves in our current activities as acting 'into' our own present situation, in terms of the opportunities and barriers, the enablements and constraints that it offers. Mead (1934: 140) – to note his continuing relevance to these issues once again – provides the following example of such a process in the short term: "being aware of what one is saying to determine what one is going to say thereafter – that is a process with which we are all familiar." More long-term examples have in fact been already discussed: by divine providence Vico means precisely the fact that our current communicative activities contain within themselves the provisions or resources required to 'shape' our activities in such a way as to ensure their own further continuation. In the past, says Vico (1968: para. 342),

> the philosophers have been altogether ignorant of it [divine providence], as the Stoics and the Epicurians were, the latter asserting that human affairs are agitated by a blind concourse of atoms, the former that they are drawn by a deaf (inexorable) chain of cause and effect . . . They ought to have studied it in the economy of civil institutions, in keeping with the full meaning of applying to providence the term "divinity" [i.e., the power of divining], from *divinari*, to divine, which is to understand what is hidden *from* men – the future – or what is hidden *in* them – their consciousness.

What unfolds or is made explicit in our practical social activities at any one moment is, suggests Vico, already present, implicitly, in the "organized setting" created by our past activities. Although we may have no plan, purpose or intention, explicitly, to do certain things, nevertheless, only certain kinds of consequences can at any one time ensue, that is, those for which a provision exists in our current social context. There is, as it were, to repeat a point made earlier, a 'grammar' to our social activities: in the ordinary flow of activity between people, a changing sea of resources is created. But the 'grammar' at issue is not just a mere practical grammar, a matter of sustaining a technique or skill, it is a grammar of a *practical-moral* kind (Bernstein, 1983). For, not only is it to do with others sensing whether an individual's behaviour is fitting in the 'situation' or not; but it is also to do with an individual acting in the situation in such a way that his or her actions contribute to sustaining an important social resource (as a dynamic, continuously reproduced stability). In this sense, such resources are "moral sources," to use a term central to Taylor's (1989) account of social life.

The growing, historical nature of a *sensus communis*

Such sources, such a common sense, then, can work to shape ways of knowing of a practical and sensuous, passionate and emotional kind, even though they may only be known to us in how they 'in-form' our actions in the course of their performance.

As a set of "sensory topics," it provides a means by which people can coordinate their activities together in a way which has, says Vico (1986: para. 141), "respect for human needs and utilities;" they provide a *sensus communis*, which, he says, is a means of "judgement without reflection, shared by an entire class, an entire people, an entire nation, or the entire human race" (1986: para. 142). As societies develop, however, such a *sensus communis* is overlaid by intellectually and reflectively constructed devices and procedures. Highly developed social organizations come to work by reference to rules rather than sensory topics and the presence of an underlying common "sense" is lost. It is to the recovery of that 'lost' or 'hidden' sensory basis to our common sense, to our social life together, that Vico's work contributes. The importance of this endeavour lies, not just in recovering a lost basis for a more mutually satisfying form of communual life,[6] but in once again getting 'in touch' with the sources of growth and change available in a society. For – to return to the *temporal* nature of the activities constituting such sources mentioned above – it is in their very nature as stabilities within a flow, that they only retain their unity in relation to a whole range of unpredictable changes in their surroundings, by being continuous sources of novelty.

Although there is not space to pursue the issue in any detail here, it perhaps worth examining briefly the connection between this and Heidegger's (1967: 188) claim that, "as understanding, Dasein projects its being upon possibilities." In attempting to explicate what Heidegger might mean by this claim, we again make contact, of course, with one of our recurrent themes: the commitment 'embodied' in modern philosophy to approach such claims as this, just as much *ahistorically* as *theoretically* (Scharff, 1992). However, to interpret possibilities ahistorically is to interpret them as merely factual or empirical possibilities, as already existing possibilities. The extraordinary nature of a *sensus communis* is that it contains possibilities, *topoi*, that are not at any one time all already there. But they only come into existence to be sensed as such, as a providential result of certain historical occurrences within it – where, yet again, such developments may be seen as 'created' in joint action. Thus, as such, they have not only a dialogical, 'developmental', non-planned quality, but also intentionality, in the sense of specifying a 'space' that is open both to further action and to yet further specification and interpretation, that is, it is a space with a 'horizon' to it.[7] I shall call it a 'providential space'.

The case is also similar on a smaller scale: hence, people's task in *developing* their understanding. This "development of understanding," says Heidegger (1967: 188), "we call 'interpretation' . . . [where] interpretation is [not] the acquiring of information about what is understood; it is rather the working-out of possibilities projected in understanding" (1967: 108–9). And later (see Chapter 6), in discussing the nature of conversational realities compared with academic discourses, the distinctions drawn here between empirical and historical possibilities will be crucial. For unlike an undisciplined conversation, a disciplinary discourse by its very nature (as we shall see) precludes such historical 'developments'. While discourses support inquiries into already existing possibilities, conversation is to do with the 'working-out' of novel possibilities. Here, for the moment, it will be useful to explore further the meaning of our common-sense understanding being of a historical or 'developmental' nature.

In discussing what is involved in people developing their understanding ("interpretation") of their circumstances, that is, what he calls "the ready-to-hand" for them, Heidegger (1967: 191) remarks that such an understanding "is grounded in *something we have in advance* – in a *fore-having*." We are not free to conceive of our circumstances just as we please. Beyond any conscious control of our own, how we see and act, how we talk, think, and evaluate, the manner of our being in the world is a matter of the 'world' we are within. "Whenever something is interpreted as a something, the interpretation will be founded essentially upon fore-having, fore-sight, and fore-conception. An interpretation is never a presuppositionless apprehending of something presented to us" (1967: 191–2). But it cannot be emphasized too strongly that this is *not* because we are all acting and perceiving *from within* a common framework, system, schematism, structure, or whatever other ahistorical entity one wants to use as a metaphorical 'container' for our ways of knowing and being. If Vico and Heidegger are right, it is because we are all involved 'in' a common history, and our task is that of attempting to reveal its nature by the use of a set of very different, much more history-friendly set of metaphors – but still metaphors for all that.

Recapitulation and conclusions

To recapitulate: we have been concerned, at least in a preliminary way, with what might be involved in formulating an account of practical-moral sociality, where by sociality we mean the generative properties of the relational field within which persons are situated. We began by noting the results of Ingold's textual investigations: that current discourses only establish 'positions' within a dialogue, representing one or another side of an opposition, whereas life and living seems to involve a form-creating 'movement' between such positions. Current discourses thus fail properly to represent either the phenomenon of life or the living origins of their own formation as discourses. Differences can give rise to distinct representations only *within* already existing discourses, they thus fail also to account for the relations which link discourses together within a unity as intelligible responses to each other. Because of these difficulties, we turned to certain positive and negative methodological maxims offered by Vico. In line with his positive maxim, that "doctrines must take their beginnings from that of the matter of which they treat," we turned to a study of what he called 'sensory topics', the 'places' within the flow of sensuous awareness we have in the living of our own lives to which we can return and refeel (sense, intuit) a past circumstance. However, the negative maxims recommended by Vico (the two 'conceits') alerted us to the fact that such entities could not be *represented* within a discourse (any discourse). They are extraordinary entities, 'outside' the common sense of any nation or culture.

This may tempt us to say that they exist in an extra-linguistic reality, outside of all socio-historical circumstances. Such a reality may be extra-linguistic, but it is in no sense an extra-relational reality. Its socio-historical character stretches back to the beginnings of (our) time. For us, the set of sensory topics, the loci of continuously novel activities in which our linguistic realities are 'rooted', are dynamically sustained and reproduced now in our daily social activities. Following Prigogine, it is at the boundaries between flows of different activity that they are created. They 'subsist' in the "bustle," or "hurly-burly" (terms used by Wittgenstein, 1980: II, nos. 624–9) of everyday social life, as continuous unforeseeable or contingent sources of originality, historically changing (but retaining their identity) as their surroundings change. They are the origins or 'seeds' from which acts or utterances *belonging* to a social group can be fashioned.[8]

To apply such 'developmental' knowledge practically, or to give it linguistic form, further *metaphorical* activity is required: for Vico, this is the primary operation productive of the different, distinctive forms of human mentality – hence his claim that early peoples were poets who spoke in poetic characters. The root sense of metaphor here is in the activity of 'carrying over, or transferring something,' from the Greek *metapherein*. In practical affairs, this means a 'giving' or a 'lending' of significance to sensory perception, a 'bridging' of the gap between human beings and their circumstances. Language in such a view as this ceases to be a neutral medium for the representation of, and reference to, events and things somehow already grasped as such non-linguistically; it characterizes language as being *constitutive* or *formative* of what it represents. It involves *tropes*, figurative and formative ways of communicating and speaking, at every level. It is everywhere rhetorical in the sense that in their contingency, sensory topics are 'given' or 'lent' a determinate form one way or another within different forms of talk. Hence my claim, above, that we need not only a poetics but also a rhetoric of relationships, where a rhetoric is concerned with the giving of a first linguistic form to the 'feelings' to be found again in topics. But here, our concern has been just with beginnings.

So, to repeat our formulation, our 'story' again: the hero of the story is "divine providence;" as the first outcomes of joint action, sensory topics are as sources of continuous unforeseeable originality that constitute the beginnings of language. And they are also the beginnings from which a 'theory' of the generative loci in the relational fields between people, the 'providential spaces' in which they live, can be fashioned. But to characterize them in a way which captures their nature, as it might have been for the first peoples, we have had like them to resort to a poetic, metaphorical approach. Others may still want to offer what, they claim, are yet further revealing metaphors.

FOUR

Wittgenstein and psychology: On our 'hook-up' to reality

We must do away with *explanation*, and description alone must take its place. And this description gets its light, that is to say its purpose, from . . . philosophical problems. These are, of course, not empirical problems; they are solved, rather, by looking into the workings of our language, and that in such a way as to make us recognize those workings: *in spite of* an urge to mis-understand them. The problems are solved, not by giving new information, but by arranging what we have already known. Philosophy is a battle against the bewitchment of our intelligence by means of language.

(Wittgenstein, 1953: no. 109)

Here, I want to discuss Wittgenstein and psychology. The stance taken in this book is that central to an understanding of anything psychological is an understanding of the role of language in human affairs. But what *is* the part it plays? As we know, Wittgenstein thought of it in his earlier and later work in two distinctly different ways: in the *Tractatus* (Wittgenstein, 1922) its role was representation, that is, language functions to provide 'pictures' of states of affairs in the world; while in the *Investigations* (Wittgenstein, 1953) its role is communication – it is *used* within certain, circumscribed ways in people relating themselves to one another in particular *forms of life* – for, as we shall see, when all the testing and checking of people's claims comes to an end, "[w]hat has to be accepted, the given, is – so one could say – *forms of life*" (Wittgenstein, 1953: 226). If in this view it still seems that words *are* used to represent things, then that is only because 'representation' is one of the many uses to which one can put one's language in sustaining the forms of life in question.

Modern psychology and mental representations

At the moment in the landscape of modern psychology, there are a number of different movements of importance, which relate to these two phases in Wittgenstein's work. The mainstream is following through all the implications of what it calls 'the cognitive revolution': the idea that everything intelligent we do involves a 'cognitive process' working in terms of 'inner' *mental representations* of the 'external' world, and that the way to study such processes is by modelling them in computational terms (see, for example, Boden, 1982; Johnson-Laird, 1983). But there are also, in fact, quite a number of other movements in opposition to this approach. Among them are: the ecological approach to perception of the Gibsonians (Gibson, 1979); the rhetorical and discursive approaches to social psychology being pioneered by Billig (1987) and Edwards and Potter (1992); the socio-cultural approach of Cole (1990), Wertsch (1991) and Valsiner (1988); as well as a whole social constructionist approach to psychology (Coulter, 1979, 1983, 1989; Harré, 1983, 1986a; Gergen, 1985; Shotter, 1984; Shotter and Gergen, 1989). Wittgenstein's philosophical investigations are, I feel, relevant at a number of points in this landscape: first, they offer good reasons for thinking that the current 'cognitive' orientation in psychology is radically misconceived, and the idea, that computer models (or supposed 'mental representations') are relevant to a general understanding of human activities, will eventually lose its credibility – indeed, it will show up the degree to which we have misled ourselves by fictions of our own making (see Chapter 8) while at the same time, Wittgenstein's investigations also offer many helpful hints towards the development of all the new movements I have just mentioned – as I shall show in a moment.

In developing my argument, let me begin with a quotation, not from Wittgenstein, but from someone who had a major influence upon him (Janik and Toulmin, 1973; Wittgenstein in *Culture and Value*, 1980b), the great nineteenth century physicist Heinrich Hertz – the discoverer (or should we say, inventor?) of radio waves. Right at the beginning of his *Principles of Mechanics*, in introducing an important discussion of certain problems, to do with the use of symbolic representations in science, Hertz (1954: 1) described their role thus:

> In endeavouring . . . to draw inferences as to the future from the past, we always adopt the following process. We form for ourselves images or symbols of external objects; and the form that we give them is such that the necessary consequents of the images in thought are always the images of the necessary consequents in nature of the things pictured. In order that this requirement may be satisfied, there must be a certain conformity between nature and our thought.

In other words, we say our theories are true theories if the *predictions* we derive from them match or 'picture' the *outcomes* of the processes we study. So, although we can bring off some quite spectacular results in the sciences, it is just *in terms of such results*, not the whole structure of a theory, that we think of a theory as a *true* theory. Our knowledge, as Quine (1953) said later, "is a man-made fabric which impinges on experience only along the edges."

This 'instrumental' criterion of truth, as I shall call it, however, allows for a considerable degree of loose-jointedness in the relations between our theories and the character of our surroundings – what we uncritically call our reality.[1] "As a matter of fact," says Hertz (1954: 2), we do not know, nor have we any means of knowing, whether our conceptions of things are in conformity with [the things themselves] in any other than this *one* fundamental respect. The images we may form of things are not determined without ambiguity by the requirement that the consequents of the images be the images of the consequents.

This lack of a *direct* 'hook-up' between theory and reality may not worry most natural scientists, but it should, I think, worry a psychologist. For in studying people, one should be concerned not just with truth in an 'effective' or 'instrumental' sense, achieved by the use of *models*, but with the 'adequacy' of such models, with whether they do justice to *the being* of a person (see Chapter 8). But to be able to judge that, we must know what a human being 'is'. And that problem, as Hertz makes perfectly clear, cannot be solved (without undecidable ambiguities to do with 'appropriate-ness') by formulating models and looking for 'conformities' between their products and human products. The discovery of what something 'is' for us can only be discovered from a study, not of how we talk about it in reflecting upon it, but of how 'it' necessarily 'shapes' those of our everyday communicative activities in which it is involved, *in practice*; an influence which is only revealed in the 'grammar' of such activities. Hence the relevance of Wittgenstein's (1953: no. 373) claim to us here, mentioned already before, that: "Grammar tells us what kind of object any-thing is."

To some extent, then (but only to an extent), the problem of *what it is for us to be a human being* is a philosophical problem, and, in Wittgenstein's terms, there are two interlinked aspects to its philosophical study: besides investigating the (in fact very many different) ways in which our *image*(s) or *concept*(s) of ourselves are implicitly involved in our everyday activities and practices, we must also study the degree to which our explicit *formulations* or *accounts* of them actually accord, or not, with our practices (Wittgenstein, 1980a: I, no. 548). For it is there, Wittgenstein felt, in the formulations we use to specify the nature of our knowledge, that mis-understandings of the 'link' between them and the reality they are meant to rep-resent arise. Indeed, to point straight away to what might be argued *is* just such a misunderstanding, in the Preface to the *Tractatus*, Bertrand Russell states the then standard philosophical view of language: "The essential business of language is to assert or deny facts" (Wittgenstein, 1922: 8). But is it? Does such a claim represent, that is to say, accord with, what 'is' in fact the nature of our linguistic practices?

The view that Wittgenstein later came to hold, which I now believe is the correct view, is the one which I have already mentioned: that, if it does seem that words can be used to *represent* things, to 'picture' facts, then that is just *one* of the uses of language possible for us from within a form of life *already constituted* by the previous uses to which those words have been put.

Hence the interlinked nature of the two aspects of Wittgenstein's study. First, by being content merely to describe rather than to explain the nature of our mental activities, he shows how indefinitely various their nature is. For example: many instances of what we call "remembering," or what we call "recognizing," are all in fact very different from one another. While they may all *in their context* be called cases of remembering or recognizing, when they are examined in themselves, we find they have no properties in common among them at all. Second, by exposing the temptation we feel to *explain* so-called 'mental processes', he shows how we fall victim to the need to find a single *basic* process in each case, which will show us 'how' remembering or recognizing occurs, or is done.

For instance, about "recognizing" – and this is a central case, for it involves the important part he sees 'pictures' as playing in our reflective thought about things that I will discuss more extensively in a moment – Wittgenstein (1953: no. 604) says:

> It is easy to have a false picture of the processes called 'recognizing'; as if recognizing always consisted in comparing two impressions with one another. It is as if I carried a picture of an object with me and used it to perform an identification of an object as the one represented by the picture . . . .

For surely, recognizing a voice, a smell, a feeling, an emotion, or a person's legal rights, is done in some other way than by comparing a state of affairs with a picture. Such circumstances, one might say, are the other side of the picture. Thus, as he saw it: "A main cause of philosophical disease – a one-sided diet: one nourishes one's thinking with only one kind of example" (1953: no. 593).

In coming to this view of philosophy, as entailing a critical description of language use, Wittgenstein was again deeply influenced by Hertz's comments to do with a special set of problems in science: those which arise, not out of any lack of empirical knowledge, but out of "painful contradictions" in our ways of *representing* such knowledge to ourselves. About such problems, Hertz (1956: 8) had said:

> It is not by finding out more and fresh relations and connections that [they] can be answered; but by removing the contradictions between those already known, and thus perhaps by reducing their number. When these painful contradictions are removed . . . our minds, no longer vexed, will cease to ask illegitimate questions.

And this was the method Wittgenstein turned to when, in the Preface to the *Philosophical Investigations*, he was to write of the "grave mistakes" in "my old way of thinking" that talks with friends had forced him to recognize.

As it is Wittgenstein's "old way of thinking" which is currently at the heart of mainstream psychology, before turning to the relevance of his later work for a new psychology, let me first just say a little more about the view of the relation between language and reality which it incorporates, the view which he later came to think of as a "grave mistake." In psychology, the view in question is attributed by many cognitive psychologists to Kenneth Craik (1943), who stated it thus:

> My hypothesis is that thought models, or parallels, reality – that its essential feature is not 'the mind', 'the self', 'sense-data', nor propositions but symbolism, and that this symbolism is largely of the same kind as that which is familiar to us in mechanical devices which aid thought and calculation.
>
> (1943: 57)

Thus, for instance, Johnson-Laird (1983: 2) explicitly follows Craik in suggesting that "the psychological core of understanding . . . consists in your having a 'working model' of the phenomenon [in question] in your mind." Boden (1982: 224) also makes essentially the same claim: that artificial intelligence research "studies not the world itself, but the way representations of the world can be constructed, evaluated, compared, and transformed." This is "the old way of thinking" central to Wittgenstein's approach in the *Tractatus*. There, he made such claims as: "We make to ourselves pictures of facts" (1922: 2.1), and "The picture is a model of reality" (1922: 2.12). Further, such a model is "linked with reality" (1922: 2.1511) by being "like a scale applied to reality" (1922: 2.1512). And what "every picture, of whatever form, must have in common with reality in order to be able to represent it at all – rightly or falsely – is the logical form, that is, the form of reality" (1922: 2.18). It is this latter claim that 'mirrors' Craik's, so to speak.

The 'grounds' of our agreements

But what is that form?[2] What counts as *appropriateness* here? What is the character of the 'link' or the 'hook-up' between phenomena and their representations? Here is a central weakness, for the trouble is, as Wittgenstein (1922: 2.172) says in the *Tractatus*: "The picture . . . cannot represent its form of representation." How can we get to know its form, then? Well, the picture itself "shows it forth," he says (1922: 2.172). Thus, to the extent that its *form* is *shown* in its structure, its correspondence to reality is something which one must 'just see'. As Lewis Carroll realized (in the tale of Achilles and the Tortoise), we cannot be cognitively (or physically) coerced through irrefutable reasoning to accept it. In other words, as Wittgenstein (1969: no. 215) also realized, "the idea of 'agreement with reality' does not have any clear application."[3] But if we do not always check our claims to truth by a procedure of formally comparing theory and reality in terms of their 'pictured shape', how can they be checked? For sooner or later, one's claims have to be publicly accepted or not by others, and, for that to be possible, others have to be able to apply the same kinds of procedures and criteria in judging them as oneself. Thus, "if language is to be a means of communication," says Wittgenstein (1953: no. 242), then, "there must be agreement not only in definitions but also (queer as this may sound) in judgments."

Indeed, whatever kind of utterance one makes, one must be able to judge the nature of its relation to its surroundings, how it is linked to the world. And in particular, if it is a claim to knowledge, then one must ask: How might such a claim be 'rooted' or 'grounded'? For, although Wittgenstein rejected 'picturing' as the only way in which representing was done, this did not mean to say that he rejected the whole idea of being able to justify one's claims to knowledge in some way or other: they must be such that they are 'permitted', 'allowed', or 'afforded' as representations of reality, of *our* circumstances.

> Giving grounds . . . , justifying the evidence, comes to an end; – but the end is not certain propositions striking us immediately as true, i.e., it is not a

kind of *seeing* on our part; it is our *acting*, which lies at the bottom of the language-game.

(Wittgenstein, 1969: no. 204)

No matter how we might twist and turn, and attempt to find somewhere a fundamental, 'naturalistic', or 'logically necessary' foundation – which can be explicitly formulated in stable, unequivocal, formal terms – we always run up against the question: How can you justify your claim to others? This, however, always occasions the prior problem of how one can make one's claims intelligible to others. In other words, the 'grounds' for our claims to knowledge ultimately are to be found in who we 'are', in our forms of life. For it is in our socialization into a certain way of being that we learn how to do such things as making claims, raising questions, conducting arguments, sensing disagreements, recognizing agreements, and so on. These *ontological skills* – these ways of being a certain kind of socially competent, first-person member of our society – are necessary for there to be any questions, or arguments, at all (Shotter, 1984).

> 'So you are saying that human agreement decides what is true and what is false?' – It is what human beings *say* that is true and false; and they agree in the language they use. That is not agreement in opinions but in form of life.
>
> (Wittgenstein, 1953: no. 241)

What this means then, to repeat, is that in actual fact there are an indefinite number of ways in which the connection between an utterance and its circumstances is, or can, be literally, 'made' and – if the utterance is a claim to knowledge – justified. Indeed, if we ask, how many kinds of uses for our utterances there might be, the reply we receive is:

> There are *countless* kinds:[4] countless different kinds of use of what we call 'symbols', 'words', 'sentences'. And this multiplicity is not something fixed, given once for all; but types of language, new language-games, as we say, come into existence, and others become obsolete and get forgotten.
>
> (1953: no. 23)

The 'logical' form used in a 'picturing' relation to our supposed 'reality', is thus only one such way; other ways of formulating claims to knowledge about one's circumstances, such as narrative, metonymic, or even ironic forms, are also possible. Indeed:

> It is interesting to compare the multiplicity of the tools in language and of the ways they are used . . . with what logicians have said about the structure of language. (Including the author of the *Tractatus Logico-Philosophicus*.)
>
> (1953: no. 23)

The trouble is, in science as in logic (as also in psychology), because we mistakenly "*compare* the use of words with games and calculi which have fixed rules" (1953: no. 81), we always think that words *must* have stable, unequivocal, already determined *meanings*. But in the openness of ordinary everyday life, in comparison with the closed world of logic, this is precisely *not* the case.

To state now explicitly the well-known Wittgensteinian slogan: in everyday life, words do not in themselves have a meaning, but a *use*, and furthermore, a *use only in a context*; they are best thought of not as having already determined meanings, but as *means*, as tools, or as instruments for use in the 'making' of meanings – "think of words as instruments characterized by their use," he says in *The Blue Book* (Wittgenstein, 1965: 67). For, like tools in a tool-box, the significance of our words remains open, vague, ambiguous, until they are used in different particular ways in different particular circumstances. "When we say: 'Every word in language signifies something' we have so far," says Wittgenstein (1953: no. 13), "said *nothing whatsoever*; unless we have explained exactly *what* distinction we wish to make," and we make different distinctions (with the same word) in different situations – "our talk gets its meaning from the rest of our proceedings" (Wittgenstein, 1969: no. 229). This is utterly to repudiate the assumption that words in language *already* have a meaning independent of the circumstances of life in which they are used.

The renunciation of analysis and (explanatory) 'theory'

Here, then, we have a very different view of the nature of language and of the function of words and symbols from that still held by most psychologists (and by most scientists in general, for that matter). How did Wittgenstein ever come to this view of words as 'instruments' and of meaning as 'always situated'? What was his 'method' or 'methods', so to speak? First, as I have already remarked, he resists the temptation to rush to an explanation or understanding of something too early; we must first be clear about *what* is it that really puzzles us. Indeed, every time he hears the claim that something *must* have a certain character to it, he says (and you can almost hear him *shout* it in anger): "Don't think, but look!" – don't think what *must* be hidden, within us somewhere, but look at the *circumstances* of our talk. This is because our ways of talking "tempt" us into thinking that what we say *must be justified* by reference to what the talk is about;[5] they tempt us into thinking that because we talk of certain 'things', the things we talk of '*must*' actually exist.

In psychology, for example: suppose we were to observe a person A writing down a series of numbers 1, 5, 11, 19, 29, watched by a person B who then tries to continue the series. If B succeeds, and exclaims 'Now I can go on!', we say that B has *understood* the series, and we are tempted to try to discover the mental process of understanding which seems to be hidden behind what B has done. But, as Wittgenstein points out, in solving the series B may do any one of a number of different things: tell of inventing and confirming a general formula; tell of discovering the sequence of differences (4, 6, 8, 10); simply say that the series is one already familiar to him; or say nothing, and simply continue the series. Behind all these different activities, we are tempted to say that there *must be* a single, essential process of understanding, and it is our job as psychologists to discover its nature.[6] But, says Wittgenstein (1953: no. 154):

If there is any thing 'behind the utterance of the formula' it is *particular circumstances*, which justify me in saying I can go on – when the formula occurs to me.
Try not to think of understanding as a 'mental process' at all. – For *that* is the expression which confuses you. But ask yourself: in what sort of case, in what kind of circumstances, do we say, 'Now I know how to go on', when, that is, the formula *has* occurred to me?

And he also adds elsewhere:

That way of speaking is what prevents us from seeing the facts without prejudice . . . *That* is how it can come about that the means of representation produces something *imaginary*. So let us not think we *must* find a specific mental process, because the verb 'to understand' is there and because one says: Understanding is an activity of the mind.
(Wittgenstein, 1981: no. 446)

We have here, then, an example of one aspect of his method at work. But because of all the temptations to which we fall victim, it is not easy to implement. For the trouble is, if one does just 'look' at everyday human social activity, all one sees is its "bustle" (Wittgenstein, 1980: II, nos. 625, 626), its variability; indeed, "variability itself is a characteristic of behaviour without which behaviour would be to us as something completely different" (1980: II, no. 627). We seemingly need something to help us 'see' its nature. But if its nature really is disorderly, how can we form ahead of time an agreed framework within which to conduct our investigations of its nature? The answer is, we cannot.[7] And this is one of the reasons why he was unable to supply a coherent, systematic treatment of language. As he says in the Preface to *Philosophical Investigations*, "my thoughts were soon crippled if I tried to force them on in any single direction against their natural inclination" (Wittgenstein, 1953: ix). But what part did the "natural inclination" of his thoughts play in his investigations? It is here, I think, that we can find another aspect of his method. For, if it is the case (as I shall suggest in Chapter 6 it is) that the saying of a sentence, or the doing of a deed, in a practical context, originates in, and is guided by, a person's vague and unordered *sense* of their relation to that context, then whatever they do or say can be judged in terms of its adequacy to that sense. Indeed, if we read Wittgenstein (1953: 192) we do find him saying, "how do I myself recognize my own disposition? – Here it will be necessary for me to take notice of myself as others do, to listen to myself talking, to be able to drawn conclusions from what I say."[8]
Indeed, about the 'tendency' he felt as a philosopher to solve problems by *analysis*, among other comments, he said this:

We feel as if we have to *penetrate* phenomena: our investigation, however, is directed not towards phemomena, but, as one might say, towards the *'possibilities'* of phenomena. We remind ourselves, that is to say, of the *kind of statement* that we make about phenomena.
(1953: no. 90)

In other words, in countless 'thought' ("inner speech") experiments, he 'sensed' the 'inclinations', the 'tendencies', the 'order of possibilities', created by attempts to *use* words practically in various particular contexts.[9] This, I think, is clearly another aspect of his method.

But it is still not yet enough to enable us to get by without explanatory theories. For the final aspect of his method, we must return to the prosthetic function of words (and images created by words) mentioned in Chapter 1. There, it was suggested that by acting or perceiving prosthetically 'through' our speaking, we seem able to specify the 'content' of our perceptions (and actions), to fashion a "way of looking."

This is where Wittgenstein's (1953: no. 122) "perspicuous representations" play their part (Edwards, 1982): In breaking away from explanatory theory, he set up the metaphor of language games, not to serve as an idealization (as a usual first move, prior to the production of a rigorous theory) but for another reason altogether:

> Our clear and simple language-games are not preparatory studies for a future regularization of language – as it were approximations, ignoring friction and air resistence. The language-games are rather set up as *objects of comparison* which are meant to throw light on the facts of our language by way not only of similarities, but also of dissimilarities.
>
> (Wittgenstein, 1953: no. 130)

We must not begin with a preconceived idea to which the reality of our language *must* correspond (if our idea of it is to be correct);[10] what we want is something with which to contrast it, some measuring rod or instrument which, by its very existence, serves to create a dimension (or dimensions) of comparison, a way of talking about the character of what it is we want to study, where each 'instrument' reveals interconnections between aspects and characeristics otherwise unnoticed. Thus all the metaphors used by Wittgenstein (such as "the ancient city," the "tool-box," the "handles and levers in a locomotive cab"), bring to our attention aspects of language, and of our knowledge of language, that were previously rationally invisible to us, for example, its 'rule-like' features, the characteristics of its 'boundaries', its 'archeology', and so on. They serve the function of creating

> an order in our knowledge of the use of language: an order with a particular end in view; one out of many possible orders; not *the* order. To this end we shall constantly be giving prominence to distinctions which our ordinary forms of language easily make us overlook.
>
> (1953: no. 132)

Such metaphors cannot *represent* any already fixed orders in our use of language, for, by their very nature in being open to determination in the context of their occurrence, they do not belong to any such orders. But what they do do for us, in artificially creating an order where none before existed, is to make an aspect of our use of language 'pictureable', that is, both to make that aspect of our language use "rationally-visible" (in Garfinkel's terms) and thus publicly discussable and debateable, and to make it into a "psychological instrument" (in Vygotsky's terms) and thus into something, a practical resource, that we can think, act and perceive with and through.

Critical description not explanation

This, then, is the task he set himself: simply to describe what actually 'are' our everyday linguistic practices. And if there is a key to Wittgenstein's later philosophy, then I think that it is this: the raging determination to renounce all explanatory theory, and "to put all this indefiniteness, correctly and unfalsified, into words" (1953: 227). Where, as he said: "The difficulty of renouncing all theory: One has to regard what appears so obviously incomplete, as something complete" (1980: I, no. 723). Indeed:

> Mere description is so difficult because one believes that one needs to fill out the facts in order to understand them. It is as if one saw a screen with scattered colour-patches, and said: the way they are here, they are unintelligible; they only make sense when one completes them into a shape. – Whereas I want to say: Here *is* the whole. (If you complete it, you falsify it.)
>
> (1980: I, no. 257)

So, if we take it that one of Wittgenstein's major insights in his later philosophy is that the idea of 'agreement with reality' lacks any clear application, then I think this counts as another: that everyday human activities do not just *appear* vague and indefinite because we are still as yet ignorant of their true underlying nature, but that they are *really* vague.

> We are under the illusion that what is peculiar, profound, essential, in our investigation, resides in its trying to grasp the incomparable essence of language. That is, the *order* existing between the concepts of proposition, word, proof, truth, experience, and so on.
>
> (Wittgenstein, 1953: no. 97; emphasis added)

But the fact is, there is no order, no already determined order, just an "*order of possibilities*" (1953: no. 97),[11] an order of possible orderings which it is up to us to make as we see fit. And this, of course, if we are to act in the world and be able really to influence what happens there, is exactly what we require of language as a means of communication: we require the words of our langauge to give rise to vague but not wholly unspecified 'tendencies', which permit a degree of further specification *according to the circumstances of their use*, thus to allow the 'making' of precise and particular meanings appropriate to those circumstances.

We are tempted in the example above to put the coloured patches into an order, because only that seems to give them a meaning. But that is not the case. What they then take on is not so much a meaning as *intelligibility*, that is to say, they become capable of being grasped reflectively and intellectually, that is, represented as having a place within a closed and orderly language game. But in such circumstances, as we know from works of science fiction, it is possible for syntax to masquerade as meaning to such an extent that it is possible to create a 'sense' of a 'reality' that does not in fact exist. And the fact is, in their *incomplete* state, within a particular context of action, they possess a perfectly clear meaning, according to the particular exigencies of that context; "the circumstances decide whether, and what, more detailed specifications are necessary" (1953: 199). They take on their meaning according to how they are used in the context. Because of this, though:

> The *facts* of human natural history that throw light on our problem, are difficult for us to find out, for our talk *passes them by*, it is occupied with other things. (In the same way we tell someone: "Go into the shop and buy . . ." – not: "Put your left foot in front of your right foot etc. etc., then put coins down on the counter, etc. etc."
>
> (1980: I, no. 78)

Mostly we talk with the aim of creating and sustaining various forms of life, with the aim of 'going on', and not with stopping to contemplate its 'facts'. For the really important knowledge for us in all of this, is to do with us "knowing our way about"[12] within the indefiniteness of our ordinary, everyday human affairs. And that is obtained from an investigation of how we do actually do it, in practice. Hence, the methodological importance for Wittgenstein of the sense of wrongness in certain usages of words. For, in his attempts to give descriptions of word use, his aim was *not* to describe established usages – that is an approach that gives rise to *theories* of language. For him, a 'wrong description' is one "which does not accord with the practice of the person giving the description" (1980: I, no. 548). A 'right' description, a critical description, is one that does not impose a pre-existing theoretical order on the phenomena in question.

The rhetorical constitution of psychological 'processes'

What, then, does all this mean for psychology, and for our attempts to understand what is involved in remembering and recognizing, in thinking, perceiving and acting? What actually should we investigate, in wanting to say something sensible about feelings, about emotions and about motivation, and in what way should we try to communicate our results? It means that we should "take the various psychological phenomena: thinking, pain, anger, joy, wish, fear, intention, memory etc., – and compare the behaviour corresponding to each." But, Wittgenstein (1980: I, no. 129) asks: "What does behaviour include here? Only the play of facial expression and the gestures? Or also the surrounding, so to speak, the occasion of this expression?" He later says: "the word 'behaviour' as I am using it, is altogether misleading, for it includes in its meaning the external circumstances" (1980: I, no. 314). But it is precisely these circumstances – our shared practices, our embodied ways of judging, discriminating, and reacting, our ontological skills at being who we 'are' – which are not amenable to systematic description.

This does not mean, however, that we should give up psychology and turn to a study of computer models of either the brain, or of supposed 'mental processes'. Far from it. Indeed, about the resort to such approaches Wittgenstein (1981) made comments like the following. First, about thinking:

> No supposition seems to me more natural than that there is no process in the brain correlated with associating or with thinking . . . [W]hy should the *system* continue further in the direction of the centre? Why should this order not proceed, so to speak, out of chaos?
>
> (1981: no. 608)

Second, about remembering:

> Why must something or other, whatever it may be, be stored up [in one's nervous system] *in any form*? Why *must* a trace have been left behind? Why should there not be a psychological regularity to which *no* physiological regularity corresponds? If this upsets our concepts of causality then it is high time they were upset.
>
> (1981: no. 610)

Now it is not that Wittgenstein wants to deny that there is any process at all involved in thinking and remembering, and such like; he only wants to deny that an orderly 'picturing' process lies at the bottom of it.[13] In other words, as Wittgenstein sees it, what we as human beings seem able to do (and here I am repeating my piece of theorizing above!), is to take vague and unformulated, possible forms of order, and to 'give' or to 'lend' them a socially intelligible and legitimate order, hence to assign them a *use* or *significance* within the contexts belonging to one or another of our forms of life.

Within the sphere of remembering, Sir Frederic Bartlett (1932) studied the process in exactly these terms, in his classic book *Remembering*. There he says this about people attempting to remember a complex situation:

> In all ordinary instances he [the person] has an overmastering tendency simply to get a general impression of the whole; and, on the basis of this, he constructs the probable detail. Very little of his construction is literally observed and often, as was easily demonstrated experimentally, a lot is distorted or wrong so far as the actual facts are concerned. But it is the sort of construction which serves to justify his general impression.
>
> (1932: 206)

If asked to characterize this nature of the *general impression* functioning as the origin of the process, as he says, the word which is always cropping up is 'attitude':

> Attitude names a complex psychological state or process which is very hard to describe in more elementary psychological terms. It is, however, as I have often indicated, very largely a matter of feeling, or affect. We say that it is characterized by doubt, hesitation, surprise, astonishment, confidence, dislike, repulsion and so on. Here is the significance of the fact, often reported in the preceding pages, that when a subject is being asked to remember, very often

the first thing that emerges is something of the nature of an attitude. The recall is then a construction, made largely on the basis of this attitude, and its general effect is that of a justification of the attitude.

(1932: 207)

In other words, the mental process in question is of a two-way kind. In the agent–attitude direction, the act of recall 'constructs' the memory; but the agent cannot construct the memory just anyhow. Thus in the other, attitude–agent direction, the attitude acts back upon the agent and determines the 'grounds' for the construction. The agent can only construct what the initial 'attitude' will permit or afford. Thus, in no way is remembering for Bartlett a matter of 'retrieving' an already well-formed memory trace from a 'memory store'. Whatever is 'stored' in one as a result of one's past experiences need have no discoverable *order* in it at all; its order is something constructed during the process of remembering.

But we face a further task in our claims to be remembering something other than being able to check 'within ourselves', so to speak, whether our formulations are permissible or not; we must also check them for their social function as intelligible and legitimate *accounts* – for verbally recounted 'memories' do not just occur in a social vacuum. Indeed, although Bartlett does not in fact reflexively explore the implications of his own theories for the gathering of his results, it is clear that people are not just providing neutral statements, but feel their conduct 'questioned' in some way. Thus, as he says,

the confident subject justifies himself – attains a rationalization, so to speak – by setting down more detail that was actually present; while the cautious, hesitating subject reacts in the opposite manner, and finds his justification by diminishing rather than increasing, the details presented.

(1932: 21)

In other words, not only are we working here within a framework of social account-ability, such that we have a responsibility to others (and to ourselves) to formulate in our "efforts after meaning" a justifiable memory account – one which the circumstances 'afford' (Gibson, 1979) – but the accounting practices involved have a *rhetorical structure of (implied) criticism and justification*.

Here, then, is where we make contact with some of the current approaches in psychology which are in opposition to the mainstream, cognitive, mental representations approach. Gibson (1979), in his *ecological* approach to perception, has emphasized – not unlike Hertz, in talking about 'permissible' formulations (see note 2 to this chapter) – what particular behaviours an organism's surroundings or circumstances will *afford*, given the kind of organism it is. Like Wittgenstein – who, as we have seen, points out that it is not 'seeing' but our 'acting' which grounds our ways of talking – so Gibson (1979: 239–40) also makes it clear that:

Perceiving is an achievement of the individual, not an appearance in the theatre of his consciousness. It is a keeping-in-touch with the world, an experiencing of things rather than a having of experiences . . . [P]erception is

not a mental act. Neither is it a bodily act. Perceiving is a psychosomatic act,
not of the mind or of the body but of a living observer.

In other words, Gibson provides the possibility for an account – similar to the two-
way flow account I provided above – of a much closer form of 'hook-up' between
us and our surroundings than that provided in previous (merely causal) theories of
perception. But what he clearly lacks in his theory of perception is any account of
how any checking or testing might occur as to whether one's perceptions not only
made sense *within a form of life*, but can be evaluated as intelligible and legitimate.
It is here, I think, that Billig's (1987) recent work on a rhetorical approach to
arguing and thinking becomes relevant.

Beyond the mainstream of modern science

Clearly, the major revolution in accounts of human action introduced by Wittgenstein,
Austin and Ryle, unlike the implicit assumption in modern scientific psychology
that ethics is an applied science based upon psychology and biology,[14] assumes that
in anything intelligible we say about human conduct, we express or at least pre-
suppose judgements of good/bad, appropriate/inappropriate, skilful/clumsy, etc.,
judgements which are grounded in reasons, which in turn may be grounded in one
or another form of life. But what this means is that one must be aware, in all of
one's behaviour, of its fittedness to its circumstances, especially if one wants to act
in other than a routine manner: for although we are free to act as we please, as long
as we make use of the ways of acting and speaking accepted in our society, we must
apply them with care in negotiating with the others around us lines of action
acceptable to them. Hence Billig's claim that all properly *social* contexts are *contexts
of argumentation*, that is, contexts structured by the possibility of the activities within
them allowing criticism and/or requiring justification, perhaps interminably.[15]

But this view, to be quite explicit about it, leads to the following very radical
claim: that our *psychological being* derives its nature from whatever 'rooting' we might
have in various forms of life, with some forms having more historical continuity and
social extent than others. And that we would not be 'us' except for the 'parts' we
play in the talk constituting them. Which means that whatever misunderstandings
there might be in our society's ways of talking, *philosophical investigations alone cannot
disentangle us* from our involvement in them – hence my comment, at the beginning
of this chapter, that the problem of what or who we 'are' is only *to an extent* a
philosophical problem, and that other aspects of the problem are practical-ethical
and political. Thus "the sciences of man," as Charles Taylor (1971: 51) then called
them:

> cannot be *wertfrei*; they are moral sciences in a more radical sense than the
> eighteenth century understood . . . [T]heir successful prosecution requires a
> high degree of self-knowledge, a freedom from illusion, in the sense of error
> which is rooted and expressed in one's way of life; for our capacity to understand
> is rooted in our own self-definitions, hence in what we are. To say this is not

to say anything new: Aristotle makes a similar point in Book I of the *Ethics*. But it is still radically shocking and unassimilable to the mainstream of modern science.

But this, I think, is *precisely* the relation of Wittgenstein's work to current psychology: for the claim that understanding the nature of mind is *not* simply a 'scientific' matter of 'discovering' its properties, but *is* a moral and a political problem, to do with how we *should* relate ourselves to one another, *is* a radically shocking claim and unassimilable to psychology in its current guise as a modern science.

But gradually, views of this kind – that people's worlds cannot be understood in terms merely of abstract, decontextualized, non-social, non-historical principles – must, I think, be assimilated and understood, for surely their time has now come. For times now are, perhaps, just as in Wittgenstein's "dark" but "interesting times" in Vienna, in which there was a loss of confidence in the power of the intellect to help shape one's future; a feeling that the conditions for honesty in social debate no longer existed; and of a precariousness in both social and international relations. These feelings, which *some* of us have now (for they are not necessarily shared by all) were also, as Janik and Toulmin (1973) point out, experienced by many in Wittgenstein's Vienna (1890–1919). Then, just as now, attention came to focus upon an analysis – upon a critical description – of communication, upon a critique of language. And it is Wittgenstein's achievement to have shown how the 'tools' we (and he) had previously thought adequate to the conduct of meaningful discussion of real and urgent problems fail us; and to have provided the basis for the fashioning of more adequate alternatives – alternatives which this time, I think, *can* help us to face and to cope with the uncertainties and fluidities of life in an 'open' and honest way, instead of trying once again to defend ourselves against them by entrapping ourselves within one or another 'closed' form of life, blind to what is going on about us.

FIVE

Rom Harré: Realism and the turn to social constructionism

Conversation is to be thought of as creating a social world just as causality generates a physical one.

(Harré, 1983: 65)

In the two-sided, dilemmatic scheme of things that I want to explore in this book, one of the major sharp *oppositions* would seem to be that between social constructionism and *realism* – where realism, in one or another of its versions, is the claim that not just anything goes, and that what the limitations to action are can in fact be *discovered* prior to the proposed action being taken. Indeed, as I mentioned earlier, there is currently something of a 'flight' into realism.[1] For one of the major objections to the whole social constructionist movement is as follows. Its claim that there is no independent reality to which claims to truth may be compared or referred – for all human 'realities' (*Umwelten*) are only known *from within*, so to speak – means that there are no independent standards to which to appeal in their adjudication; thus 'anything goes!', and we slide into a relativistic nihilism.

Although I shall not examine 'realism', as a philosophical position, any further at this point (I shall return to it at the end of the chapter), I do want to note that, in all its varieties (Harré, 1986b), it itself is born out of an attempt to provide a principled solution to a dilemma. The dilemma arises out of the following two points. First, as a structured scheme of necessary dependencies between a certain set of supposed entities, a theory has two functions: it functions as a larger, calculational context for the orderly production of representations of lawful, possible reconfigurations in the supposed entities; and it is a structured 'container' into which to fit 'data' supposedly indicative of such reconfigurations in reality. As such, as Einstein (1979: 312) remarked, "it is a work of pure reason [a 'free invention of the mind']; the empirical contents and their mutual relations must find their representation in the *conclusions* of the theory." Second, scientific theories are not, therefore, as in the classical empiricist view, deduced from experience or based in observations, for theories which are merely structured 'containers' for observations do not function as calculational devices for the production of *possible* reconfigurations, and thus cannot provide *predictive explanations*. In short, the dilemma, called the theoretician's dilemma by Hempel (1963), is this: if theories are defined in terms only of observations, they cannot function as explanatory; if, on the other hand, they are not, how did they have empirical support?

As I see it, politically, the dilemma is this: do we attempt to resolve such dilemmas as this, ahead of time, by in-principle policy solutions, and if so, *whose* policy should we accept, and on what 'grounds'? Or do we simply accept their existence, and agree to resolve them whenever they appear in terms of local, contextual 'grounds', argued for as such by those concerned? Earlier (with just questions of this kind in mind), I drew a distinction between that strand of the social constructionist movement with a practical, dialogic interest in 'words in their speaking', and that with a theoretical, monologic interest in systems of 'already spoken words' – where the former strand (seemingly) avoids relativism. For speakers in a dialogue or conversation are 'committed' not only to responding to each other by their 'acceptance of dialogue', so to speak, but also to their own earlier utterances. Thus, if participants 'sense' in an utterance (or action), a lack of 'fittedness' to the situation in which it occurs – recollect the *intentionality* of joint action here – this may variously be an 'opportunity', that is, 'grounds', for objection, correction, sanction, breakdown, etc. Thus there *are* 'standards', but they are only of a momentary kind to be found within the practical context the speakers occupy. But doesn't this mean that the 'standards' they accept are still only relative to the conversation they are 'in'?

An exploration of how one might respond to this question entails a study of the nature of conversational realities, and a study of what happens when they breakdown and are repaired. For those involved in such breakdowns must, to effect a repair, now appeal to resources in the larger context in which the conversation was embedded. It is the nature of this conversational context *at large* that I intend to begin to explore in this chapter. In doing this, I shall make contact with the work of Rom Harré, for he has wrestled with this problem for some time. I have know Rom for many years, and the body of this chapter was first written as part of an edited tribute to him (in Bhaskar, 1990). But now I can benefit from his replies to his (critics) friends (Harré, 1990), and so develop those views further here. Thus, compared with its original version, the chapter will be extended to included an examination of *realism* and its current standing. It begins, however, with material to do with certain matters in Rom's and my personal history. As, however, I think that this material is relevant to the issue of realism that concerns us here, I have left it in the text untouched.

In what follows below, then, I want to explore the tensions in Harré's work in the political dilemma I outlined above. They show up between the tendencies to naturalism occasioned by his realist stance, and the anti-naturalistic tendencies occasioned by his concern, in his recent socio-psychological writings, with the intricate workings of *moral* orders in the structuring of people's social activities. This gives rise to a tension between, on the one hand, the claim that there is (or can be) no essential difference between conducting investigations and warranting their results, in both the natural and the social sciences (his realism); and, on the other hand, if one takes his concern (in, for example, Harré, 1983, 1986a) with one's location in a moral order seriously, the implication that quite different ways of formulating and warranting claims to knowledge would seem to be required in the social sciences, when compared to the natural sciences (his turn to social constructionism). In other words, I want to uncover some of the unresolved oppositions present in Harré's socio-psychological writing – to do both with the relation between individualism *and* collectivism; and with that between attempts by experts to settle things in terms of *principles*, ahead of time, and attempts to settle things by public debate on the spot; as well as many other such unresolved dilemmas which we all face in characterizing and coping with our relations with those around us – which open it up to yet further development and provide it with its dynamic.

Powers

I would like to begin to outline these polarities in greater detail by first mentioning a bit of personal history and the part played by Rom in it. In 1969, after becoming depressed by the intellectual barrenness (though not, I hasten to add, the enormous challenges to one's ingenuity) in attempts to simulate by computer supposed processes of language acquisition (Shotter, 1969), I turned from an interest in machines and mechanisms to a study of agency. What depressed me about a mechanistic psychology was the way in which it suppressed genuine individuality, and led to us all being treated as indistinguishable atoms; but what also depressed me (to perhaps an even greater extent) was the way in which appeals to mechanism were used as a device to disclaim responsibility and to avoid accountability for what were (to my mind) obviously political (and often morally obnoxious) proposals.[2] While there was a good deal of dissatisfaction with this kind of academic psychology in those heady days around 1968–9, and many acquaintances who shared my feelings abandoned it because of this, few within academic psychology itself were admitting the fact, let alone attempting in any serious way to formulate a more adequate alternative – indeed, a vigorous and quite aggressive defence of the status quo was mounted, both academically (Broadbent, 1970, 1973) and institutionally.

A friend in Nottingham, attending one of Rom's philosophy of science courses in Oxford at the time, told me of Rom's similar worries about psychology, and took along to him an early paper of mine which Rom read, commented upon, and sent back with an invitation for us to meet. Straight away I was enlivened by Rom's tenacity, energy and verve, and by his determination to get some debate, somewhere, about psychology's fundamentals put on the agenda; and although Rom's own (official) situation in Oxford also had its rough sides (and has never, it seems to me, reflected the credit due to him), he was still none the less generous in his attention to my predicament as well. And that mattered and has continued to matter a lot to me.

At the time, Rom was still fairly heavily involved with his 'first love' – his realist philosophy of the natural sciences (Harré, 1970a, 1972) – and he gave me a paper of his on "Powers" (Harré, 1970b), a 'generative' concept in both senses of the word, both in itself and for me in my thinking. And I set to work, trying to apply it in the new context in which I was now studying language acquisition: the (videotape records of) interactions between actual (!) mothers and children. And it was within this context that Harré's formulation of the concept of powers came to play a most important part. Influenced to an extent by Saussure's (1960) and Chomsky's (1957) claim that linguistics could only become 'autonomous' and prosper academically if it could take as its subject matter a circumscribed, humanly constructed product, it seemed to me that "personal powers" could serve that same purpose in psychology. For the new 'twist' in Harré's way of formulating agency in terms of powers, worked to separate the unlimited task of describing the whole of an agent's nature from the limited task of describing its powers. As he put it:

> To ascribe a power to a thing or material is to say something specific about what it *will* or *can* do, but to say something unspecific about what it *is*. That is, to ascribe a power to a thing asserts only that it can do what it does in virtue of its nature, whatever that is. It leaves open the question of the exact specification of the nature or constitution in virtue of which it has the power. Perhaps that can be discovered by empirical investigation later.
>
> (Harré, 1970b: 85)

Furthermore, in relating 'power' to the notion of 'capability', he said:

> 'Capability' as a positive concept expresses something of this idea: a capability is a power which can be acquired (or lost) without there being a change in the fundamental nature of the thing or material in question.
>
> (1970b: 93)

For those with developmental concerns, this formulation seemed to provide a way in which they could be articulated: the nature of the development involved could be seen as a transformation of "natural powers" into "personal powers." The possession of natural powers is, one can say, in the 'nature' of the child, and what requires explaining is how children are helped by those around them, to 'appropriate' their own natural powers and to bring them under their own control as personal powers. And that is how I formulated the matter at that time (Shotter, 1973a, 1974a).

From the natural to the societal

However, although sharing an interest in agency and meaning, Rom and I almost straight away found ourselves with a difference. Harré centred his initial attention upon what might be called the *already* socially aware person. And, influenced by the whole movement in the philosophy of human action in support of the supposedly Wittgensteinian, "rule-following model," and Chomsky's brilliant work on syntax, he took it that self-directed and self-monitored behaviour, performed by reference to rules, "is the prototype of behaviour in ordinary daily living" (Harré and Secord, 1972: 9). For me, however, one of the reasons for my depression with the computer metaphor was the feeling that the rule-following model of meaning was inadequate: people do not just follow rules; they also create them (as well as challenge, change and correct them; and, in applying them, check out with others whether they have applied them correctly). Hence, in this respect, I was thinking along very different lines to Harré at this time.

Furthermore, given my concerns with how one became able to take *responsibility* for the outcome of at least some of the actions in which one is involved (Shotter, 1970), and influenced among others by the Kantian, John Macmurray (1957, 1961), I was worrying about *moral* issues and how they affected what Macmurray called the (logical) form of the personal. I was concerned to formulate a *developmentally sensitive* account of it, to provide an opening for rule-creation, meaning, at that time, not so much the creation of rules *de novo*, as the re-creation in the child of already existing rules in the possession of adults. And Macmurray's Kantian influence is apparent in the formulation I produced. But so also are Harré's thoughts about *negotiations*, and it is these which, in the end, emerge as of central importance. In taking a genuinely personal, as opposed to a mechanical or organic approach, it seemed to me that

> psychology is removed from the realm of the natural sciences and placed among the moral sciences. This alters its character entirely. It becomes concerned with *negotiations* . . . Values, opinions, beliefs, feelings, intentions, etc., once again assume a crucial role in human affairs . . . While classical science demands that everything be studied as if it were matter in motion according to an absent God's pre-established laws, *persons* seem able on occasions to act from a belief, a mere *conception* of a law . . . and in attempting to live thus, according to the conception of a law, people may fail; they may act inappropriately, rightly or wrongly, legitimately or illegitimately, etc., for conceptions decree only what *should* or *might be* the case, not what is. Attempting to live according to laws inevitably involves the judgement of other people.
> (Shotter, 1974a: 217–18)

In other words, how the source of an action is ascertained, and how the attribution of a moral responsibility for it influences future action, struck me as a fundamental, ineradicable, and irreducible part of any proper characterization of the nature of any genuinely *social* activity.

The next step was that, developmentally, the view that the growth of social awareness and the self-determination of action could be seen as the appropriation of powers from a 'natural' into a 'personal' realm gave rise to a number of problems. One was that in assuming essentially a rationalist formulation of the developmental process – that the task of those around children is seen as being merely that of helping to reveal what in some sense is already (innately?) in them – almost everything of historical, moral and political importance is omitted. It is not a genuinely *social* account of development, but an inter-individualistic one, taking place within a featureless context, devoid of psychological resources and valencies, that is to say, in such a non-specific context that it could be situated anywhere.

However, the basic approach contained a number of conceptual Trojan horses which, happily, when they began to discharge their contents, changed its nature entirely. They were the claims which I have already mentioned: first that psychology must be seen as essentially a *moral* science, because all our actions (even when acting all alone) must be performed with an awareness of how they will be *judged by others*; and second, Harré's claim that such judgements involve *negotiation*. To these must be added: Harré's Wittgensteinian claim that mental activity is not private, but available publicly in the activities in which people are involved with each other; hence, the problem of identifying it is not a matter of *access*, but of *authority*, and is to do with who has what rights in negotiating an account of its nature, and how that nature should then be attributed (Harré and Secord, 1972: 121–3). And finally, there was both my own and Harré's adoption of Vygotsky's (1962, 1966, 1978) notion of 'appropriation', and a concern with what is involved in the process of one person, who lacks a skill, acquiring a mastery of it from those around him.

Vygotsky: from the individual to the collective

As Vygotsky's views have come to play a central part in Harré's more recent expositions of his social constructionist stance (Harré, 1983, 1986a,c,d), it will be useful at this point to give their flavour by stating what might be called Vygotsky's two major laws of development. One is that

> consciousness and control appear only at a late stage in the development of a function, after it has been used and practiced unconsciously and spontaneously. In order to subject a function to intellectual control, we must first possess it.
>
> (Vygotsky, 1962: 90; 1986: 168)

Thus instructors do not face the task of attempting to teach us how to do something *de novo*, their task is only to 'stage manage' a context of joint action which 'calls out' what in some sense we can already do, and thus to help us recognize how to call it out for ourselves. And the source of what we can already do spontaneously (what previously I called our 'natural powers'), where is that to be found? The answer is that it is 'in' the general social activity in which we are all embedded. This is expressed in what Vygotsky calls "the general genetic law of development" which can be, he says, formulated as follows:

> *any function in the child's cultural development appears on the stage twice, on two planes, first on the social plane and then on the psychological*, first among people as an intermental category and then within the child as an *intramental category*.
>
> (Vygotsky, 1966: 44)[3]

What Harré has drawn from these laws is, as he puts it, "the insight (which history must surely ascribe to L.S. Vygotsky)" (Harré, 1986a: 120), that the personal psychology of each individual is created by their 'appropriating' the conversational forms and strategies available to them in the general clamour of everyday conversational

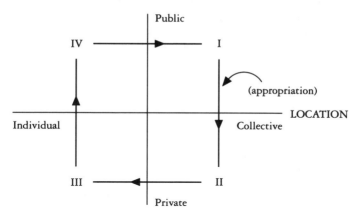

Figure 3 Vygotskian 'space'.

activity around them. And, "insofar as individual people construct a personal discourse on the model of public discourse, they become complex 'mental' beings with unique 'inner worlds' " (Harré, 1986a: 120).

In developing his formulations in this sphere, Harré has set them out in terms of two polarities: one dimension he terms a mental activity's *manifestation*, and distinguishes between whether its performance is *publicly* available or occurs *privately*, that is, in a way we make inaccessible to others; and the other he terms the activity's *location*, and distinguishes between whether it is located in the *collective* or in the *individual*. The two dimensions form what he calls a two-dimensional "Vygotskian space" of four quadrants (Figure 3). And, to quote him (Harré, 1986a: 121–2),

> according to the constructionist viewpoint, 'development' must occur through the transfer of rules and conventions that govern public conversation and other social practices from Quadrant I, via Quadrant II, to Quadrant III . . . The first step is the privatization of the language of the local social group.

But in fact, "the Vygotskian space allows us to think of the mind of another person as spread out over all four quadrants" (1986a: 125–6).

But what I think Harré has done here, in adopting this thoroughgoing social constructionist stance, albeit somewhat implicitly, is to have abandoned what might be called the 'things-ontology'[4] he introduced in his original formulations of the concept of powers – and along with it, what is seen as one of the strengths of the realist position: the possibility of appealing, in warranting our claims to knowledge, to structured entities which exist independently of our knowledge or of our experience of them. It is no longer the case that mental powers are or can be ascribed to locatable things or entities in virtue of *their* natures (whatever they are). Their developmental trajectory must be thought of as originating in (and perhaps as terminating in) the diffusely spread-out activities already existing within a collective. Even when they become privatized and localized within an individual, they can never be thought of as consisting of *complete* and hence describable structures, that is, structures to which to refer in enabling and constraining the performance of actions. For all our actions must, if they are to have any proper social currency, be *open* in their performance to interpretation and evaluation by others (see, in this connection, the comments later about the necessary incorporation in one's talk of a "rhetoric of reality").

But just to illustrate the depth of Harré's present commitment to this view, let me point to how in more recent writings he gives it further articulation. Harré (1986c: 288), declares his Wittgensteinian stance on mental phenomena as follows:

> Wittgenstein's philosophy of language has prompted, directly or indirectly, the daring suggestion . . . that much, perhaps all of the *fine grain* of human psychological functioning is a product of the language that a person has acquired. For that reason psychology must from now on be thought of as much a collective as an individual phenomenon. The revival of interest in the theories and empirical researches of Vygotsky has added a further impetus to this movement.

Thus, as he now sees it (see, for instance, Harré, 1983: 58), "the primary human reality is persons in conversation." But this raises quite a few questions for the realist philosophy of science he had previously helped to found.

From a things-ontology to a moral activities-ontology?

Let me try to be more specific about what I think some of those questions are. Given his turn to a social constructionist stance, and given his current claims that many of "the powerful particulars" of social life – like people's beliefs, their identities, and even their minds – are socially constructed, and only have a continuously negotiated and reproduced existence in certain of our social activities, can his conception of the world as "an interacting system of powerful particulars" (Harré and Maden, 1975: 7) be sustained? To what extent does it still make sense for him to maintain that causal powers should be seen (for the purposes of scientific investigation), not only as *located*, but also as actually located in *things*, which provide *in their natures* a basis for such powers? While the rhetoric of realism suggests the possibility of constructing and testing theories about the "generative mechanisms" which are said to be the *causes* of the behaviour observed – the programme set out in Harré and Secord (1972), and still not wholly abandoned (Harré *et al.*, 1985) – by comparison, his social constructionist rhetoric is less clear-cut. Rather than a world of locatable, powerful particulars, it implies – I shall argue – a world of much more diffusely distributed, non-locatable, morally structured activities, which can only be investigated from a position of involvement within them. And this immediately raises the question of how the character of the involvements in which one is placed should best be characterized: in terms just of a structure of locatable powers and competencies, or in terms of diffuse, non-locatable powers, which are open to morally and politically significant *attributions*, which are contestable as to their nature and location?

The strength of the realist's position in psychology – to quote Manicas and Secord (1983), who have attempted to set out its implications for psychological research – is that realists accept that "knowledge is a social and historical product; . . . [and] that there is no preinterpreted "given" and that the test of truth cannot be 'correspondence'." Nevertheless, they insist that

> it is precisely the task of the sciences to invent theories that aim to represent the world. Thus in the spirit of Kuhn . . . the practices of the sciences generate their own *rational* criteria in terms of which theory is accepted or rejected. The crucial point is that it is possible for these criteria to be rational precisely because on realist terms, there is a world that exists independently of cognizing experience. Since our theories are constitutive of the known world but *not* of the *world*, we may always be wrong, but *not* anything goes.
>
> (1983: 401)

By comparison, a thoroughgoing social constructionist stance seems to lack such anchor points. It seems to suggest that not only our knowledge of the world but the world itself is a social construction, and this seems to leave social constructionists whirling in a maelstrom of total relativity, bankrupt of any standards against which to judge the worth of their claims to knowledge.

Below, in a moment, I shall argue (again the claim I have already made above) that the world in question for social constructionists, our *Umwelt, is* socially constructed: for it is a world of mental powers and capacities, of mental liabilities and tendencies; of 'places', 'positions', and 'providential spaces'; of rights, duties, obligations, and privileges; of identities, roles, personalities, and selves; of different forms of human association – dyads, groups, institutions, bureaucracies, governments, industries, and so on. Such a social reality is articulated in terms both of the ways people can devise for relating themselves to one another, and of the kinds of people those modes of relationship allow or invite. But this does not means to say that just 'anything goes'. And we *can* in fact find (prefigured in Harré's recent work in a social constructionist vein) *standards* in such constructions, in what can be called an *ethics of communication*, or a *relational ethics*[5] – where such an ethics is to do with the responsibilities between the people involved, in maintaining their social constructions as the constructions they are. Here, however, let me continue with what I see as one of the main problems with a realist stance.

Rhetoric and the cunning of language

As I see it, the trouble is that a realist rhetoric or idiom authorizes a way of talking about certain 'things' and 'entities' – such as, "basic human powers and competencies and the structures that underlie them . . ." (Manicas and Secord, 1983: 411) – when no such things, entities, or structures as such may actually exist! Indeed, as Manicas and Secord (1983: 412) themselves state it, the advantage of the approach is that "it allows scientists to *believe* that they are grappling with entities that, although often not directly observable, are real enough" (emphasis added). Precisely! It allows scientists to warrant a way of talking about human mental phenomena *as if* they consisted in things like powers and competencies with describable underlying structures, without first questioning whether the source of their beliefs (about the existence of such locatable *entities*) is to be found solely in the nature of their talk, in the character of their own (non-locatable) communicative *activities*. They do not know whether the things they take to be 'real enough' are in fact *false*, and/or *imaginary*. Furthermore, in treating language as primarily referential, they ignore its rhetorical power to 'move' us in our feelings, to create a sense of *commitment*, and make us feel that we *must* proceed in a certain way – that *this* is how something has to *be*.[6]

Various comments of Wittgenstein's already mentioned are relevant here: As we have already seen, Wittgenstein (1980: I, no. 257) warns against the unwarranted completion (in our descriptions) of essentially incomplete human activities still in progress: "If you complete it, you falsify it." In other words, the unwarranted treatment of what is essentially ongoing activity as a completed object of knowledge, *falsifies* its historical (intentional) relations to other activities, past, present, and future: this makes it impossible to understand how, besides having a meaning, one's speech has a 'directionality', thus to 'move' those to whom it is addressed in a particular way, as well as making it impossible to understand the *possibilities* it makes available for the constitution of 'fitting' responses to it. In another comment, taking as given that our ways of talking create certain 'urges' or 'tendencies' within us, he remarks "that is how it comes about that the means of representation creates something *imaginary*" (1981: no. 446) – we come, as in a piece of science fiction writing, to *treat* certain entities as real, for after all, we have a 'sense' (in the movement of our thought about them) of their nature. However, the question as to whether, at least in the realm of mental phenomena, realists are victims of grammatical distortions or illusions generated by the nature of their own talk 'about' them, not only does not arise, it *cannot* arise and be investigated within a realist methodology. (Indeed, a Wittgensteinian would want to add, while beliefs may seem real if people believe they are real, that is not because believing is done by a special effort of will; it is because it is a special social practice, which is maintained by a particular pattern of social, political, economic and linguistic relations; it is a matter of how one lives one's life.)

Furthermore there is a difficulty to do with the implicit theory of human nature and action such a way of talking *commits* one to. Witness, for instance, how Manicas and Secord (1983: 406) describe psychology's task:

> Chomsky's generative grammar is seen (rightly or wrongly) as a theoretical structure that enables persons to generate sentences, and thus provides a core explanation of linguistic competence ... We believe that psychology as an

experimental science is best understood in analogous terms – as concerned with the structure of our competencies and not our realization of them in our everyday behaviour.

But what is it that warrants the claim that a theoretical structure is, in itself, enabling? And what suggests the thought that once a "competency" has been described (that is, represented) in terms of its "structure," a result of some psychological worth has been attained? Whence comes the complexly structured nature of Manicas and Secord's proposals? For surely, no one in psychology at the moment would claim to possess already a body of clearly organized empirical knowledge, or a set of generally effective experimental methods?

Again, a remark of Wittgenstein's (1953: no. 308), already mentioned, is, I think, appropriate here (and its application to Harré's (1970b) formulation of powers will not escape notice either). In talking of how philosophical problems arise about mental processes and states, he says:

> The first step is the one that altogether escapes notice. We talk of processes and states and leave their nature undecided. Sometime perhaps we shall know more about them – we think. But that is just what commits us to a particular way of looking at the matter. For we have a definite concept of what it means to know a process better. (The decisive movement in the conjuring trick has been made, and it was the very one we thought quite innocent.)[7]

In other words, the complexly structured nature of Manicas and Secord's proposals for the conduct of psychological research can be seen as issuing not from an empirical knowledge of successful research projects in psychology, but from the nature of their *talk* about 'powers' and 'competencies'. It is the talk that generates the feeling as to what *must be* the case – talk which is in fact only formulated in this way to make people's behaviour amenable to naturalistic methods of experimentation.

Conversational realities

But, it might be argued, aren't what I am calling grammatical distortions, illusions and commitments, just the kind of things realists think of as real anyway? Indeed, we all know W.I. Thomas's dictum "If men define things as real, they are real in their consequences," and isn't this all that matters? Aren't the activities going on between people real material activities, with real material bodily *consequences* in how they actually live their lives? Don't they contain historically developed, reproduced stabilities which, while enabling certain activities, also place real constraints upon what can be said and done? And, if we want to understand the determinants of people's actions, aren't these the structures we should attempt to describe? Yes . . . but! Are there any such *structures*, really? And, given the historical character of the enablements and constraints clearly operating in our communicative activities, is that how they are *best* characterized?

For what is in question here, is not whether people can exert a material effect upon one another in their communications, nor whether they can create certain forms of order (and then submit themselves to their reproduction) in their activities – realists and social constructionists alike accept both these claims. The question is, in what do such orders consist? And the question arises, because, as I see it, what is at issue is not just the proper characterization of the 'shape' or the structure of people's social activities, but the nature of their *moral* involvements with each other in the conduct of the historically formative processes concerned. In other words, do we require an ontology of already existing things, or an ontology of ethically significant, developmental activities? Harré has not answered this question, but has simply set his recent work, as I said above, in what he now sees as "the primary human reality," that of "persons in conversation."

Some of the things Harré (1983: 58–66) has argued about the nature of our conversational involvements, and I think quite correctly and most importantly, are the following:

1 That a "space," or a "referential grid," or what one might call an *intralinguistic reality*, is constructed in such talk, which functions (among other things) to provide a set of 'locations' or 'places' structured by *moral and political* considerations.
2 That the use of such pronouns as "I" (and "you") are empirically non-referential, that is, they do not refer to any empirically identifiable object, but work to index *momentary* status locations in such a space.
3 That other kinds of indexical expression, such as 'here', 'now', 'then', there', function to locate, root, or anchor such an intralinguistic reality in a larger, more publicly accountable world.
4 That the actions or utterances occurring in such a space can function both to refer to states or entities specified within the space, and to change its nature and, in particular, to change the array and nature of status locations, that is, the range, distribution and interrelation of the conversational rights and duties momentarily available to those conversationally involved.
5 That while in such contexts, people are in a sense *simple* beings, that is to say, they 'move' and are 'moved' by one another's immediate saying and doings. But they can change from simple into complex beings, and 'move' from the immediately interpersonal realm into the realm of public affairs in an instant. It is when the interpersonal flow of activity between them breaks down and they must *account* for, that is, justify, their conduct to one another, that the 'situation' of such interpersonal exchanges in a larger social scheme of things becomes apparent. It is through the necessity for *accountability*, as Harré (1983: 121) points out, that the social gets into the personal. For it is at a point when 'repairs' are necessary, that a publicly agreed form of order can determine the nature of the repairs made. And it is this which ensures that personal affairs retain a 'rooting' or 'anchoring' in a public order of things.

It is in this last point that we make contact with the primary issue set our above. What happens when such conversational realities are disrupted, to what do those involved in them appeal in effecting a repair? What is involved in their saying

"Now we know how to go on"? What is involved, both Harré and I would argue, is something to do with knowing how to be publicly accountable. But in what does such an ability consist?

From generative mechanisms to ethical logistics

Although human beings who are already constituted as morally accountable, self-conscious human beings can go out and gather, in a wholly autonomous and individualistic way, what counts in their society as 'information' about the things and events around them, they cannot gain their knowledge of how *to be* such individuals in this way. Indeed, to an external, third-person observer, it is not at all clear what would constitute the relevant 'information'. For it is not to do with what something '*is*' but with how it *should be* judged. And, what Wittgenstein (1953: 224–5) says about learning to judge people's motives:

> There is such a question as: "Is this a reliable way of judging people's motives?" But in order to be able to ask this we must know what "judging a motive" means; and we do not learn this by being told what '*motive*' is and what '*judging*' is.

or, simply about determining the length of a rod:

> What "determining the length" [of a rod] means is not learnt by learning what *length* and *determining* are; the meaning of the word "length" is learnt by learning, among other things, what it is to determine length.

applies here also. In other words, incorporated in all of what is accounted as human knowledge, is an evaluative or corrigible aspect. Thus, in acquiring any 'information' about one's circumstances, one must know how what one encounters *should* be accounted – for not *everything* one encounters in one's surroundings can be accounted as information by any means.[8]

Hence, among many other things, what is involved in gaining one's autonomy and learning how to learn by acquiring 'information', is grasping the 'methods' of checking applied by others to what are counted as claims to knowledge, and applying them in one's own attempts to learn. Hence Harré's (1986c: 288) rejection of what he calls the "Cartesian answer" to how such knowledge is acquired. An educative task of this kind cannot be accomplished simply by the transfer of a subjectively known body of knowledge, through some communicative 'channel', into the subjective contents of another being – for, among other things, there would be no way of knowing that the transfer had been accomplished correctly. What must be involved, he says, is the appropriation by an individual of a *resource* made available (under the restraints, quite often, of a certain political economy to do with scarcities of access) in certain regions of public, social activity at large. But what is the character of that resource?

Actually, paradigms of its nature are not at all difficult to identify and articulate.

Let us explore for a moment what happens as our linguistic competencies increase, and as adults we become more adept at constructing the whole network of *intralinguistic* references constituting a "linguistic reality." Now, instead of to an immediate, extralinguistic context, our utterances can refer to entities constructed within this intralinguistic context. But, as we begin to talk more about entities and states of affairs not immediately present, there is a decrease of reference to what 'is', and an increase to what 'might be'. In other words, there is an increase of reference to a hermeneutically constructed, potentially fictitious (or theoretical) world. Such a way of talking, if it is to have any factual status, requires the development of *methods* for warranting, in the course of such talk, one's claims about what 'might be' as actually being what 'is'.

In other words, morally responsible and autonomous people, if they want to be seen as talking factually, must incorporate in their talk a number of procedures or 'methods' (Garfinkel, 1967). In addition to the fact that these procedures must establish that the structure of the state of affairs in question must be seen as fitting into a certain 'basic' reality – the way we see 'things' in the West, in fact, as 'things' rather than 'activities' (Whorf, 1956)[9] – they must also establish that such facts are, for instance, the same for everyone, independent of people's wishes and opinions, and that knowledge of them was based upon personal observation, communicated by an authority, etc. And further, if their talk is to pass as factual, they must make opportunities in it for their claims to be challenged, and to be able to meet such challenges when they occur, on the spot. It is by the use of such methods and procedures that adult forms of speech can function with a great degree of independence from their immediate linguistic context. In other words, as adults we have learnt to incorporate in our speech what might be called a "rhetoric of reality," a way of talking which gives a sense, or a feel, for the reality we are taking about.

Here, then, is a paradigm which represents something of what is involved in talking with a sense of how what one is saying is going to be judged by others. But still more needs to be said, for we are still not yet wholly in the realm of the public: for the 'procedures' of warranting we include in our talk only set out *accounts* of the ways in which our claims were supposedly checked. Yet more needs to be done if we are to have our claims *actually* 'rooted', if not in the real world, then at least in what counts for all of us as the real world, our *Umwelt*. And *whose* task is it to do that work?

As Harré (1983: 58–66) points out, the 'locations' created in a conversational reality specify a set of rights and duties, privileges and obligations, as to who may speak to whom and in what manner. In other words, among other activities, they can be seen as specifying or directing who should do what at what moment, in the processes involved in the social construction of meaning. This is what it means to say that meanings are socially negotiated; a kind of *ethical logistics* is required – a skill at *coordinating the management of meaning* (Pearce and Cronen, 1980). But it is most important to add here a another point Harré (1983: 65) makes about the *unequal* distribution of such rights and duties.

In pointing out the need for our interpersonal exchanges to be located not only in the larger public sphere but also in "the continuous space and time of physical reality," he goes on to say:

> The relation between the consequences of our joint location in both manifolds is mediated by the local moral order, particularly the unequal distribution of rights upon which I have already remarked. For example, one may be physically present with others in the same space and time of a meeting, but, in the position of secretary, may not have the right to contribute to the cognitive processes proceeding in the flow of conversation.

Or, by contrast: one may be involved in the flow of conversation, but have no right to ask a high-status speaker for clarifications, it being assumed that it is the duty of the listener. Indeed, it is precisely children's misunderstanding of what are the reciprocal (and possibly asymmetrical) rights and duties of speakers and listeners, as to who should do what at what moment in making sense of a communication, that Rommetveit (1985) has been exploring to such brilliant effect recently. But much more is possible. In fact, such an account opens up a massive field of possible research topics to do with what I earlier called a political economy of communicative and developmental rights: to do with social identities in general, and gender identities in particular; to do with the unequal distribution of developmental opportunities; with rights of expression; with devices of accountability and warranting; with silences and the repair of misunderstandings; with closures, that is, who has the right to define otherwise ambiguous expressions clearly: and so on. In short, a study of the cultural politics involved in one's rights of access to, and duties for the provision of, the psychological resources available to others and oneself in the public sphere.

Conclusions: ethics of communication and realism

As I said at the beginning of this chapter, I wanted to explore some of the tensions between Harré the realist and Harré the social constructionist. And the question we now face is whether he has lost, by his turn to social constructionism, the very gains he sought by espousing realism: namely, the construction of some *impersonal* standards, independent of the wishes or desires or opinions of any particular individuals, against which claims to knowledge could be judged? And finally the answer, I think, is "no."[10] For, if it is the case that the world of all the differently morally managed ways of relating ourselves to one another – our different forms of social life – *is* socially constructed in our self–other relations, then, as I maintained earlier, we *must* observe certain standards in our conduct – or else we will destroy the very 'foundations', the 'basic' ways of making sense, upon which the intelligibility (and legitimacy) of our actions rests. Indeed, others will hold us to them. Or, to put it another way: if we do accept that our forms of rationality are socially constructed, then we cannot rationally deny in our talk the (moral) grounds upon which our rationality depends – while still claiming, at the same time, that our denials are rational. Although our denials would not, perhaps, be logically (or theoretically) self-defeating, they would certainly be, ultimately, rhetorically and thus practically self-defeating.

For example, it makes no sense to offer, as a justification for the assertion that all people's actions must be caused by their external circumstances, the fact that it is possible to *doubt* their capacity to act freely. "One simply tends to forget," says Wittgenstein (1980: II, no. 342), "that even doubting belongs to a language game." Thus even the expression of a doubt, if it is to be properly understood, involves one respecting what might be called *the ethics of communication*. So, although we may, in a Cartesian sense, raise 'supposed' doubts, that is to say, theoretical doubts, about people's rights and capacities to act freely, we cannot in any practically effective sense deny them these rights and capacities, if, that is, we want those who listen to our claims to take them seriously. Only a genuine doubt, a practical doubt which actually disturbed the 'ethical logistics' of the social relations involved – one in which in practice, say, we treated those to whom we were talking as entities incapable of understanding us – would destroy the pattern of social activities which makes our opportunities for communication possible. Thus, as Wittgenstein (1980: I, no. 548) says, what is at issue is a matter of whether our descriptions accord, not with what we claim our customs and conventions to be, but with how we actually act, in practice.

However, the methodological maxim I stated above only claims that *ultimately*, if rigorously sustained, such self–other orderings will prove self-defeating. Thus, it cannot in any way be interpreted as an invitation to quiescence. For, in the meantime, it is perfectly possible for societies to impose, or attempt to impose, single (or limited) orderings upon their members, who are then also constrained to reproduce such orders in their daily lives. For, from within the person–world dimensions to which such orderings give rise, people can only very gradually discover the 'infections' in those dimensions occasioned by the communicational biases, inequalities and injustices in the self–other relations they are constrained to live out in their daily lives. After all, the person–world dimension is *nearly* independent of the self–other dimension of interaction. Indeed, as we have already seen, concerning the entrapments discussed by Stolzenberg and Fleck, the professionalized incompetencies outlined by Feyerabend, the conceits discussed by Vico, the grammatical illusions discussed by Wittgenstein, and, no doubt other biases and distortions for which others can make a case, a great deal of metamethodological work is required to cure ourselves of all these ills of our own making.

These ills 'infect', so to speak, the person–world dimensions of interaction we produce in our self–other, joint actions. In that sense, they are indicative of the fact that, within our *Umwelten*, our person–world interactions are *not independent* of the interests, desires, opinions, etc., of particular persons or groups within them. To the extent that there is an ordering among them, it favours a particular ordering in our self–other relationships. Or, to put it the other way around, to the extent that a certain, single ordering of interests exists in our self–other relations, *that* ordering will be reflected in our person–world relations in some way; and to the extent that a multiplicity of differing orderings are struggling in contest with each other, we will face in the person–world dimension irresolvable dilemmas – the situation I think realism, as a philosophy of science, now faces (Shotter, 1992a).

As I said at the outset, as I see it, the dilemma for realism is this. One alternative is to attempt ahead of time, to resolve these dilemmas by in-principle, policy or theoretical solutions – as in Harré's (1990) "policy realism", or Bhaskar's (1989) and Eagleton's (1989), "realist theorizing" (as I shall call it). Although, if the views offered here (and the reasons for them) are accepted, then we can see that the 'convictions' that different realists feel, that there just *must* be a reality 'out there', will take on different forms in different communicational contexts. Thus this solution will, as I see it, still give rise to interminable debates about *whose* principles, policies, or theories should be followed. For, at least in social theory – the case is clearly different in the natural sciences where communicative practices revolve around a limited set of practical activities – there will be almost as many varieties of realism as realists. An alternative possibility is simply to accept the existence of such dilemmas, and turn instead to a study, when they appear, of the local 'grounds' in terms of which in fact they are resolved – thus to reveal the local cultural politics at work, where this, in fact, is the continuation of (realist's) politics by other means: instead of theory in the scientific sense of explanatory theory, what we shall require is theory in Wittgenstein's (1953: no. 122), sense[11] that is, in terms of "perspicuous representations" that produce "just that understanding which consists in 'seeing connections'."

But how can we know, ahead of time, what actually constitutes a *destructive* inequality in our ethics of communication? For inequalities are inevitable: if anybody is ever to tell us anything, then they must be allowed a right or a privilege to 'move' us with their words, and we have a duty or commitment to 'make sense' of the 'movements' their utterances produce in us. In the joint actions between people, first-person rights and duties are different from second-person ones, while those of third persons, 'outside' the situation in question, are quite different again, and all must be 'managed' in appropriate ways as the circumstances change (Shotter, 1984: 15–16). Only as a communicative situation develops do the providential possibilities within it become apparent. Thus the problem here is not easy to solve. But it is one thing to point to inequalities *within* a communicative practice; it is quite another to find standards which allow one to judge *between* communicative practices. The answer to these two problems can only be found, it would seem, by situating the practices concerned in a yet larger public context. Thus, rather than a theoretical problem, they give rise to a practical problem: that of constructing those larger public contexts. In other words, genuinely political problems about actual practical social arrangements face us at every turn – and cannot be solved in general theory ahead of time. But that does not mean that we cannot be more certain about particular things at a more local level, if larger public contexts *do* exist.

Clearly, not only are rights of access to communication, rights of access to developmental opportunities, and rights to closure (of the openness making for ambiguities in meaning) all unequally distributed in our society at the moment, but so also are the rights of accountability, the right to make or to call for 'repairs' which work to 'anchor' a discourse in a larger context, beyond its current 'reality'. It is not at all clear, however, whether this is as it should be or not. But what *is* clear is that hidden in the current rhetoric of individualism and the privatization of resources in the public domain, is a destruction of that larger public sphere to which, as an otherwise powerless individual, one can address claims about the negative effects of such inequalities and expect to have the rational force of one's claims felt, and their justice judged. But the tendency in science, no matter how much the degree of its backsliding in its more technological and instrumental manifestations – a tendency that I hope is still evident in the studies in this book, however 'merely rhetorical' they may seem – is in the opposite direction: towards the enlargement of the sphere of public accountability.[12] And this also, I think, has been one of the effects of Rom Harré's work. As he put it in *Social Being* (Harré, 1979: 3), "people have a deep sense of their own dignity, and a craving for recognition as beings of worth," and it has been Rom's project to show the worth of energy, tenacity, wit, and intellectual and academic skill, in helping to keep that sense of human dignity alive.

SIX

Vygotsky, Volosinov, and Bakhtin: 'Thinking' as a boundary phenomenon

By its very existential nature, the subjective psyche is to be localized some-where between the organism and the outside world, on the *borderline* separating these two spheres of reality.

(Volosinov, 1973: 26)

In this chapter, I want to explore two new and hitherto ignored themes in the study of Vygotsky's account of what he calls either the *internalization of higher psychological functions* (1978: 52), or the *sociogenesis of the higher forms of behaviour* (1966: 45), and I shall call the 'social construction of mind'. I want to sound a responsive or rhetorical as well as an ethical note.[1] My point in doing this, through an examination of Vygotsky's, Volosinov's, and Bakhtin's writings, is to explore the nature of what is said to be our 'inner' lives. And the conclusions for which I want to argue are as follows. The process of internalization is not, as the term may seem to suggest, a process in which what is at first outside us simply comes to be incorporated within us. For such a view would assume that we all already possessed a well-developed individuality; that we already knew how *to be* thoughtful and autonomous members of our society, and faced only the task of gaining information about our surroundings relevant to our goals — whereas the development of this kind of practical-moral knowledge (of how to be a certain kind of individual) is, I think, a major part of what is involved in what Vygotsky calls 'internalization'.

Instead, I want to argue that people's private 'inner' lives are neither as private and inner, nor as merely logical or as systematic as has been assumed. Indeed, rather than functioning mechanically and systematically, according to a unitary order, I want to argue that they reflect in their functioning essentially the same ethical and rhetorical considerations influencing the transactions between people, out in the world. And furthermore, instead of being organized at the centre of our being (thus to be given orderly expression or not as required), they are organized peripherally, in a moment-by-moment process of 'ethically sensitive negotiations' at the boundaries of our being, where the negotiations involved are as varied in their form, say, as those between intimate lovers, parent and child, those between distant strangers, those between poets and logicians, or those between different social classes, and require equally varied skills in their 'management'. By examining the structure of our 'minds' in this way, we can begin to see how we come to embody in our very ways of 'thinking' certain patterns of social relations.

What it means to say that our 'inner' life is a 'boundary' phenomenon

There is no doubt that currently nothing seems more natural to us as individual adults than that our thought goes on inside our heads. Indeed, we take it that it goes on within the neurological networks in the cortex of our brains, doesn't it? Where else could it be located if not there? Well, Wittgenstein voiced his disquiet with this claim in many ways. Here is, perhaps, one of his most dramatic expressions of it:

> No supposition seems to me more natural than that there is no process in the brain correlated with . . . thinking . . . I mean this: if I talk or write there is, I assume, a system of impulses going out from my brain and correlated with my spoken or written thoughts. But why should the *system* continue further in the direction of the centre? Why should this order not proceed, so to speak, out of chaos?
>
> (Wittgenstein, 1981: no. 608)

In other words, rather than issuing mechanically from already well-formed and orderly cognitions at the centre of our being, why shouldn't the expression[2] of a thought or an intention − the saying of a sentence or the doing of a deed, for example − originate in a person's vague and unordered *feelings* or *sense* of the context they are in? And their appropriate *orderly* realization or formation be something that people 'develop' in a complex set of temporally conducted negotiations between themselves (or their 'selves'), their feelings, and those to whom they must address themselves? Indeed, why shouldn't the processes 'within' people be similar to the transactions 'between' them, in which speakers' attempts to realize their thoughts are *negotiated* in a back-and-forth process, involving their listeners' attempts to understand, with each challenging the other as to the social appropriateness of their realizations and understandings, respectively − challenges which evoke sanctions, of course, if failed?

If this seems to be a strange proposal, then we must say straightaway that Vygotsky's psychology is a strange and surprising psychology, for this *is* precisely the relation between thought and word that he proposes:

> The relation of thought to word is not a thing but a process, a continual movement backward and forth from thought to word and from word to thought. In that process, the relation of thought to word undergoes changes

that themselves may be regarded as developmental in the functional sense. Thought is not merely expressed in words; it comes into existence through them. Every thought tends to connect something with something else, to establish a relation between things. Every thought moves, grows and develops, fulfils a function, solves a problem.

(Vygotsky, 1986: 218)

And, at a later point in the text he adds: "the structure of speech does not simply mirror the structure of thought; that is why words cannot be put on by thought like a ready-made garment" (p. 219). "Behind words, there is the independent grammar of thought, the syntax of word meanings" (p. 222). "Precisely because thought does not have its automatic counterpart in words,[3] the transition of thought to word leads through meaning. In our speech, there is always the hidden thought, the subtext" (1986: 251). The unique *sense* of our words in the context of their use is 'shown' in our saying of them, in our intoning[4] of them, not in the words we say; in our speech, we 'show' more than we are ever able to 'say' (Wittgenstein). What we 'show' is there in the 'movement' of our words.

Further, there is a 'subtext' because every utterance constitutes only *an attempt* (which is hardly ever completely satisfactory) to 'develop' a sensed thought-seed into an utterance-flower. What we try to say, and what we are understood as meaning, are often at odds with each other. Hence the necessity for the realization of a thought to be 'successively developed' (and checked), and for the transition of thought to word to be through meaning. Indeed, Vygotsky (1986: 255) feels that what can be said about the long-term relation of thought to language, can be said equally well of their short-term, momentary relation:

The relation between thought and word is a living process; thought is born through words. A word devoid of thought is a dead thing . . . But thought that fails to realize itself in words remains a "Sygian shadow" [O. Mandelstam] . . . The connection between thought and word, however, is neither preformed nor constant. It emerges in the course of development, and itself evolves.

It emerges in the course of a dialogic process of what Vygotsky calls "inner speech," a process, as I mentioned above, which can vary in its character according to the 'others' involved in the thought's 'development' – those with whom, about whom, and to whom, in one's inner speech one speaks.

If the relation between thought and words is a living process not an automatic one, if our thoughts do not have an orderly form before they are realized, if we do not know precisely what our thoughts are until we attempt to formulate them in some way (in actions or in words), where should we 'locate' our mental activities if not at the centre of ourselves? Bakhtin (1984: 287) answers this question as follows:

I am conscious of myself and become myself only while revealing myself for another, through another, and with the help of another . . . every internal experience ends up on the boundary . . . The very being of man (both internal and external) is a *profound communication. To be* means to *communicate* . . . To be means to be for the other; and through him, for oneself. Man has no internal sovereign territory; he is all and always on the boundary . . .

And indeed (along with Vygotsky, Volosinov, and Bakhtin), this is what I want to argue: that our 'inner' lives are structured by us living 'into' and 'through', so to speak, the opportunities or enablements offered us by the 'otherness' both around us, and within us. Thus our mental life is never wholly our own. We live in a way which is both responsive, and in response, to what is both 'within us' in some way, but which is also 'other than' ourselves. Why? Because dialogic inner speech is *joint action*, and joint action always creates that third entity – the context, situation, circumstance, etc., that the action is 'in' and must 'fit in' with.[5]

In this *communicational* view of ourselves, then, the current view we have of persons, as all equal, self-enclosed (essentially indistinguishable) atomic individuals, possessing an inner sovereignty, each living their separate lives, all in isolation from each other – the supposed experience of the modern self – is an illusion, maintained by the institution between us of certain special forms of communication. It is an illusion which, besides misleading us about our own nature as human beings, also misleads us about the nature of thought and of language – we have come to think about both as if they are like the closed, unitary systems of signs in mathematics rather than as a heterogeneous set of means or devices for us to link ourselves to our surroundings.[6] This is precisely the assumption Vygotsky (1986: 1–2) challenges at the very outset of his work:

> The unity of consciousness and the interrelation of all psychological functions were, it is true, accepted by all; the single functions were assumed to operate inseparably, in an uninterrupted connection with one another. But this unity of consciousness was usually taken as a postulate, rather then a subject of study . . . It was taken for granted that the relation between two given functions never varied; that perception, for example, was always connected in an ideal way with attention, memory with perceptions, thought with memory.

Yet, as he goes on to say, "all that is known about psychic development indicates that its very essence lies in the change of the interfunctional nature of consciousness" (1986: 2).

In other words, Vygotsky opened up 'gaps' between all the different psychological functions, 'responsive gaps' that we can bridge in different ways, at different times, in different circumstances, by the use of various "mediatory devices." A series of questions (as in a mnemonic, say) provokes within us a series of responses, a dialogic sequence of questions and answers; the mnemonic provides us with an organized scheme of 'reminders', thus aiding us to remember events, happenings, etc., that would otherwise be lost to us. The bridging of the 'gap' between question and answer, the responding 'into' the context fashioned by the asking of question, *is* the making of the link. But, as for Wittgenstein, so for Vygotsky, there are countless ways in which such links might be made. And it is treating the 'links' between thoughts and words as having a 'developmental' or 'providential' character, rather than as being related in a systematic, mechanical, or logical manner, that leads, as we shall see, to the introduction of an *ethical* and *rhetorical* (justificatory) note into accounts of how people organize and 'manage' their own mental activities – as well as, of course, to a much less systematic and less unified view of language itself.

Language and thinking: dialogue and ethics

I want to turn first to a consideration of ethical issues for three major reasons. Firstly, because Vygotsky himself, in his own talk about internalization, makes a central distinction between things people do spontaneously and those they do deliberately, and thus he himself, if only implicitly, hints at such a concern. My second reason is connected with what I said above about our learning how *to be* a proper member of our society. Indeed, I want to point out that the consequences of conceptualizing human activities in moral terms have not yet been fully recognized and explored in psychology. If we were to treat social relationships ethically rather than causally (which we do not at the moment in social theory do), this would change their character entirely. As we have already seen, rather than things happening in an input-output, one-pass, causal and systematic manner, all human activities (within a culture) would have to be seen as 'developmental': they would have to be seen as involving in their *proper* conduct, a *socially negotiated or negotiable*, dialogically structured process of formation, a process which in its conduct or 'management' must, moment by moment, take into account the changing character of what is morally permitted and what is not. Indeed, even fully 'internalized' (cognitive) processes, taking place wholly 'within' individuals, if they are to be accounted as socially appropriate, that is, as both intelligible and legitimate, must also honour in their formation certain moral privileges and obligations. Thirdly, as the *ethical* aspects of interaction only hinted at by Vygotsky are central to both Bakhtin's and Volosinov's[7] accounts of language, it is thus interesting to try to develop some of Vygotsky's notions about the relation of thought and language with the help of the further resources they provide.

While most other psychologies are concerned, as we know, with determining the conditions controlling people's behaviour, Vygotsky is concerned to study how people, through the use of their own social activities, by changing their own conditions of existence can change themselves. Our higher mental functions can be developed, he suggests, not by developing more fully any 'natural' potentials we may contain within ourselves as individuals, but by our first discovering how to make use of what he calls "psychological tools or instruments" – quite artificial aids or devices of our own invention – and then how to incorporate (or embody) the functioning of such devices within ourselves. The major 'tool' for influencing people's behaviour is language: this is his central and most important notion. For, in the development of behaviour, says Vygotsky (1966: 39–40), "the child begins to practice with respect to himself the same forms of behaviour that others formerly practiced with respect to him." Hence, he continues, "we may say that *we become ourselves through others* and that this rule applies not only to the personality as a whole, but also to the history of every individual function" (1966: 43) – thus, what at first appears on the social plane as something intermental, between people, later appears as something psychological, as an intramental category within the child (1966: 44) – where, to repeat, the same ethical concerns which held in the social realm are still of importance in the 'inner', psychological realm of the individual.

The special nature of this ethical concern, perhaps, becomes more apparent if, in exploring what Vygotsky actually means when he talks of the process of *internalization*, we ask: 'Is he talking about it as a *physical*, or a *psychological* movement inwards?' In other words, is he talking about how what is 'outside' us geometrically or geographically, so to speak, gets 'inside' us; or is he using the word 'internalize' to characterize something not essentially spatial at all, but to do with a transformation in our *responsibility* for things? To put it yet another way, is he talking about a merely cognitive[8] process, in which what was at first inside only the adult's head is transferred into the child's head, or, is he talking about a process in which things which at first a child only does spontaneously and unselfconsciously, under the control of an adult, come under the control of the child's own *personal agency*? Although, as I said above, Vygotsky never explicitly made the distinction in ethical terms, I think he clearly means the second of these two possibilities. For we must be impressed by his claim that one of the basic laws governing psychological development is that "awareness and deliberate control appear only during a very advanced stage in the development of a mental function, after it has been used and practiced unconsciously and spontaneously. In order to subject a function to intellectual and volitional control, we must first possess it" (Vygotsky, 1986: 168). Clearly, for him, a central criterion in our mastery of a function is our being able to perform it, as he says, consciously rather than unconsciously,[9] as we ourselves rather than as our circumstances require.

As an example of such a process, he discusses the development of the child's ability to pronounce individual speech sounds upon request as a result of the child learning the grammar[10] of his or her native tongue while learning to write in school. If, before the young pre-school child learns to write, he points out, you ask him or her to produce a combination of separate speech sounds, for example *sk*, the task is usually too difficult. Yet within the context of a familiar word – such as *Moscow* – the child finds the task easy. But through learning to write, the child

> may not acquire new grammatical or syntactic forms in school but, thanks to instruction in grammar and writing, he does become aware of what he is doing and learns to use his skills consciously. Just as the child realizes for the first time in learning to write that the word *Moscow* consists of the sounds *m-o-s-c-o-w* and learns to pronounce each one separately, he also learns to construct sentences, to do consciously what he has been doing unconsciously in speaking.
>
> (Vygotsky, 1986: 184)

We have here, then, a process of 'instruction' in which certain invented devices – in this case, certain written forms of language, whose formal significance can be 'visualized' – are made use of, as Vygotsky says, not necessarily to teach the child any new speech skills, but which do function none the less to transform a child's own relation to his or her own acts of speaking. What actually is happening here?

The 'cultural' use of artificial signs in the control of a function

Of help here, I think, is a study of the use of artificial signs in the development of self-controlled remembering (Vygotsky, 1978: 38–51). Here, he discusses a game where children had to answer a number of irrelevant questions, among which were interspersed a series of relevant colour-questions ('What colour is . . .?') – where the 'rules' of the game were to do with what colours they were allowed to use in their answers (certain colours being completely forbidden, while others could not be used more than once). The artificial 'signs' made available to the children were simply a set of cards coloured upon one side, cards which the children could, of course use (by turning them over as they said the colours, to indicate to themselves the 'answers' still left available to them at any point in the game). Without going into the details of the different ways in which the cards were actually used (or not), the following comments are relevant.

Firstly, as Vygotsky notes, that there are two forms of remembering, 'lower' or 'elementary' forms and 'higher' forms: elementary forms of remembering are unmediated and direct – there are some things we do just remember – while other, higher forms make use of mediatory aids serving as organized reminders. Secondly, these two qualitatively different lines of development, one which is biological in origin and the other which is socio-cultural, are interwoven:[11] we can make use of what we *just* remember to control what we in our culture *must* remember. While thirdly, the process of interweaving is not in any way a 'natural' process – "the child does not suddenly and irrevocably deduce the relation between the sign and the method for using it" (Vygotsky, 1978: 45). A number of 'stages' of development seem to be involved: At first, with pre-school children, the performance with and without the cards is the same, they perform badly. The cards do not seem to have any kind of 'instrumental' function at all; only older children are able to use the cards as external aids, as a means for the control of their remembering; without the cards, though, they still perform badly. With adults, however, a stage is reached where the performance with or without the cards is similarly high, the presence of the actual cards themselves is unnecessary. Now it seems that "the external sign that school children require has been transformed into an internal sign produced by the adult as a *means of* remembering" (1978: 45, emphasis added).

Indeed, we might go a step further and claim that the external signs 'mastered' by the child have, in the adult, become embodied as prostheses *through* which to sense the nature of the problem – that is, in their embodied form they come to function as 'mental organs' in the sense discussed in Chapter 1 (although, in a moment, I shall want to extend the account offered there). Thus as socially competent adults, if appropriately 'instructed' as children, they come to act as 'the task' seems to require. In other words, as the children of a particular culture, they learn how to appropriate capacities both from their own biology *and* from the culture's socio-cultural history, appropriate to life in that culture. As adults, these capacities have become reincorporated into their being, that is, embodied, and they come again to react to their circumstances in a spontaneous and unthinking manner, but now in ways which make sense within the terms of their culture. As a result, as adults, they find themselves confronting a 'given' but unique situation, a situation which, given what and who they are (as members of and as individuals in their culture), is *their* situation and no one else's. They cannot wish it away. To act upon it, they must themselves respond to it personally. But now it is 'given' them in socially intelligible terms.

What changes as the child grows up, then, according to Vygotsky, is not simply a matter of the child's being simply able to remember more things, along with a larger number of connections between them. But the child is 'instructed' in the use of various, culturally invented, mediational means, and enabled, in developing various *interfunctional* relations between them, to develop an ability to interweave mediated and non-mediated functions into an organized plan of action. First listen to the question; then look at the cards for an available answer; then select the best answer; then turn the card over so it cannot be selected again, and so on. By 'thinking', that is, by 'instructing' herself with the help of the cards, she can put her remembering into an appropriate order, thus to control it, to bring her innate capacity to remember things to bear on the task in the appropriate way, at the appropriate (cultural) moment. Indeed, in this situation as the child develops, the interfunctional relations involved in the child's learning a 'higher' form of remembering – the relations between thinking and remembering – completely reverse their direction, Vygotsky (1978: 51) claims:

> *For the young child, to think means to recall; but for the adolescent, to recall means to think.* Her memory is so 'logicalized' that remembering is reduced to establishing and finding logical relations; recognizing consists in discovering that element which *the task indicates* [emphasis added] has to be found . . . When a human being ties a knot in her handkerchief as a reminder, she is, in essence, constructing the process of memorizing by forcing an external object to remind her of something; she transforms remembering into an external activity. This fact alone is enough to demonstrate the fundamental characteristic of the higher forms of behaviour. In the elementary form something is remembered; in the higher form humans remember something. In the first case a temporary link is formed owing to the simultaneous occurrence of two stimuli that affect the organism; in the second case humans personally create a temporary link through the artificial combination of stimuli.

This, I think, is a very cogent account of the nature of 'instruction' leading to mediated remembering. However, there is still, I think, not only something missing from it, but also something wrong with it.

What is missing from it is what I alluded to above: that when Vygotsky says that human beings create a temporary link *personally*, he fails to explicate what it means to do things 'personally', that is, what it is to be and to act as a person within a particular culture. Further, what I think is wrong is that he claims that the child, in discovering what he or she must do, discovers, like the adults I mentioned above, what 'the task indicates' has to be done. How should we react to these deficiencies?

Clearly, what Vygotsky means in saying that people come to remember something 'personally' is that, as their skill at using mediational devices develops, they become able to subject remembering to intellectual and volitional control; they become able themselves *to be responsible* for the way in which it is done – where an important part of what it is to be responsible for something is, as Winch (1958), following Wittgenstein, points out, knowing how to correct oneself if one goes wrong. In other words, what Vygotsky does not make clear is how the child learns, not only *in what way* a task *must* be done, but also in what way mistakes must be corrected. For the task in the cards experiment is, for the children, not just learning *a* way of using the cards, but to make use of them in the *right way* at the *right time* – according to how the adults (who are teaching them) have arranged the task. Thus at first, it is not 'the task' itself which indicates what children have to do, and which corrects them if they go wrong, but *the adults around them* to whom they are responsible; they are the ones who can and do *judge* whether the child is acting correctly or not. They are the 'keepers', so to speak, of the culture which the child must acquire.

Thus, in learning how to make appropriate use of the coloured cards, children do not simply learn the 'logical' relations between the cards and the questions, in general – for indeed, there are no such relations in general and none as such are taught to the child. Different cards must be used in different ways in different situations, and the children themselves must work out how to apply the cards to the task. It is this which Vygotsky misses when he talks of the child's memory becoming 'logicalized'; he misses the importance of the fact that the children's initial grasp of what the task 'is' is not in itself immediately obvious – it is something culturally defined. The children gain a grasp of it in their conversations with their adult teachers; and both at the start of the experiment and right the way through it the adults continue to correct the children in their attempts to do the task, until a point comes at which (presumably) no further corrections are necessary. At that point, the children do not just know 'personally' how to create an appropriate 'temporary link', but also how to 'see' what the problem 'is' for which they must create a solution, and how to justify their actions to others if asked to do so. It is the development of this 'way of seeing' the problem situation that is, I think, almost more important than the development of the personal ability to solve it. For it is "by means of words [that] children single out separate elements, thereby overcoming the natural structure of the sensory field and forming new (artificially introduced and dynamic) structural centres. The child begins to perceive the world not only through his eyes but also through his speech" (Vygotsky, 1978: 32) – this is a paradigm of the kind of embodied, practical-moral knowledge that I think is involved in becoming a member of a culture. And it is this kind of knowledge that I would now like to discuss.

"Psychological tools"

We now turn, I think, to the most important innovation in Vygotsky's work: the idea of the word as a tool, the idea that in the speaking of words, people can 'shape' each other in their psychological being. In studying the development of 'higher' forms of socio-cultural mental activity from 'lower' biological abilities, Vygotsky asks, how is it possible? What is it one seeks? "The main question", says Vygotsky (1986: 102),

> about the process of concept formation – or about any goal-directed activity – is the question of the *means* by which the operation is accomplished. Work, for instance, is not sufficiently explained by saying that it is prompted by human needs. We must consider as well the use of tools, the mobilization of the appropriate means without which work could not be performed. To explain the higher forms of human behaviour, we must uncover the means by which man learns to organize and direct his behaviour.

In portraying the nature of the means used in the mediation of 'higher forms' further, it is important as I mentioned in Chapter 1, to distinguish *prosthetic* and *indicative* functions in the devices mediating our investigations: the means used may serve a function like the blind person's stick, enabling us in actively investigating our situation *through* it in ways which would otherwise be inaccessible to us; or they may be like the pointers on dials, indicating some remote state of the world. But now further functions need to be added to these: I have not yet made any clear distinction between 'investigatory devices' and 'tools', nor between 'tools' and linguistic 'signs'.

Here again, we shall find it useful to refer to Vygotsky's account before suggesting modifications to it. In discussing the development of two different lines of mediated activity, he distinguishes between signs and tools, saying:

> A most essential difference between a sign and a tool, and the basis for a real divergence of the two lines, is the different ways that they orient human behaviour. The tool's function is to serve as the conductor of human influence on the object of activity; it is *externally* oriented; it must lead to change in objects. It is a means by which human external activity is aimed at mastering, and triumphing over, nature. The sign, on the other hand, changes nothing in the object of a psychological operation. It is a means of internal activity aimed at mastering oneself; the sign is *internally* oriented.
>
> (1978: 57)

But what we must add to Vygotsky's account is that linguistic signs themselves can also have both a 'tool' and a 'prosthetic' function, as well as sign functions (in the sense of these terms outlined above). Indeed, I have tended to talk indiscriminatively of all 'tools' as having a 'prosthetic' function, which of course they do: as one hammers a nail in, one 'feels' the hardness or softness of the wood *through* the hammer's handle. Similarly, linguistic signs exhibit both 'tool' and 'investigatory' functions. Nevertheless, the 'tool' and the 'prosthetic' function of signs need to be distinguished.

Although both influence our social ontology, the kind of people we *are*, the 'tool' function of language extends our capacities to act, to 'move' others, and our selves, in particular ways, while the 'prosthestic' function of language extends our perceptual skills at being a certain kind of listener, speaker, disinterested observer, storyteller, thinker, etc. With regard to the 'tool' function of language, Vygotsky (1986: 106) himself remarks that "our experimental study proved that it was the functional use of the word, or any other sign, as means of focussing one's attention, selecting distinctive features and analyzing and synthesizing them, that plays a central role in concept formation." "Learning to direct one's own mental processes with the aid of words or signs is an integral part of the process of concept formation" (1986: 108). In other words, what one has learned to do in thinking conceptually, is, in Vygotsky's terms, not to compare the configuration of a supposed inner mental representation with the configuration of a state of affairs in reality, but something else much more complicated: one has grasped how to organize and assemble in a socially intelligible way, one which makes sense to the others around one, bits and pieces of information dispersed in space and time in accordance with 'instructions' they (those others) provided, and which now a supposed 'concept' provides.

At first, the child may be influenced by the externally oriented language of others; they can use it in a 'tool'-like way to influence his or her activity, to 'move' the child to certain actions. Later, this interpersonal function of language can be transformed into an intrapersonal one: children may come to use the words used by others to control them, to control themselves. What they learn in the course of being 'instructed' by adults becomes incorporated into their very being as members of their society.

Having made these distinctions above, the point to emphasize here is that all these functions are in play at once in our speaking. Usually, if asked to reflect upon the process of speaking, we 'see through' the speech we use, that is, we see 'from' what we say 'to' either its effects, or 'to' its meanings; its prosthetic functioning remains 'invisible' to us. We fail to notice it because, in speaking, we act 'through' our utterances in 'making sense'. But clearly, if this account is correct, as a very special form of "psychological instrument", linguistic signs possess what might be called a 'prosthetic–tool–text ambiguity', the three different aspects each becoming visible according to the different 'direction' of our view: Acting towards the future, prospectively and creatively, in the *saying* of an utterance, we attempt to use it both prosthetically, as a device 'through' which to begin to express our meanings, and, as a tool-like means to 'move' other people. Indeed, we can go so far here as to say that this prosthetic–tool function of speech, or words in their speaking, works on one's surroundings formatively, to specify them further (see Shotter, 1984). Retrospectively, however, what we (and others) have already *said* remains 'on hand', so to speak, as like a 'text', constituting a given aspect of the situation between oneself and one's interlocutors, into which they (as well as oneself) must direct their speech. Thus, in using words (as Bakhtin makes clear below), we have to take into account *whose* words they are. Indeed, it is in the tensions between the retrospective and the prospective, the given and the created, the form and its use, between 'finding' and 'making', in the expression of an utterance, that the 'mental movements' it represents can be shaped.

Rule-following

It is the socio-cultural, socio-historical nature of this *intralinguistically created* textual context, as it is temporally (and spatially) developed[12] by what is said, that everyone involved must take into account (when it is their turn to speak or act) – if, that is, their actions are to be judged as appropriate to it. It is this, the realization that as one speaks, a temporal-spatial network of intralinguistic references is developed into which one's future speech *must* be directed, that I think is the key to the further understanding of the ethical nature of our mental processes. For this network is a 'providential space' of joint action with two major properties: first, it carries within it the traces of one's socio-cultural history, and one *ought* to act within it in such a way as to sustain the resources it contains; but second, in *responding* to the 'invitations', etc., available to one from one's place or position within it, one acts in it in one's own unique, creative, novel way. However, if one respects its providential nature, then one's creativity is always intelligible creativity, because it takes place within the *forms* of the 'providential space' in question. To see how this can be, we must turn to a discussion of Bakhtin's concepts of the utterance and speech genres. But before doing so, I first want to say something about rule-following, and what is involved in our reflexively grasping the conditions of our own historical origins and growth. For I want to combat the still almost hegemonic notion that rules and conventions, or, systems of conventionalized meanings, are constitutive of our being to such an extent that there is no way we can move beyond them to grasp the historical grounds of our own being.[13] In fact, the invention of a methodology for the grasping of these grounds is precisely the metamethodological problem Vygotsky wrestled with.

In the course of developing higher abilities, as a child, one comes to embody within oneself certain practical-moral ways of 'instructing' oneself in how to act, speak, perceive, and evaluate; they are practical-moral ways because in being instructed in them, one learnt not just how to go through certain motions, to supposedly follow certain rules, but how to employ one's own, basic, biological abilities in a *right* way, that is, in a personally responsible way, a way that sustains the culture of which one is a part. And the point I want to make here is a point made quite some time ago now by Winch (1958) – even though he said that "the *analysis* of meaningful behaviour must allot a central role to the notion of a rule" (1958: 51–2, emphasis added). The point he made is as follows: after repeating Lewis Carroll's tale of how the tortoise tricks Achilles into an infinite regress by getting him to commit himself to following a rule for every step in a logical inference, he went on to make the point that

> the actual process of drawing an inference, which is after all at the heart of logic, is something which cannot be represented as [itself] a logical formula[14] . . . To insist on any further justification is not to be extra cautious; it is to display a misunderstanding of what inference is. Learning to infer . . . is learning *to do* something.
>
> (1958: 57)

Human activity can never quite be summed up in a set of explicit precepts. The activity 'goes beyond' the precepts (Oakeshott, quoted in Winch, 1958: 55). Indeed, as Garfinkel (1967) found, no matter how clearly a set of rules may be formulated, discussion of *ad hoc* considerations relevant to their application is still necessary among those who must use them. For those using a set of coding procedures to select cases for treatment in a clinic, it was

> not the case that the necessary and sufficient criteria are procedurally defined by the coding instructions . . . Instead *ad hoc* considerations are consulted by coders and *ad hocing* practices are *used in order to recognize what the instructions are definitely talking about.*
>
> (1967: 22; emphasis in original)

Thus, in some way, as Wittgenstein (1953: no. 242) also makes clear, *judgements* are involved. We must possess some way of grasping the socio-historical grounding of our own actions, some way of sensing the socio-historical nature of the *intra-linguistically created* textual context into which we must direct our own actions, if we want them to be appropriate to it. And methodologically, we must seek a way of sensing also what it is that the people involved the situation sense.

In facing this problem, Vygotsky (1978: 63–5) discussed the problem of "fossilized behaviour". By that, he meant behaviour at its very highest stage of development, when it has become so automated and mechanical that it is impossible to distinguish between it and similar biological forms. And he suggested that if we are to understand the socio-historical conditions of its origins and growth – the contexts that first 'invited' it as a spontaneous response, and the words others used as 'instructions' to 'move' us to function in certain orderly ways – then we must study those points of trouble and difficulty in its development when it is undergoing change, before it reaches its final state of development. For "to study something historically means to study it in the process of change" (1978: 64–5). In other words, instead of systems of already said words, ways of talking that have already been accepted as having meaning, what we must study are those moments of trouble and difficulty when meaning is coming into existence. We must study words in their speaking, in the contexts in which their speaking occurs, and focus upon those moments of hiatus when the 'gap' between one speaking subject and another must somehow be bridged. And we must study the resources available for people's use in their fashioning those 'bridges'.

Utterances not sentences

While the claim by such linguists as Saussure (followed by Chomsky, of course) that the single *sentence* should be the basic unit in an *analytic* understanding of language may be true, it cannot be regarded as a basic unit for studying the practical working of language. For Bakhtin (1986: 81) that unit can be found in the *utterance*.[15] The utterance is a real responsive-interactive unit for at least two major reasons. First, it marks out the boundaries (or the gaps) in the speech flow between different speakers: "The first and foremost criterion for the finalization of an utterance is *the possibility of responding to it* or, more precisely and broadly, of assuming a responsive attitude to it . . ." (Bakhtin, 1986: 76). But second, in its performance an utterance must take into account the (already linguistically shaped) context into which it must be directed:

> Any concrete utterance is a link in the chain of speech communication of a particular sphere. The very boundaries of the utterance are determined by a change of speech subjects. Utterances are not indifferent to one another, and are not self-sufficient; they are aware of and mutually reflect one another . . . Every utterance must be regarded as primarily a *response* to preceding utterances of the given sphere (we understand the word 'response' here in the broadest sense). Each utterance refutes affirms, supplements, and relies upon the others, presupposes them to be known, and somehow takes them into account . . . Therefore, each kind of utterance is filled with various kinds of responsive reactions to other utterances of the given sphere of speech communication.
>
> (1986: 91)

Indeed, even as we speak, as we formulate our utterances, we must take account of the 'voices'[16] of others, that is, the gap between what we feel we want to say, and *can* say (which is in our control), and how we feel they (the 'others') *might* respond to it (which is not in our control).

> For each word of the utterance that we are in the process of understanding, we, as it were, lay down a set of our own answering words. The greater their number and weight, the deeper and more substantial our understanding will be . . . *Any true understanding is dialogic in nature.* Understanding is to utterance as one line of dialogue is to the next.
>
> (Volosinov, 1973: 102)

It is these different gaps, the 'distances' between the 'positions' of all those who might respond to what we say, and the struggles to which they give rise, which constitute the 'semantic landscape', so to speak, into which our attempted formulations must be directed. And these are the considerations to which, even when 'thinking' all alone, we must address ourselves (if, that is, we want what we write to be acceptable and to have point). It is in this sense, that Bakhtin's account of thinking parallels Billig's (1987) – that our practical thinking is rhetorical in the sense of involving a developmental, dialogic process of criticism and justification – and why I call the stance I have taken in this book a 'rhetorical-responsive' stance.

As Bakhtin (and Billig) continually remind us, then, our mental life is neither wholly under our own control nor filled with our own materials. We live in a way that is responsive both to our own position and to the positions of those who are 'other than' ourselves, in the semiotically created 'world' in which we are 'placed'.

Bakhtin's claim above, then, that we have no internal sovereign territory of our own, arises out of his *responsive*, non-referential approach to language.[17] For him, people's linguistic task is not in any way like that depicted in Saussure's (1960: 11–12) classic, paradigmatic account of the communicative situation, in which an immaterial idea or concept in the 'mind' of one person (a speaker or writer) is *sent* into the mind of another, essentially similar person (but now in the role of a listener or reader), by the use of material signs such as vibrations in the air or ink-marks on paper. Indeed, the speaker

> does not expect passive understanding that, so to speak, only duplicates his or her own idea in someone else's mind. Rather, the speaker talks with an expectation of the listener preparing a response, agreement, sympathy, objection, execution, and so forth (with various speech genres presupposing various integral orientations and speech plans on the part of speakers or writers).
>
> (Bakhtin, 1986: 69)

In other words, the utterance is a real social psychological unit in that it marks out the boundaries (or the gaps) in the speech flow between different 'voices', between different 'semantic positions', whether between people or within them. This is not the case with sentences: "the boundaries of the sentence as a unit of language are never determined by a change of speaking subjects," says Bakhtin (1986: 72). The trouble with the sentence is that "it has no capacity to determine directly the *responsive position* of the other speaker; that is, it cannot evoke a response. The sentence as a language unit is only grammatical, not ethical in nature." For him, the process is just like Vygotsky's process of 'instruction', in which an embodied person of one kind 'makes' something known to another of a (usually very) different kind (for example, an adult to a child) by 'instructing' that person in its construction. Thus everything of importance goes on in the gaps or the zones of uncertainty, so to speak, between utterances. For it is there, at the boundaries between the different, unique positions in existence, that everyone is responsible for the constructions they make in bridging them. Nothing in Bakhtin's world is tightly coupled or pre-determined, a degree of loose-jointedness prevails everywhere.

Speech genres and the attainment of
linguistic autonomy

The existence of gaps, the lack of necessary, mechanistic connections does not, however, mean that everything is totally unconnected either. As each utterance is responded to, what has already been said remains 'on hand', so to speak, as a 'text' to form a context (of enabling constraints) as to what may next be said – a property, as I have already suggested, of joint action. Or, to put it another way, the different linguistic 'spaces' we occupy are 'providential spaces' that provide different kinds of linguistic or architectonic resources to their inhabitants. Bakhtin (1986: 78) captures their character in his notion of speech genres:

> We speak only in speech genres, that is, all our utterances have definite and relatively stable typical *forms of construction of the whole*. Our repertoire of oral (and written) speech genres is rich. We use them confidently and skilfully *in practice*, and it is quite possible for us not even to suspect their existence *in theory*.

What is constituted (and reproduced) in the use of a particular speech genre is, among many other aspects of an 'ongoing social world', a particular set of interdependently related but continually changing speech 'positions'. These are positions, on the one hand, for which we are *answerable*, and on the other, which permit us as speakers certain forms of *addressivity*, that is, to aim our speech at the positions of others. Hence, in this sense, responsivity equals answerability plus addressivity. It is in their permitting of some speech forms but disallowing others that the social institutions constituted by particular speech genres are maintained, repaired, and transformed.

Any utterances occurring within a given sphere of communication, in taking into account the (already linguistically shaped) context into which they must be directed, become filled with responsive reactions to what has already occurred within that sphere.[18] Thus, in this sense, each sphere is a particular 'providential sphere', a historical sphere, full of all the results of the past 'condensed' into the present, even though, by the different spheres in which we communicate, Bakhtin means nothing more than, say, our family, our work, in banks and post offices, in official documents, our intimate relations, and so on. All the ordinary spheres of activity in everyday life that have been, or are, maintained in existence by an ongoing communicative process of a particular kind – it is their historical nature that gives them their particular character as the spheres they are, and structures what we are permitted to do in them. Thus:

> Speech genres organize our speech in almost the same way as grammatical (syntactical) forms do. We learn to cast our speech in genetic [developed and developing] forms and, when hearing other's speech, we guess its genre from the very first words; we predict a certain length (that is, the approximate

length of the speech whole) and a certain compositional structure; we foresee the end; that is, from the very beginning we have a *sense* of the speech whole, which is only later differentiated during the speech process.

(Bakhtin, 1986: 79, emphasis added)

As we become more and more adept, then, at the use of various speech genres, at participating in already constructed networks of *intralinguistic* references to function as a context into which to direct our own further utterances – as well as adept at constructing our own – then we become increasingly capable of acting within a context, independently of its immediate, momentary structure. In such a development, there is a transformation from being 'answerable' for our own immediate position to being answerable for our 'position' in an alternative, intra- linguistically constructed context, claimed to be a *representation* of it. Thus, here we can begin to see how an 'official' ideology can come to supplant the 'living' ideology present in the activities of everyday social life. One relies, for the justification of one's actions, not upon common sense, upon a sense of the disorderly, communal speech whole in which one is embedded, but upon an orderly network of links between what has been already said by a special group. In such circumstances, as there is in fact a decrease of reference to what 'is', there must in consequence be an increase of reference to what 'might be' – an increase of reference to a hermeneutically constructed *imaginary* world (see the account in Chapter 1 of the imaginary nature of hermeneutical constructions). As a result, what is said requires less and less grounding in a shared *sense* – for it can find its 'roots' almost wholly within the new, linguistically constructed context. Thus it is that one can justify one's actions to people in terms of circumstances not actually at the moment present to them, circumstances which are not, so to speak, their own circumstances.

Such a way of talking requires, however, especially in the light of the expected responsiveness of listeners, the development of methods for *warranting* in the course of one's talk, that is, giving *good reasons* for one's claims about 'might be' as being what 'is' . . . unless, that is, one can avoid the need for such warranting by learning to speak *authoritatively*, meaning, within the accepted idiom or genre of the social order within which one is acting. In the former situation, one would speak with a great deal of uncertainty and hesitancy, with an expectancy of challenge (see Chap- ter 10). In the latter, as with the upper classes in Britain, one could speak without fear of challenge. To be wholly linguistically autonomous, to speak without a care for people's *sense* of the immediate situation, one must have a sense of the 'basic' or 'dominant' speech genre in operation in one's society. This is not to say, however, that when one talks in this way one's speech is wholly one's own, for, in the very nature of speech genres, they pre-exist the individual; furthermore, not all are equally conducive to reflecting the individuality of the speaker.[19] But it does mean that in using certain forms of words, psychologically, one is drawing upon the support of all those in one's group who have used them in the past. If we do try to take the words of others to make them our own, it is in their response to our usage of them that they can exert their power – for they can refuse to respond to us with understanding, refuse to accept us into their group, they can deny us the use of *their* words.

Conclusions: the political ethics of speaking and thinking

What are the conclusions we arrive at, then, in reformulating our approach to the understanding of our 'inner' lives in terms of processes, semiotically mediated in terms of ethically responsive (rhetorical), socio-culturally developed signs? For Vygotsky, such signs play the role of psychological tools or instruments, and make an 'inner' life possible. For Bakhtin, the social nature of these signs makes it impossible for me to know whose side 'I' am on. The 'movement' of my 'inner' life is motivated and structured through and through by my continual crossing of boundaries; by what happens in those zones of uncertainty where 'I' (speaking in one of my 'voices' from a 'position' in a speech genre) am in communication with another 'self' in another position within that genre, where it is at first unclear which position I should be in, that is, which side of the boundary *I* should be on. In this scheme of things, I come to know myself as who and what I am, in terms of how, until now, I have resolved all the 'differences' that have arisen in me – the differences between me (as I have become) and what I experience as 'other than' me.

All of this, however, is to introduce into modern psychology issues of quite a revolutionary kind, ones which would completely undermine the currently popular conceptualizations of cognitive psychology – as concerned as it is to model all our supposedly 'inner mental processes' upon what might be called 'unquestioned routine processes of information communication'. If we were to take it seriously, we would have to develop a wholly different approach to the study of cognition. One must be more concerned with the social and historical conditions within a social group which make various routines possible and gives them their warrant – an issue I shall explore further in Chapter 8.

If, as Vygotsky says, the relations between the higher mental functions were at one time real relations among people, then at that moment of appropriation, what precisely these relations were, or still are, is important. In particular, we can ask, what were or are the ethical proprieties which must be negotiated moment by moment in sustaining them; and how is it possible for words to have, so to speak, ethical currency?

In my view, what it is for words to have *ethical* currency is, as I said before, for them to be used 'providentially', that is, in a way that respects the 'space' in which they are being used, in a way that works to sustain it as a cultural resource. Or, to put it another way (see Chapter 8), it is to speak in a way that respects the *being* of the person to whom one is speaking in that context. For, in the Bakhtinian/ Vygotskian scheme of things I have outlined here, what makes one unique is the unique place or position one occupies in existence, and the degree to which one is allowed to be answerable for it to, and by, the others around one. And one can only be answerable for it, to the extent that it is unique, if one can be an *author*. Authoring, in the sense of creating a novel linguistic formulation of one's own position, is necessary, as one cannot simply describe one's position from within an already existing scheme of factual or empirical possibilities. After all, one does not occupy a non-historical space, a simple order of possibilities, one occupies a 'providential space', in which the possibilities inherent it only become apparent as they are developed in joint action with others. Hence, the violation of one's being when one is denied such opportunities.

What is crucial, of course, is what has been emphasized in this book at every turn: a certain sensibility, a particular stance or attitude, is required if one is going to notice what is shown in people's speakings, to *sense* what is shown in its movement rather than constructing the product of what is said. And this, as Bakhtin makes clear, can only be studied at the point of action, so to speak, from within the 'movement' of the communicative act. For, although normatively identical forms exist in the 'tool-box' of language – just as normatively identical tools exist in the actual tool-boxes of carpenters, say – it is in different particular contexts (like the carpenter's tools), that, as an author of their own lives, people put a word or words to use in creative and novel ways. Thus:

> the word is expressive, but, we repeat, this expression does not inhere in the word itself. It originates at the point of contact between the word and actual reality, under the conditions of that real situation articulated by the individual utterance. In this case the word appears as an expression of some evaluative position of an individual person . . . .
>
> (Bakhtin, 1986: 88)

It is only in a speaker's particular use of a particular word at a particular point in time – like, say, the carpenter's particular use of a chisel stroke to slice off a wood sliver at a particular point in a piece of joinery – that the speaker can sense what its use achieves in the construction desired. Clearly, from a practical-moral point of view, what is involved in 'making sense' of words used in particular concrete communicative contexts, amounts, says Volosinov (1973: 68), "to understanding [a word's] novelty and not to recognizing its identity."

Thus also, it is precisely here, in this zone of uncertainty as to who can do what in the construction of a word's significance, at the point of contact between my creative use of it in an attempt to reshape the social reality between myself and another, that I can exert my power, and the other can exert theirs. It is in what Holquist (1983: 307) very aptly calls "the combat zone of the word" that the struggle over the question of the speaker's rights and privileges compared with those of the listener takes place. And the importance of these rights and duties should not be underestimated, for even apparently simple situations, objects, events, states of affairs, remain in principle enigmatic and undetermined as socially agreed realities until they are talked about – where what is enigmatic is essentially the question: who should live in whose reality?

· SEVEN ·

Conversational realities and academic discourses

I want in this chapter to draw an important distinction: that between conversation and academic or disciplinary discourses – a distinction roughly similar to that between playful activity and the playing of games *as if* according to rules (Shotter, 1973b). There will be a number of interesting spinoffs from such an endeavour, most of which will become clear as I proceed, but the central reason why I want to make this distinction I will state now: our search, not just for explanatory theories, but for predictive ones, at least within one of the "grand narratives" (Lyotard, 1984) of the West, has often been for emancipation.[1] And rational frameworks, in being both explanatory and predictive, seemingly allow us to aim at the future, by manipulating the present, on the basis of understanding the past. We have wanted to understand the 'machinery' of emancipation, with the hope that once we had its plan of operation, we could consult it when necessary to choose the right buttons to press or levers to pull, thus to set emancipatory activity upon its right course. Without a rational framework, as an aid to carry around with us, how else might we proceed in our emancipatory endeavours? How otherwise can we understand how to bring about *in the future* what at present we lack?

The answer is, I suggest: by understanding how conversation works. For 'providentially' (as Vico in fact claims), it contains more possibilities for our own future development than we have ever before imagined. But grasping them requires us to grasp them not as static, spatial forms, but in their dynamic, temporal formative 'movements'; not from a position of detached observation, but from a position of involved participation. Thus, if we can *critically describe* the social conditions conducive to emancipation in *this* Wittgensteinian sense, then – although we will not then be able to stand aside to watch it happen, because rather than theoretical knowledge, practical-moral knowledge will be involved – we will *nevertheless* know how to distribute and apportion our own responsibilities better in the processes involved.

A Vygotskian study of the form of 'instruction' involved in enabling, say, a middle-class child to become linguistically autonomous, and that involved in disabling[2] a working-class child so it remains subservient to external authorities, would (very roughly) consist in *descriptions* of the different instructive words used, in what contexts, and at what times, that is to say, an account of what, socially, brought the difference about. "Is that all that happens?" Wittgenstein (1981: no. 314) spoke of the difficulty here of not seeking further.

> The difficulty is not that of finding the solution but rather that of recogniz-ing as the solution something that looks as if it were only a preliminary to it. 'We have already said everything. – Not anything that follows from this, no, *this* itself is the solution'.
>
> This is connected, I believe, with our wrongly expecting an explanation, whereas the solution of the difficulty is a description, if we give it the right place in our considerations. If we dwell upon it, and do not try to get beyond it.
>
> The difficulty here is: to stop.

A description is 'instructive' *if* – take Wittgenstein's notion of language games as an example – it is given at an appropriate point in a conversation, at a moment of sensed difficulty: through it, prosthetically, one can see 'connections' not previously grasped. A description is also 'instructive' *if* – in one's inner, dialogic speech – one continually 'gives it' to oneself (as handing oneself a tool) as an aid in 'think-ing through' many different, problematic circumstances: then it enables one to make comparisons, see differences, arrange the different cases in an order, etc. (see Chapter 4).

'Basic' ways of talking

As I mentioned earlier, Harré (1983: 58) claims that "the primary human reality is persons in conversation." In Harré (1990: 345), he goes on to criticize a certain model of conversation – Argyle's (1990) coordinated interaction model (CIM) – by claiming that

> conversation cannot itself be something to be understood under [such a model] because it *is* itself that model. By that I mean that so far as anyone has ever been able to ascertain, there are only two human realities: physiology and discourse (conversation) – the former an individual phenomenon, the latter collective.

Now I think Harré is trying here to say something similar to what I am claiming above: that conversation cannot itself be something to be understood in terms of a model because it itself provides the 'grounds', or works to create the 'space', in terms of which *all* supposed 'models' in science are in fact seen as such. But he is experiencing a degree of difficulty, he oscillates between conversation and discourse, and one senses something of a strain in logical grammar in claiming conversation itself to be a model. If it is a 'model' of itself, then it lacks precisely those charac-teristics that make a model useful in science: the possession of a surveyable order making it possible for us to contemplate an overall 'mental picture', or a *mental representation*, of a problematic state of affairs. The trouble is that, in terms of our present cognitive-representational construal of the nature of knowledge, our knowledge of a conversational reality is utterly *strange* to us – even though, remarkably, it is the world of our own everyday life. For if to imagine something is to contemplate it in the sense I outlined above, then it is a world that we cannot even imagine, for it is the primary 'background' of human activity from which mental representations emerge and in which they are grounded.[3] Yet without some kind of shared textual account of *its* nature to carry about with us, how are we to compare the worth of different kinds of human *Umwelten*, and the different forms of human being they might and do make available to us? Without an account of how the lives of different peoples are 'rooted' in different 'backgrounds', we have no way of investigating further the crucial anthropological, political and ethical questions we now face.

To begin to outline how such an account might still be possible, let me begin with some reminders about the relation of language to perception. One is Rorty's (1980: 12) remark that

> it is pictures[4] rather than propositions, metaphors rather than statements, which determine most of our philosophical convictions . . . [And] without the notion of the mind as a mirror, the notion of knowledge as accuracy of representation would not have suggested itself.

Another is, as Billig *et al.* (1988) and Volosinov (1973) have pointed out, that a way of talking and communicating 'shapes' not only our ways of looking at the world, but also our ways of thinking, speaking, acting, and evaluating, and in fact provides a whole "living ideology." Indeed, by the time we develop into socially competent adults, it is as if a 'semantic engine or mill' of some very general kind is at work within us somewhere, homogenizing everything we encounter to fit it into a particular world order, into 'our' world. It is, and this my final reminder, as Garfinkel (1967: vii) has put it, our ways of talking and acting come to work, from within themselves, to make "those same activities visibly-rational-and-reportable-for-all-practical-purposes, that is, 'accountable', as organizations of commonplace everyday activities."

My reasons for beginning with these comments are three. The first, simply, is to emphasize Rorty's and Garfinkel's claims above: that certain 'basic' ways of knowing and talking – our 'embodied' ways – primarily work to create, maintain, reproduce and transform certain modes of social and societal relationships, to 'open up' to us, so to speak, different forms of human being (and by the same token, 'close off' others). In this view, as I have said before, it is *not* the primary function of these forms of talk to *represent* the world. If, in our experience, it seems undeniable that at least some words do in fact stand for things, they only do so, I have argued, *from within* a form of social life already constituted by ways of talking in which these words have been already used in some other, non-representational way – as 'tools' to 'shape' people (Bakhtin, Volosinov, Vygotsky). Thus the entities they represent are known, not for what they are in themselves, but in terms of their 'currency' or their significance in our different modes of social life, that is, in terms of what it is deemed sensible for us to do with them in the everyday, linguistically structured circumstances of their use. They have their *being*, they have their 'life', only within the form of life we (the whole community) conversationally sustain between our-selves. Hence the difficulty we have in formulating and testing any "theories" of the nature of these 'basic' ways of talking; we do not know properly how to doubt them. That is, we do know how to formulate any intelligible doubts about their nature without relying upon them for the intelligibility of our formulations.

Secondly, in such a view as this it is assumed that the primary function of these ways of talking is to 'give shape' to, to coordinate, and to account for, diverse social action (Mills, 1940). Indeed, at any one moment, these 'basic' ways of talking seem to be so pervasive (and persuasive) that, although there are clearly many other important spheres of human activity, they *dominate* our form of life in the following (judgemental) sense: given that people must mutually judge and correct each other as to the 'fittingness' of their actions to what they take their ultimate reality to be – if, that is, they are to sustain those realities in existence by continually remaking them in their everyday social activities – then, it is in this 'basic' kind of talk that all such ultimate judging and evaluating, that is, final accounting, must take place. Indeed, as we know, and as Wittgenstein (1953: no. 242) insists, "if language is to be a means of communication there must be agreement not only in definitions but also (queer as this may sound) in judgments," and we can now see that without such judgements, the culture would not of itself settle and endure (Vico).

My third reason for mentioning Rorty's and Garfinkel's claims above, is simply to ask the following questions: What must we, and the nature of our 'basic' ways of talking (and knowing), be like, for it to be possible for us to find ourselves limited by the 'pictures' implicit in our ways of talking, and for 'metaphors' to be influential in and upon our philosophical convictions? What is the nature of the urge we feel, as academics, to arrive at a supposed accurate 'picture' of an event or circumstance? How do ordinary people, without the supposed 'disciplines' available to us academics, make what they are talking about "rationally-visible" to themselves? I raise these questions because the answer to them, I feel, is not to be found in any academic discourses, but *doubly* in the nature of everyday conversational realities themselves: in describing how and why such forms of talk are so fundamental to our form of being in the world, and in finding within conversation itself – but not a disciplinary discourse (Foucault, 1972)[5] – the resources required for the description of its own nature (cf. Harré's comment, above, about conversation being its own model).

In discussing the nature of conversational realities and their distinction from (disciplinary) discourses, I want to argue for the importance within them of the third, extraordinary form of non-representational, embodied or sensuous, practical-moral knowledge I have introduced above. Given our current 'basic' ways of talking, however, we cannot easily grasp the nature of such knowledge. Indeed, to the extent that we cannot "command a clear view" (Wittgenstein, 1953: no. 122) of its overall nature, we cannot rationally imagine it. Further, because it cannot be represented (or formed) as an object of knowledge within a normative or disciplined form of talk, that is, within a discourse, its nature, for us, is *extraordinary*. Yet, even so . . . if not as a "model" of itself (note the terms of Harré's claim above), then at least as a metaphor of itself . . . if not from within a discourse, then at least from within conversation itself (note Harré's equivocation between discourse and conversation) . . . it is still possible, I think, to elucidate its nature. And that is what I want to attempt to do below.

The sensuous, non-cognitive nature of everyday, human conversation: knowing of the third kind

At this point, I want to return to Vygotsky's work to begin to introduce a further problem, to do with the activities at work within the voicing of words, a problem that Vygotsky touched on in a number of ways: the socially *evaluative* attitude embodied in a word in its speaking. In broaching this problem, let me first remark that Vygotsky sought to emulate Marx's method in *Capital*, which is, as he saw it, of focusing upon a single living "cell" of capitalist society, such as the nature of value (a microcosm of the macrocosm), thus to discover within it the whole system (Vygotsky, 1978);[6] he spoke against that method which

> analyzes complex psychological wholes into *elements* . . . It leads us into serious errors by ignoring the unitary nature of the process under study. The living union of sound and meaning that we call the word is broken up into two parts, which are assumed to be held together merely by mechanical associative connections.
>
> (Vygotsky, 1986: 4–5)

Given, as we have now seen, that words as single units only have their life, so to speak, within utterances within speech genres, I now want to point out that although Vygotsky spoke of people using words as 'tools' in organizing the structure of their own activities, he also saw *words* as providing the investigatory unit we need. "What is the unit of verbal thought that is further unanalyzable and yet retains the properties of the whole? We believe that such a unit can be found in the internal aspect of the word, in *word meaning*" (1986: 5).

Here, then, I would like to return to examine further the idea of words as 'tools', to give yet more prominence to the formidable range of formative activities at work within them, in their voicing – for words themselves are a source of ceaselessly unforeseeable originality.[7] Indeed, at the moment of its uttering, a word itself is the site of joint action – and thus formative of a providental space in miniature. "The word is a thing in our consciousness", as Ludwig Feuerbach (1986: 256) put it, "that is absolutely impossible for one person, but that becomes a relation for two. The word is a direct expression of the historical nature of human consciousness." In bridging the 'gaps' between voices, words link 'me' with what is 'other than' me; a word is interindividual and cannot be assigned to a single speaker; 'I' can be 'moved' even in my own speech by the influences in a word of 'others'. Words can thus function for us also as investigatory units. And, we should feel no disquiet now in focusing on words and not on utterances as aids in our investigations, for why shouldn't we have different tools in our tool-box for different purposes? Our tools themselves do not have to interlock into a system.

The fact that words work in non-cognitive, formative ways to 'shape' our unreflective, embodied or sensuous ways of looking and acting, speaking, feeling and evaluating, has in fact always been one of Vygotsky's main themes. But, held 'captive' by the picture of knowledge as inner representation, there has been a widespread failure to appreciate this – and a tendency to interpret his talk of 'tools' in only an instrumental sense – even to the extent of suggesting Vygotsky himself failed to appreciate the importance of sensuous, embodied knowledge also (Takatori, 1992). This is not so, and in fact cannot be so. In developing from creatures functioning under the control of our surrounding (social) circumstances to functioning under our own control, more is involved than incorporating within ourselves just the instrumental aspect of the words that others first use in controlling, directing, and organizing our behaviour for us. Indeed, even a cursory reading of *Thought and Language* (Thinking and Speech)[8] makes it clear that Vygotsky took seriously Marx's first thesis on Feuerbach – that reality has been incorrectly "conceived only in the form of the *object or of contemplation* not as *sensuous human activity, practice*" (Marx and Engels, 1970: 121). Indeed, without the sensory, sensuous or affective function of words, to 'move' people to perceive and act in different ways, his whole project falls to the ground.

Thus it comes as no surprise, in attempting at the outset to clarify the nature of the problem as he sees it, to find him saying that "when we approach the problems of the interrelation between thought and language . . . the first question that arises is that of intellect and affect" (Vygotsky, 1986: 10). If they are separated, then, he says, "the door is closed on the issue of the causation and origin of our thoughts", for we are unable to understand "the motive forces that direct thought into this or that channel." Hence, the approach he adopts "shows that every idea contains a transmuted affective attitude toward the bit of reality to which it refers." If we add to this his reminder that "all the higher functions originate as actual relations between human individuals" (Vygotsky, 1978: 57), then we can claim that the affective attitude which provides the thoughts and ideas of an individual with their dynamic, that is, with their particular motives and valencies[9] linking them to each other and their surroundings in a particular way, is a transmuted version of a social relationship. But of what kind?

Well, quite literally, as we have already seen, of an "instructional" kind; we come to 'instruct' ourselves as others instruct us. But now we must see those instructions as occurring in a real social context of asymmetrical power relations. Thus, although people do do a large number of instrumental things to each other in their talk, they do other things besides. Before focusing upon that, though, let me just offer some reminders of the nature of 'instructive' talk: People 'point things out to us' ("Look at this!"); 'change our perspective' ("Look at it like this"); 'order' our actions ("Look at the model first, then at the puzzle pieces"); 'shape' our actions ("Turn it over, then it will fit"); 'remind' us ("Think what you did last time", "What do you already know that's relevant?"); 'encourage' us ("Try again"); 'restrain' us ("Don't be too hasty"); 'evaluate' for us ("That's not right", "Don't do that, that's greedy"); 'set our goals' ("Try to put these pieces together to match that [pointing at a model]"); 'count' ("How many will it take?"); make 'measurements' ("Will that fit properly?", "Just compare"); make us 'check' our descriptions ("Is that right?", "Who else says so?", "What's the reason for your belief?"). But in doing so, they voice their 'instructions' in a certain tone, a tone that is 'shaped', among other things, by how they see themselves 'placed' in relation to whom they are addressing. And on occasions, of course, they utter explicit evaluations: 'they distance themselves from us' ("Don't do that, it's crazy"); or 'they affirm they share our world' ("Wow, that's great"); and so on. And so on, for no doubt a countless number of instrumental functions, and, if not countless, at least a large number of possible social relations.

With these issues in mind, it is perhaps worth returning for a moment to what Vygotsky had to say about there always being a 'hidden' thought in our speech, its 'subtext'. Here we might mention two examples: The first (1986: 250–3), is from a play in which Stanislavsky listed characters' supposed hidden motives in saying what they said. In the play, Chatsky comes across Sophya unexpectedly, and she, in her confusion, seems insufficiently pleased to see him. She tries to tell him that she is *always* pleased to see him. He answers: "Well, let's suppose it's so. Thrice blessed who believes. Believing warms the heart." As Vygotsky remarks, Stanislavsky interprets this as "Let us stop this talk." He himself suggests, among a number of other possibilities, that it could equally well mean "I do not believe you. You say it to comfort me." Whatever . . . it is a question of the intonation adopted by the actor that will determine whether it suggests distancing offence, accepting resignation, or a hopeful suggestion of a new start, and the play's director must choose according to how it fits in with the rest of the proceedings. Another example (pp. 241–2) is one Volosinov (1973: 103–4) also reports: Dostoevsky relates a conversation between six drunks that consists entirely of one unprintable word said six times in succession by each of them. In its context, the conversation is perfectly intelligible. Without quoting the whole piece, it will be enough to note that the sequence goes as follows: the first is a disdainful denial of a previous point; the second, a doubted veracity of previous denial; then, indignation at the first's denial; then, indigence at the third drunk butting in; an exclamation by the fifth, 'I've got it'; while the sixth pours cold water on the fifth. Volosinov's interest in this example is that it illustrates that the word in this instance was only a vehicle for intonation, and that in this case the intonation was wholly indicative of the different evaluative positions between the speakers in the dialogue, and of the struggles between them. Vygotsky's interest here, is to show how in our inner dialogues with ourselves, "inner speech," our sense of what we are 'talking' about may be as vague and ill formed as the words in this drunken conversation, and yet still serve their purpose perfectly well.

Now, with our more academic concerns in mind, let us turn our attention towards *concepts* to see how they are transformed when viewed with this scheme of things. Again, words are the *means* Vygotsky has in mind when he says that

the main question about the process of concept formation – or, about any goal-directed activity – is the question of the means by which the operation is accomplished . . . To explain the higher forms of human behavior, we must uncover the means by which man learns to organize and direct his behavior.
(Vygotsky, 1986: 102)

And "our experimental study proved that it was the functional use of the word, or any other sign, as means of focussing one's attention, selecting distinctive features and analyzing and synthesizing them, that plays a central role in concept formation" (1986: 106). "Learning to direct one's own mental processes with the aid of words or signs is an integral part of the process of concept formation" (1986: 108). But now we must think of *who*, at each dialogical point in the organization of our 'thinking', when we must issue the next reminder, the next directive to pay attention, etc., is voicing the relevant word? And, perhaps, what dissident voices might be heard also! In other words – Vygotsky's words – what one has learned to do in thinking conceptually is not to compare the configuration of a supposed mental representation with the configuration of a state of affairs in reality, but something else much more complicated. One has grasped how to organize and assemble in a socially intelligible way, a way which makes sense to *certain of the others* around one, bits and pieces of information dispersed in space and time in accordance with 'instructions' they provided, and which now a supposed 'concept' provides.

On this view, rather than a self-contained, simply subjective activity within an individual – dealing with merely inner, cognitive 'pictures' which may, or may not, be accurate representations of an outer reality – thinking conceptually becomes a special social practice. And furthermore, it becomes a practice in which speech, thought and feeling are, at least at first and for the most part, interlinked with their surrounding circumstances in "a dynamic system of meaning" (Vygotsky, 1986: 10–11). As examples of how, in our inner speech, our use of a single word can evoke the sense of a whole world, Vygotsky mentions the titles of books and plays: *Don Quixote, Hamlet, Anna Karenina*. "Another excellent example is Gogol's *Dead Souls*. Originally the title referred to dead serfs whose names had not yet been removed from the official list and who could still be bought and sold as if alive" (1986: 247). Only gradually, and probably as a result of the effects of becoming literate – in which, "in learning to write, the child must disengage himself from the sensory aspect of speech and replace words by images[10] of words" (Vygotsky, 1986: 181) – can we learn to think like academics, and develop modes of formal, decontexualized rationality, that is, to think in wholly representational[11] terms. Influenced by this 'picture' of what thinking is, the traditional methods fail "to take into account the perception and the mental elaboration of the sensory material that gave birth to the concept. The sensory material and the word are both indispensable parts of concept formation" (Vygotsky, 1986: 96–7).

How might we do better? What kind of account of speech communication would afford us the possibility of linking words to sense, of elucidating the relation of form to feeling?

It is at this point that I would like again to turn to Bakhtin's work on the dialogical nature of speech communication, for, as we have already seen, it opens up to study those *dialogical or interactive moments* when there is a 'gap' between two (or more) speaking subjects. And, no matter how *systematic* the speech of each may be while speaking,[12] when one has finished speaking and the other can respond, the bridging of that 'gap' is an opportunity for an utterly unique, unrepeatable response, one that is 'crafted' or 'tailored' to fit the unique circumstances of its utterance.[13] Indeed, it is "on the boundary between two consciousnesses, two subjects" (Bakhtin, 1986: 106) that the *life* – whatever it is that is 'living' in the communicative act – is manifested. Thus we can appreciate, as Volosinov (1973: 68) says, that:

> What the speaker values is not that aspect of the form which is invariably identical in all instances of its usage, despite the nature of those instances, but that aspect of the linguistic form because of which it can figure in the given, concrete context, because of which it becomes a sign adequate to the conditions of the given, concrete situation. We can express it this way: *what is important for the speaker about the linguistic form is not that it is a stable and always self-equivalent signal, but that it is an always changeable and adaptable sign.*

In fact, given both Volosinov's and Bakhtin's view – that even within the speech, or the writing, of a single individual, many 'voices' can be at work, such 'gaps' can be found, prompting us to affectively react to what they have to say[14] – the turn to a 'dialogical' account of the speech process opens it up to a whole new realm of discursive activities to study. It is in the creative work of semiotically linking ourselves, meaningfully, both to each other and to our surroundings, that we also socially construct our identities – where, as we saw earlier, this is done by our being embedded in a common sense of our own making.

Conversation, *sensus communis*, and metaphor

In turning to the origins of such a sense, a culture's *sensus communis*, I discussed earlier Vico's account of the social processes involved. Here, because I want to refer to aspects of it in what follows, I want briefly to recapitulate it. The processes involved, he claims, are based not upon anything pre-established either in people or in their surroundings, but on socially shared *identities of feeling* they themselves create in the flow of activity between them. These he calls "sensory topics," – "topics" (Gr. *topos* = 'place') because they give rise to "commonplaces," that is, to shared moments in a flow of social activity which afford common reference, and "sensory" because they are moments in which shared feelings for already shared circumstances are created. The paradigm situation I mentioned earlier, involved everyone running to take shelter from thunder, where people's responsive reaction to it was fear, expressed in the character of their bodily activities. This gave a shared *sense* to an *already shared* circumstance. It is at this point that Vico introduced the idea of an "imaginative universal:" in the case of thunder, this is Jove, the image of a giant being, speaking giant words, but one can easily imagine other such shared circumstances in which shared feeling, expressed in the same responsive, bodily reactions might occur – the birth of a child, the death of a group member, and so on. And later, perhaps, on to more secondary matters, including, for instance: mutual recognition (the valuing of known over unknown persons); reverence through ritual (the value of sustaining invented social forms); truth telling (a late arrival when doubts began to set in); and so on.

Thus these first common 'places', or 'providential spaces', are to do not with 'seeing' in common, but with 'feeling' in common, that is, with the 'giving' or 'lending' of a shared *significance* to shared *feelings* in an *already shared* circumstance – thus providing, as it were, not only a sufficiently large 'container' within which a set of different activities can all fit and be seen as the same, but also a sense in terms of which to *judge* their fittingness. In other words, the first mute language is the immediate responsive representation in gesture, in bodily movement, of a moment or place of common reference, where the bodily movement functions *metaphorically*, not to refer to something already known about, but to indicate an 'is', to *establish* a 'something' with common significance.

Two points follow from this. The first is to do with the properties of joint action: its ability to generate a providential space that all those involved experience themselves as 'in'. The second is to do with, as we have already mentioned, our being able to 'look through' certain words and see connections that would otherwise be invisible to us – only now, I want to emphasize that this function inheres in the word's 'movement', not its form.

To turn to the fact that joint action seems to generate a feeling of 'being judged'. As both Volosinov and Bakhtin mention, at various points in their writing, it is in the very character of dialogue to create a kind of third containing-and-judging entity.

> Any utterance always has an addressee (of various sorts, with varying degrees of proximity, concreteness, awareness, and so forth), whose responsive understanding the author of the work seeks and surpasses. This is the second party ([but] not in the arithmetical sense). But in addition to this addressee (the second party), the author of the utterance, with the greater of lesser awareness, presupposes a higher *superaddressee* (third), whose absolutely just responsive understanding is presumed, either in some metaphysical distance, or in distant historical time . . .
>
> (Bakhtin, 1986: 126)

At other points in their writings, Bakhtin and Volosinov talk of this third entity as the author's "hero." The trouble is, authors do not just write *about* their heroes from the outside: "such is the nature of all active creative experiences: they experience their object [their hero] and experience themselves *in* their object" (Bakhtin, 1990: 7).

Regarding intonation, the outcome is the same: Volosinov (1976: 99–103) discusses a paradigm we might be tempted to substitute for Vico's. Two people, fed up with a long winter, sitting in a room in May, look out of the window, only to see it snowing. Then one of them says: "Well!" The other does not respond.[15] To whom is this reproach addressed, asks Volosinov? For it voices not only passive dissatisfaction, but also active indignation and reproach – and the speaker's friend cannot be blamed for the snow! "This tack of the intonational movement patently makes an opening in the situation for a *third participant* . . . [however] the 'hero' of this verbal production has not yet assumed a full and definite shape . . ." (Volosinov, 1976: 103). What is created here is, like Vico's imaginative universal, says Volosinov, an "intonational metaphor," an image *through* which we can begin to see the character of the hero.

The second point I want to make connects directly with this. For what Vico outlines, above, is a poetic image, a metaphor, *through* which – as in Volosinov's intonational metaphor above, in which the third participant in the joint action is seen as responsible for the snow, and thus blameworthy and reproachable like another person – one might begin to understand the *mute*, extraordinary, common-sense basis for an articulate language. Such a basis constitutes the unsystematized, primordial contents of the human mind, its basic paradigms or prototypes, its providential spaces. These are the sensory topics or commonplaces that make up the basis of a community's *sensus communis* – in terms of which our first words can have their sense, and against which, much later, the adequacy of our concepts may be judged.

Let me explore the notion of metaphor further. Vico was particularly interested in what might be called "civic rhetoric" and the problem of what constituted good government (Mooney, 1985; Schaeffer, 1990), but he developed his views against a background within which the tradition of rhetoric was under attack by the new "geometric method" of reasoning promoted by the Cartesians. And to an extent, his arguments constitute a counter-attack upon it, for he saw it as completely inimical to his concerns. In his *On the Study Methods of Our Time* (first published in 1709), he defends rhetoric on many grounds, but particularly on the grounds of the necessity for eloquence in one's speech: quoting Cardinal Ludvico Madruzzi, Vico (1965: 36) says: "Rulers should see to it not only that their actions are true and in conformity with justice, but that they *seem* to be so" to everyone. In other words, those who *are* satisfied with abstract truth alone, and do not bother to find out whether their opinion is shared by the generality of people, cause political calamities. Thus, not only should politicians judge human actions as they actually *are*, rather than in terms of what they think they *ought* to be, they should also – in terms of the *sensus communis* – be able eloquently to persuade the people of their judgement's correctness. But how might such persuading be done? What is involved in our accepting (if not the absolute truth) the truth of a claim relative to our current circumstances?

Here we are back again at our original problem – the understanding of that speech which, rather than simply influencing us in our intellects, 'moves' us to accept its claims in our very being – but now in a somewhat better position to formulate its nature. The problem arises when we attempt to give *reasons* for any claims we may make, for why should what we say be experienced as us giving reasons, let alone ones that constitute a *proof* of our claims?

They are accepted, suggests Vico (here following Aristotle 1991: 75–7), not because we as speakers supply a demonstrable proof, a full syllogistic structure which our listeners are passively compelled (logically) to accept, but because in their incomplete, enthymemic structure, we offer initially unconnected premises that (most of) our audience will be able to connect up for us – and feel that it is they who have 'seen' the point! They themselves make the connection by drawing upon the (perhaps in themselves inarticulable) *topoi* in the *sensus communis* already existing between them and us as speakers – in fact, once again, a process of joint action is involved! This is why, for Vico, in rhetoric, what he calls the "art of topics" (*ars topica*) is important. For 'argument' in this art

> is not 'the arrangement of a proof', as commonly assumed, what in Latin is known as *argumentatio*; rather, it is that third idea which is found to tie together the two in the issue being debated – what in the Schools is called the 'middle term' – such that topics is the art of finding the middle term. But I claim more: Topics is the art of apprehending the true, for it is the art of seeing all the aspects or *loci* of a thing that enable us to distinguish it well and gain an adequate concept of it. For judgments turn out to be false when their concepts are either greater or lesser than the things they propose to signify . . .
>
> (Vico, 1988: 178 – although I have preferred Mooney's (1985: 134) translation here)

So the special nature of the speech that we use here works to create the 'providential space', in which a 'proof' can come into existence as such. Grassi (1980: 20), a Vico scholar, characterizes this kind of speech as

> immediately a 'showing'[16] – and for this reason 'figurative' or 'imaginative', and thus in the original sense 'theoretical' [*theorin* – i.e., to see]. It is metaphorical, i.e., it shows something which has a sense, and this means that to the figure, to that which is shown, the speech transfers [*metapherein*] a signification;[17] in this way the speech which realizes this showing 'leads before the eyes' [*phainesthai*] a significance.

This, says Grassi, is *true rhetorical speech*; it is non-conceptual, moving and indicative; it functions not just persuasively but practically: the metaphor is central to it. In transferring[18] significance from the *sensus communis* to what is said, a metaphor makes 'visible' or 'shows' listeners a common quality that is not rationally deducible. As such, it cannot be 'explained' (either from within an academic discourse, or in any other way); indeed, it is the speech which is the basis of all rational thought. Thus, it is with such a way of talking that we must begin all our investigations.[19]

Metaphors and models: conversation and discourse

If we turn now to the task of distinguishing between *conversation* and *academic discourse*, it is perhaps already obvious in general how the two will differ. First, practical conversation works primarily in terms of *sense*, whereas academic discourses work increasingly (as they develop) in terms of forms. Second, practical conversation does not have a "subject matter," it is 'rooted' or "variously rooted"[20] in a *sensus communis*, while, academic discourses claim somehow (due, as suggested in Chapter 1, to the *ex post facto* fact fallacy) to have floated free of such an embedding and to be 'based' in certain supposedly undeniable properties of a "subject matter." Third, practical conversation need not work in terms of mental representations, while academic discourses must. I shall examine certain aspects of this whole process further in the next chapter, but I want to discuss this last property further here, that is, why it seems to be of importance for the subject matter of a discourse to be 'surveyable' (Wittgenstein) by an individual in rational contemplation.

Indeed, we can define an academic discourse as a rational body of speech or writing, a set of *ordered* statements, that provides a systematic way of representing, for the purposes of disciplined, academic inquiry, a particular kind of knowledge about an entity, that is, not just knowledge that is 'accountable', or which can be rendered "rationally-visible" on the spot when required, but also knowledge which enables us "to *see* how things [within the subject matter of the discourse] hang together."[21] Where a discourse is systematized around not just a single focal image or commonplace, but – in Rorty's (1989) terms – a 'literalized'[22] version of it, a 'picture'. Where it is a 'picture' that provides the 'basis' for a special type of representational language game, not only one 'within' which rational persuasion is possible (in a way, he claims, is impossible in ordinary conversation), but one in which one can provide both explanations and predictions. And until now, our academic discourses have been formed in this way.

But, following Wittgenstein (1953), there are not one but two ways in which we might attempt to investigate and assemble the properties of a supposed 'subject matter' to 'see' how they 'hang together': in terms of a model (or a grammatical picture),[23] or in terms of a "perspicuous representation."

Let me discuss both these in turn. The important point about a model (or a grammatical picture) is this: because one knows ahead of time that all its parts do as a matter of fact hang together in an orderly way, it seems that it is only the *laws* or *principles* of the order in which they do so that is in question. It is thus possible with a model – for example, the 'picture' of the mathematical set as a container or enclosure – to introduce an idea with a few illustrated examples, and then to assume that the idea is completely understood in its full generality.[24] But as Bloor (1975: 121–2) illustrates, this is far from the truth. Although it may seem – with the 'picture' of a bounded area as a model of the mathematical set in mind, for instance – that the assertion "the whole is greater than the part" is an undeniable conceptual truth, this is not so. For as soon as we come to consider the case of an infinitely long series of integer numbers, we realize that we can put the endless series of even numbers in one-to-one correspondence with the integers in a way which will never break down. But the series of even numbers is 'contained in' the series of integers, isn't it?

As Bloor shows, this 'contradiction' was transmuted into a 'definition' (of what it is for a set to be infinite) by a 'renegotiation': it became perfectly intelligible to think that when a part *is* 'similar' to the whole, then the set is infinite – taking the image of one-to-one correspondence now as the 'picture' of what 'similarity' is.

In mathematics, we make many such models. For instance, we can mentally 'look' at the points on a straight line and can imagine at least a number of them stretching off in either direction, and assume that wherever on the line we might look, they would be everywhere the same. Thus, as individuals, we can construct a 'view', a God's-eye view, of the line, and assume what it 'must' be like everywhere along its length, that is to say, the *order* will continue everywhere the same. These moves in mathematics, and in many other spheres, are perfectly benign as long as the phenomena being dealt with *are* in fact genuinely orderly, and the problem is just to find the form of their order; they allow us to act – indeed, they channel us (as individuals) into acting – in a way which conforms to that order ahead of time. But this is precisely Wittgenstein's point: when the phenomena of interest to us are *not* already orderly, when they are – like the everyday life of human beings – somewhat chaotic, or only partially ordered, then we run into trouble. And, of course, a significant part of Wittgenstein's philosophical effort went into showing the consequences of such 'bewitchments'.

It is not our purpose, however, to explore such 'bewitchments' further here, but to question how else might we proceed, if not in terms of 'grammatical pictures' or models. His answer is in terms of "perspicuous representations" – a way of making sense of things that we are unable to do on our own, a way that relies upon people 'seeing' things in the same way as each other by the use of metaphors.

One of the metaphors Wittgenstein introduces in *Philosophical Investigations* for our language is as a somewhat disorderly city. We can see it as an ancient city, as "a maze of little streets and squares, of old and new houses, and of houses with additions from various periods; and this surrounded by a multitude of new boroughs with straight and regular streets and uniform houses" (1953: no. 18). And that he sometimes himself saw it in just this way is evidenced by the fact that, just after saying that "a main source of our failure to understand is that we do not *command a clear view* of the use of words" (1953: no. 122), he went on to say, "a philosophical problem has the form: 'I don't know my way about'" (1953: no. 123).

But how might talk of our language as being like an ancient city be of any help to us? No identifiable ancient city is mentioned, and ancient cities in general lack any already well-known order. So, if it is the case that an ancient city is a good metaphor (one among a number of others he offers) for our language, what does it teach us about the character of language? Well, if we cannot command a clear view of its street plan (from a vantage point outside it, or from a map), we can still get to know quite a lot about it from living within it . . . Vico's point! We can get to know certain prominent landmarks and, by approaching them from different directions, use them as fixed points of reference for more adventurous excursions. To be sure of its character, however, we must fill in details of the streets and houses in between (for we cannot assume an already given order); and this will take time. We might need, in fact, to dig down and to investigate some of the archeological layers, and so on. In other words, as a metaphor of our language, it may not tell us *all* we want to know about it, but it does suggests to us – at least, to those of us who know what it is like to live in a city – quite a number of important points about how we might get to know about our knowledge of our own language better.

In Wittgenstein's (1953: no. 122) terms, it functions as a "perspicuous representation," where the point of such a representation is that it

> produces just that understanding which consists in 'seeing connections'. Hence the importance of finding and inventing *intermediate cases.*

The concept of perspicuous representation is of fundamental significance for us. It earmarks the form of account we give, the way we look at things.

And, as for Wittgenstein (and for Vico), so for us. Those metaphors which 'touch' upon the sensory topics making up our embodied common sense can, in a "joint action" between us and those who present them, open up for us a 'space' in which we can 'see' as they see, that is, make sense and give the same kind of form to our feelings as they give to theirs.

We are now in a position to distinguish between a conversational reality and the 'reality' of an academic discourse. To the individuals socialized into it, an academic discourse provides the possibility of being able (after enough hermeneutical work upon the discipline's texts)[25] to build up a systematic mental image of its 'subject matter', of being able to 'survey' it. It may be a fictitious 'reality', a possible and/ or imaginary reality, but, like any good science fiction novel, one can get a 'sense' of its nature from within the texts of the discipline. Indeed, we can get a 'sense' of what activities it would support if it were truly real; thus, from within it, we can discover further 'facts' in its support. Hence our possibility of 'testing' it. Thus it is in this sense that an academic discourse can be said to *represent* a supposedly underlying, or otherwise hidden, reality . . . a reality with an *essence*. As Wittgenstein (1953: no. 92) says, this 'essence' is

> not something that already lies open to view and that becomes surveyable by a rearrangement, but something that lies *beneath* the surface. Something that lies within, which we see when we look *into* the thing, and which analysis digs out.

Thus, academic discourses, to adapt Foucault's expression,[26] form as *systematic* objects the objects of which they speak, that is, form them as mental representations.

By contrast, the participants in everyday conversations may have a 'sense' of what they are talking about, even a 'joint sense', but speakers do not 'discipline' their talk in terms of a single grammatical picture. If one figure of speech proves unintelligible, another is tried. If there is an *order* in conversation, then it is one of a very different kind to that available in a God's-eye view, a surveyable order. In a conversation, people do know what they are talking about, but as Garfinkel (1967: 40) puts it: 'the matter talked about' is an event that is developing and developed within the course of the conversation producing it; furthermore, those producing it, know in practice, that is, *from within* this development, both the 'how' and the 'what' of its production; indeed, in being (responsively) aware of each other's (responsive) understanding in the process, they know how to play their own part in its further development. And they can do all this without any reference to any inner mental representations, to any inner theories; their 'embodied' linguistic reactions are sufficient.

Conclusion: psychology and the demise of the epistemology project

Although the "epistemology project" – the idea that knowledge is to be seen as the correct *representation* of an independent reality – is currently under attack, not all are agreed as to where, precisely, the main force of that attack should be focused. Some (such as Rorty, 1980), see epistemology as primarily concerned with providing *foundations* for claims to knowledge. Thus on this interpretation, overcoming epistemology simply means abandoning "a desire for constraint," a desire which, in the vocabulary of the epistemological project itself, is "a desire to find 'foundations' to which one might cling, frameworks beyond which one must not stray, objects which impose themselves, representations which cannot be gainsaid" (Rorty, 1980: 315). Others, and here I have in mind Charles Taylor (1984, 1987), as well as Heidegger (1967) and Foucault (1970), have a different, and ultimately more radically important focus. They see the commitment to knowledge as representation, as always involving the inner, orderly 'depiction' or 'picturing' of an outer reality, as the central feature of the epistemological tradition. As Taylor (1984: 18) points out, a corollary of this view that is important for us – given our interest in conversation – is that we "construe our awareness and understanding of each other on the same representational model . . . in terms of a *theory* that I hold about you and the meaning of your words."

With whom should we align ourselves? Well, if we do away with shared frameworks, shared beliefs, shared values; if we give up appealing to the reality of objects (that is, we stop kicking stones), if we make no more appeals to conceptual truths, can we still find some 'foundations' for ourselves? In fact, the answer seems to be "Yes. In the *sensus communis* of the human *Umwelt*." We are not limited, as Rorty seems to think, to simply trying to make the other guy's way of talking "look bad," and our own "look good." There is a 'basis' for our talk, a 'background' from within which we make sense of our lives, a realm of knowledgeable activity which is sustained, not simply by a form of practical-technical knowledge, nor by a form of theoretical-conceptual knowledge, but a third kind of practical-moral knowledge of a non-conceptual kind. The study of this third, background, sphere of human activity is not easy. "We cannot", as Taylor (1987: 477) points out, "turn the background from which we think into an object for us." We face a new task, whose excellence consists in that of attempting "to articulate the background of our lives perspicuously" (1987: 481) – where, as Wittgenstein (1953: no. 122) puts it, "a perspicuous representation [i.e., the provision of an apposite metaphor or image] produces just that understanding which consists in 'seeing connections.'"

Harré, in insisting that "the primary human reality is persons in conversation," has confronted us with a problem that will not go away, but which cannot be solved with available representational-referential 'theories' or 'methods': namely, the problem of how a common 'sense' is established and sustained, the problem of specifying its conditions of possibility. Lacking a *systematic representation* of its nature, interested only in what we, as individual academics, can 'picture', we have failed to 'see' its importance; the nature of the social process involved in its creation and sustenance has been rationally-invisible to us. It has been all but destroyed in well-meaning projects that, because they must be justified within the prevailing 'rationality', work to intensify monologic, systematic, theoretical, surveyable 'realities' of the individual mind – realities which can be thought, but in which people cannot live.

PART III

FROM CULTURE AS A SYSTEM TO CULTURAL TRADITIONS

EIGHT

Rhetoric and the social construction of cognitivism

A proof cannot dispel the fog.

(Wittgenstein, quoted in Monk, 1990: 307)

Those who grow up within the providential space of a still vital culture, experience themselves (in their very being) as living 'within' a world that contains certain kinds of entities and events, etc., to which one responds with certain evaluative orientations – with surprise, disgust, acceptance, affirmations, intransigence, resentment, resignation, puzzlement, anger, admonishment, sermonizing, blank incomprehension, disdain, horror, joy, delight, wonder, amazement, enthralment, and so on. But, as Volosinov and Bakhtin make clear, one also finds oneself animated by a complex of urges, lacks, desires, hungers, longings, cravings, yearnings, etc., that one feels one ought to satisfy, and that if one does not, then in some way one is something of a failure as a person – for within a providential space, "something absolutely new appears: the supraperson, the *supra-I*, that is, the witness and the judge *of the whole* human being, of the whole *I*, and consequently someone who is no longer the person, no longer the *I*, but the *other*" (Bakhtin, 1986: 137). One finds 'in' oneself, or, oneself 'in', a world of responses and urges, and the pursuit of certain of these urges has seemed so basic to who and what we in our culture *are* (Taylor, 1989), our cultural identities, that we have institutionalized them, professionalized them even. And those truly dedicated to their satisfaction, feel that they must – or at least that they ought to – submit themselves to special instruction, to qualify themselves to undertake the task or tasks involved. In this chapter, I want, through the study of a particular case – the case of so-called "cognitive psychology" within the academic discipline of psychology – to examine some of the pitfalls, the bewitchments and bewilderments, the entrapments, and other ills, to which we are (or can be) prone in such endeavours. If we are to examine these, we must study not just the patterns of thought involved, but the source of the urges, cravings, etc., such patterns are meant to satisfy, for:

> Thought is not the superior authority in the process. Thought is not begotten by thought; it is engendered by motivation, i.e., by our desires and

needs, our interests and emotions. Behind every thought there is an affective-
volitional tendency, which holds the answer to the last 'why' in the analysis
of thinking.

(Vygotsky, 1986: 252)[1]

Rhetoric, rational visibility, and adequacy

As I have already argued, Billig (1987: 41) has shown how a rhetorical approach,
based upon Protagoras' maxim: "that in every question, there [are] two sides to the
argument, exactly opposite to each other," can play an important and revealing role
in psychological inquiry. And in particular, in line with Protagoras' maxim, he
has criticized the model of thinking currently central to cognitive psychology – of
thinking as a mechanical process conducted according to procedural programs, rules
or instructions – as not in itself incorrect, but as a monological, one-sided, and in
fact thoughtless image of thought. For, as he points out, even bureaucrats, rather
than being thoughtless rule-followers, are often ingenious rule-appliers, as well as
sometimes imaginative rule-benders or even rule-creators.[2] In acting flexibly, they
must think about how those around them, and those with whom they must deal,
might react to what they do; they must try to be dialogically responsive in their
thoughts and actions both to their clients and their bosses. If they are to be persuasive and not to have to use force in imposing their judgements, they must act
rhetorically and adapt their behaviour to their 'audience'. In short, Billig criticizes
the model of thinking in cognitive psychology for its *inadequacy*.

With this argument of Billig's in mind, I want below to do two things. One is
to explore how the status of claims made in cognitive psychology can be illuminated
by a study of their rhetorical structure. We shall find that, like mythic beasts in
fairy stories, or the three-sexed worlds, say, in science fiction stories, the theoretical
entities central in such claims have (literally) only an *imaginary* existence, within the
texts of the discipline. Without a grasp of *what* supposed 'theories of mind' ought
to be theories *of*, neither empirical evidence in their support, nor their coherence,[3]
turn out to be sufficient for their adequacy. Indeed, on this point, Wittgenstein
(1980: I, no. 549) raised the following question: "So we form a wrong picture of
thinking. – But *of what* do we form a wrong picture; how do I know, for example,
that you are forming a wrong picture of *that*, of which I too am forming a wrong
picture?" His, answer, of course, was that we cannot know, and never will; the
problem is of a different kind altogether: it is not to do with a lack of corrrespondence
between our theories and reality, but because "we don't know our way about in the
use of our word ['thinking']." This leads me on to my second concern: if we are to
avoid chasing (saying true but useless things about) dragons of our own making,[4]
we must officially broaden the focus of methodological debate in psychology to
include, besides epistemological problems to do with justifying claims to knowledge, problems also of an *ontological* kind. We must explore both how claims of what
it is like *to be* an entity of this or that kind might be formulated – especially a being
with conscious experience (Nagel, 1981) – and how such claims might be evaluated

for the extent to which they in fact *respect the being* of the entities in question, that is, evaluated for their adequacy.

In pursuing these aims here, I want to argue not for a radical change in our practices, but for a self-conscious noticing of their actual nature: namely, the fact that before turning to test the empirical accuracy of our claims about people's psychological nature, we first 'motivate' people's interest in them by 'arguing' for their adequacy (or at least for their greater adequacy compared with past proposals). If what I suggested in the previous chapter is true, we do this by offering the non-professional people around us "perspicuous representations" – metaphors that function as arguments – that are attractive to them, because they enable them to 'see connections' they would otherwise miss. But, as we saw, in their literalized form, as 'pictures' – the form they must take if they are to 'discipline' a discourse, as I shall show – they institute *an order* in what can be said; they constitute 'procedures', organized (but limited) ways of doing things by oneself, or, getting things done (by others or by machines). These *are* significant achievements. But it is necessary to recognize the social costs involved. In other words, what I am suggesting is that not only should the kind of account (of thinking) Billig offers above be recognized for what it is, that is, as serving a rhetorical function in a context of cultural politics, but that all proposals in psychology *should* be recognized as such. And furthermore, to the extent that we professionals offer them to the others around us, that their adequacy should be evaluated in terms of whether they have been formulated in an *ontologically responsible* manner, that is to say, in a way which respects the 'being' of those others, a way 'in which' those others are, so to speak, able to 'see' themselves.

In approaching these aims, I shall first want to study: some of the rhetorical moves used by those who are advocating the cognitive approach in psychology, and how these moves sustain them as a group functioning from within a research tradition; the nature of the taken-for-granted (academic) 'background' against which their claims are made to seem 'natural' and 'unquestionable'; and the means by which *that* background is sustained – a set of exclusion practices which make it very difficult for critics to voice intelligible alternatives. In other words, I want to study the way in which cognitive psychologists both wield and hide their power. For, although some may see the cognitive revolution as curing the "chaotic" state of psychological research by providing "an adequate theoretical notation in which to formulate questions about mental processes" (Allport, 1980, quoted approvingly by Boden, 1988: 259), others, among whom I would include myself, see its institutionalization as producing both "a radical reduction of inquiry to a small range of explanatory constructs," as well as, among many other such disappearances, "the disappearance of the social world" (Gergen, 1989a: 463–5). Thus, we others would like to see at least some debate, within those of our institutions devoted to a study of psychology, about what might be a more comprehensive socially and responsive/responsible psychology; and not to have it excluded as mere polemic, as merely disputatious, and as not a proper part of the doing of scientific psychology. But what is the nature of the affirmations or acceptances here, that make it seem 'natural' to see such arguments as 'merely polemic' and not as 'real' arguments?

If we turn to the history of academic traditions, we find that the contest between philosophy and rhetoric is, of course, an old and venerable one. In its modern form, it can be characterized as an opposition between two very basic ways of knowing: between a decontextualized, systematic effort to know the essential nature of the world ahead of time, modelled (since Descartes) upon mathematics and fashioned by experts within established academic institutions, and a non-systematic way of knowing that non-professional people work out among themselves as they go along, situated within the vague, practical activities of everyday life, dependent for its standards only upon their being in dialogue and debate with each other. The contrasts involved are similar to those between science and literature and their struggle as to whether truth is 'made' or 'found'. Clearly, in the West, philosophy and science have been in the ascendancy over rhetoric and literature for many centuries, and perhaps will be again for many more centuries. For seemingly, who would not prefer order over disorder, clarity over vagueness, generality over particularity, predictability over contingency, sure-fire techniques over talk and debate, and objectivity over subjectivity? But at the moment, there are some important consequences of taking rhetoric seriously, consequences for how we think and talk about everything we investigate in academic psychology.

Especially, as I have now mentioned many time before, it orientates our attention to – and provides us with the linguistic resources required to render "visibly-rational" – the linguistic, social, and political factors we have to take into account in our formulation and pursuit of what we call in academic psychology 'an approach'. This is of particular importance for us as psychologists: for while physical scientists do not have evaluations placed upon them by their own 'subject matters', we do. Psychologists are people, too, and 'we' must live in the same world as 'those others' that we attempt to investigate. As such, if we want to have what *we* say evaluated by *them* as intelligible, rational and legitimate (and what is the point of our work if it cannot be so evaluated – is it only for initiated elites?), then we ourselves must also, eventually, evaluate our talk in the same ways they do. For, if language is to be a means of communication, there must be agreement not only in definitions but also in judgements. We cannot escape this fact. As a result, psychologists can run the risk of self-refutation in a way not possible in the physical sciences: *we* cannot ignore or deny certain fundamental forms of people's tacit or background *practical-moral* knowledge of how to be competent members of their society – for example, that they are acting, thinking, perceiving, evaluating, accountable persons – without brooking self-contradiction, without denying the very conditions making not only many other important parts of everyday social life possible, but also science itself.

It cannot be avoided by replacing common-sense concepts by scientific theories, for such theories – which claim that things are not what they seem – cannot themselves explain how they attain their own intelligibility; and any account of how they are made intelligible raises again the question of who is to judge *its* validity. So, while the validity of a theory may seem to be an empirical question, to be answered by pressing particular theories to their explanatory limits, if one is reflexive about the character of everyday social life, one can as a scientific psychologist go only so far; there are already practical-moral (ontological) a priori limits upon what one can claim the case to be. For instance, as Lopez (1991) notes, while psychologists celebrate their own high standards of rationality, they also claim to have discovered (under the artificial conditions of uncertainty they create in their experiments) that people *in general* are "irrational-and-science-has-proved-it." But, as she argues, such claims are absurd. If taken seriously, they work to render rationally invisible what we all informally take as belonging to the very conditions of possibility upon which the claimed discovery depends, namely the very notion of rational agency.

It is these issues, of rational visibility and ontological adequacy broached above, that I want to discuss below. I shall claim not simply that the cognitive approach *inadequately* characterizes its subject matter (by in fact caricaturing it), but that the very idea that an objective 'notation' (a system of marks representing quantitative values) can provide an adequate (and authoritative) medium for the characterization of the psychological phenomena involved in practical-moral practices, is fundamentally mistaken — it ignores both the role of social and rhetorical processes in its own creation and what is involved in unique, first-person individuals agreeing among themselves to treat it as an authoritative form of knowledge. Recognizing this raises the question as to where cognitive psychology does in fact draw its authority: I shall claim that, rather than a genuine appeal to reason, it 'borrows' its authority from the already established authority of mathematics in the natural sciences, and the authority of the natural sciences in academic life at large. I shall present this argument in the course of introducing certain investigatory resources made available to us in recent rhetorical and poststructuralist[5] writings, and by making use of them to examine some of the textual strategies used, as I mentioned above, in the formulation of persuasive accounts aimed at creating and sustaining a research 'tradition' within a group.

Argumentative meanings, discursive regimes, and topics

In the traditional, hypothetico-deductive view of science, what is supposed to hold a research group together, is the shared attempt to prove clearly formulated *laws* or *principles* of behaviour true (Kimble, 1989). But as Harré (1970a) has argued, this is an unrealistic view of how science actually works: orientation towards a model or an analogue is what is central, and putative laws are simply heuristic devices, useful in the discovery of the supposedly *real* nature of the mechanisms and objects pictured or modelled in one's theory. And indeed, this does seem (mostly) to be how cognitivism thinks of itself as proceeding. But this raises other problems to do with creating and sustaining a research group's identity, for it is unclear how all its members come to interpret and apply the relevant aspects of the model as they do. For instance, in cognitive psychology, as machines are not *obviously* like people, besides a selective grasp of the model itself, members must be instructed in acceptable ways of applying it. How is this instructing done?

As I have pointed out elsewhere (Shotter, 1990c), the claim that psychology is built upon particular theoretical and methodological foundations only has sense, and only makes sense, in the context of many other activities and practices, central among which is the production of *written texts*. All professional psychology begins with the reading of already written texts, and ends in the writing of further texts. Bowers (1990) has added to this that it is important that such texts have a dramatic, narrative quality, and as we shall see below, cognitive psychology is no exception to this demand. Thus, in assembling the investigatory resources appropriate to the task of understanding how a research group constructs itself, it is these textual activities that we must study. In doing so, I shall oscillate between two standpoints: that of the writer/researcher/rhetorician, who is aware of having to write within a rhetorical context of criticism and justification; and that of the reader/student/ hermeneut, who takes it that the text represents a 'reality' which he or she must accurately grasp.

The argumentative meaning of formative statements

Central to the formulation of an 'approach' in psychology, and to the binding together of a social group who all think of themselves as following it, are what one might call "formative statements," statements such as the following: "Artificial intelligence (AI) is sometimes defined as the study of how to build and/or program computers to enable them to do the sorts of things that minds can do" (Boden, 1990: 1). Among other matters, it is the functioning of such statements as these that I want to examine in this section.

The first investigatory resource I want to mention is that of *argumentative meaning* introduced by Billig (1987: 91) in his discussion of the rhetorical approach to social psychology. He points out that to understand the meaning of a statement (or a whole discourse) argumentatively, it is not enough just to examine the words said, or to infer the images in the mind of the speaker/writer at the moment of their utterance; something more and different is involved. One should also consider the other positions within the particular discourse, or the other discourses, which the statement can be seen as criticizing. Without knowing these counter-positions or counter-discourses — indeed, the whole *argumentative context* within which they play their part — the argumentative meaning will be lost. Or at least, it will remain rationally invisible to us, and will not appear on the scene as a topic of academic debate. Similarly, to understand why at a particular point a justification, or some other form of argument, is offered, one must search for the actual, or a possible, criticism that the writer is seeking to deflect. Thus a rhetorical investigation explores the meaning of a set of statements or piece of text by locating it within its context of controversy. Or (to put Billig's claim in another idiom): making explicit the absent-presence of 'the repressed other' (Derrida, 1976) is a crucial component in understanding, practically, the proper socio-political point in what someone says or writes.

In a scientific approach, such argumentative contexts, however, are not simply arenas of debate about scientific facts among a set of isolated individuals, but are also (or should be) arguments about whether the appropriate scientific values or virtues have been exercised in their supposed discovery. In such circumstances we can again follow MacIntyre (1981); I shall say that in psychology the argumentative contexts of importance constitute a *living tradition* – where a living tradition is rooted both in people's embodied knowledge and in their embodied evaluative attitudes, and is a historically extended argument, conducted both in speech and action, as to how both their knowledge and their attitudes might best be formulated. Or, in other words, it is a providential space. This is a very different idea, of course, from what we are used to thinking of as a tradition – as a hierarchically structured, *closed system* of knowledge, a framework, that is supposed to provide members with ready-made solutions to problems. Indeed, it means that arguments do not just take place *within* a tradition, but the tradition itself is constituted in a continuous argument as to what the tradition itself is or should be. And it is into just such a tradition of argumentation, I want to argue, that the beginning student (all unawares) is, in fact, being inducted into in being introduced to a particular field of research in psychology. As Best (1986: 31) says in his introductory textbook, "the revolutionary period [in cognitive psychology] is not yet over;" controversy about its proper nature still continues, and it is this that the rhetorical investigator must study.

Discursive regimes

To the beginning student, however, the task looks different. For the student, the theoretical terms mentioned in the formative statements are presented as set within a *discourse* – a disciplined way of talking constituting "the approach" as such – and it is this discourse that the student must attempt to understand. They must construct it not from the argumentative meanings of theoretical terms, but from their constitutive meanings. They must do this by reading 'around' the terms in question, and by trying to use them in ways those who are already practitioners judge as relevant to the approach. The student must begin by treating such terms (as 'computer', 'information processor', or 'mind') as representing real objects which are at first only vaguely known to them, but whose meaning they must ultimately show a systematic grasp of (if they want to qualify for membership in the profession). Thus *their* task is at first genuinely a hermeneutical one: they must try to understand the meaning of a theoretical term (a part) by the building up of a gradual grasp of its place within a particular discourse (a whole). Only later do they face the question of the place of *that* discourse within psychology, and within academe as a whole.

Their hermeneutical task is aided by a special quality supposed to be possessed by scientific texts of this kind not possessed by literary texts: for scientific texts must (in certain crucial regions at least) be *systematic*. Their systematicity is derived, as Rorty (1980, 1989) and Edwards (1982) have pointed out, both from a set of components supplied by a foundational *metaphor* literalized into a 'grammatical picture', and, I must add, from other structuring devices implicit in the *syntax* of our language (see below), which, working together, fashion these components into an orderly, intelligible whole. Where, as described in the previous chapter, the order among the components in the 'picture' is used to discipline what can coherently be said within the discourse, and thus to produce the "discipline" as such. For, unlike in everyday conversation, where a speaker may change one figure of speech for another if the first proves unintelligible, in an 'approach' in science and philosophy we must discipline our talk by relating all its terms to a single model, analogue or metaphor. Thus metaphors function to provide a set of *already formulated meanings* in terms of which all else that is said can be understood; they thus work to institute a *discursive regime*, that is, – to repeat Foucault's (1972: 49) formulation – "practices that systematically form the objects of which they speak," and which, in so doing, hold a group of researchers together as a group with a tradition, as all seemingly researching into the same thing.

Thus in psychology, we literally regiment the terms we ordinarily use for talking about mental activity, by drawing them all from the same *metaphorical* source. And indeed, this is precisely how Boden (1989) characterizes what it is that, despite the very many ways in which they might literalize the metaphor, holds computational (and information processing) psychologists together as a recognizable group: the fact that "computers – or rather, concepts drawn from computer science – play *some* central theoretical *role* in the computational psychologist's claims about what the mind is and how it functions" (1989: 5; emphasis added). The computer (or information processing system) is *the* metaphor in terms of which workers can see similarities between people's activities and the activities of machines. And it plays at least two roles in their theoretical practices: hermeneutically, it works to an extent like a telescope or microscope (a prosthetic) in enabling those who 'look through it' to see only the 'relational structure', or the 'logic' of people's behaviour, and to ignore all else; but also rhetorically, to provide members with access to what might be called the *justificational rhetoric* used by all cognitive scientists, thus enabling them all to participate as members of the same tradition of argumentation.

Narrative seduction

Where the student sees a logical *system* of thought (or at least what promises ultimately to be a well-formed system), to be mastered according to various academic norms and values, a system *representing* real things, the rhetorical investigator cannot approach the problem in this way. He or she can neither understand the meaning of a theoretical term by fitting it into a formal system, nor by interpreting it in relation to a hermeneutical whole – because the investigator begins from the knowledge that neither system nor whole as yet fully exists! Thus, the investigator does not see theoretical terms as yet having a clear meaning at all. He or she sees the statements within which the terms appear as *formulations*, as form-giving acts that play a part in a piece of persuasive writing within a tradition of argumentation; a theoretical term is thus seen as a *means* in the making of a *possible* meaning. Hence, just as a piece of well-crafted science fiction may work to tempt one to wonder whether a circumstance is truly real or not, so here as well. And, in being tempted to explore it as a possibility of that kind, so one's attention is diverted away from other possibilities in the context of controversy in which the statement first appears – but how are such temptations motivated?

As Bowers (1990) has argued, formative statements on their own do not seem to be enough to found an approach, a "narrative drama" seems to be required, not only to hold a research group together as all orientated towards the same subject matter, but also to motivate their investigation of it. While earlier discussions in artificial intelligence began with dramatic questions like "Can machines think?" (Turing, 1950), the current drama has become more complex, and Boden (1988: 1) sets it out thus: "Computational psychology today is rather like the dragon in earlier times: of the people who are seeking it, not all agree on what they expect to find or how they hope to find it – while many others doubt that it exists to be found at all,"[6] and the whole character of her book is set out as a dramatic history of the quests so far mounted in search of the still to be identified 'grail', ending with the present, still somewhat "chaotic" state of the field, but with the final 'double-bind' that, of course, "uncertainty is part of the adventure" (1988: 264). Thus, her drama can still work in seducing (some) to participate in one of cognitivism's founding tenets: which is, as we know, that it is only possible to 'see' a similar logic in the activities of computers (or information processing systems) and people, if we agree at the outset to ignore everything to do with their different material instantiations. It works because in accord with the general, taken-for-granted background assumption of theoretical thought – that in theory, things are *not* what they seem to be in everyday life – such a proposal still seems perfectly legitimate.

I say 'seductive' for, as Bowers argues, the student does not notice, or, has been trained not to treat as important, the fact that it institutes within the discursive regime a number of *exclusionary and/or dividing practices* – for the well-trained student as an objective scientist has already accepted cognitivism's founding tenet as an adequate beginning. But, concerning the "Turing test" (Turing, 1950) – a test which in any case many think is insufficiently rigorous (see, for example, Johnson-Laird, 1983: xii) – Bowers shows how it establishes what he calls both a regime of vision, and a regime of articulation. A regime of vision is set up by the test calling for those trying to decide whether they are dealing with a person or a machine, to stay in a separate room, and to communicate only by use of typewritten messages; no facial expressions, body movements, tones of voice, intakes of breath, hesitations as such (marking uncertainty or disagreement), . . . are permitted. In short, the very 'movements' of persons as the authors of their own lives are excluded; they are permitted sentences but not utterances. A regime of articulation is established by constraints being placed upon what can be said: the interrogator must articulate a certain kind of speech (questions) to which the person/machine responds with (what must be interpreted as) answers. In other words, the responsive meaning of their (not permitted) utterances, is also eliminated. The physical boundary thus divides and differentiates the participants in a way which prevents joint action, and in particular, the demand for one-pass, question–answer forms of communication excludes responsivity, and hence what is crucial in everyday communication: the negotiation of meanings.

In other words, as Foucault (1972, 1979) has shown, these regimes establish power relations that can be understood in terms of who has rights to do what to whom, and who has duties to respond to whom. Only if people were to relate themselves to each other in ways quite unlike the ways in which they ordinarily do so; only if they relate themselves to each other as if machines; only if they relate themselves to each other in the extraordinary, non-negotiable ways such as the Turing test demands, does the outcome afford us the opportunity to say that the logic in a machine's behaviour parallels the logic in the behaviour of human beings. But if being inducted into an approach in psychology requires us to see ordinary, everyday life activities in such a unusual way as this, upon what *basis* can we be tempted and seduced into doing it?

Two-sided topoi

Besides the formative statements and metaphors used in establishing an approach and binding a research group together, we must also examine the functioning of other more general sources of appeal used by researchers in warranting their claims: those taken for granted as a basis in the common sense of science itself. For example, Johnson-Laird and Wason justify their turning away from the "methodological obsession with experimentation" (1977: 2) and towards an interest in AI, by first discussing existing criticisms of experimentation – that psychologists often waste time testing inconsistent and intuition bound theories, and so on – and then by saying: "An obvious advantage of expressing a theory in the form of a computer program is that it is rendered entirely explicit and its logical coherence is put to a stringent test" (1977: 10).[7] In saying that the advantage is "obvious", however, they are making a rhetorical appeal to a two-sided, scientific "commonplace," something so basic that one cannot be said to have a scientific orientation at all without adherence to it: for in science one wants *both* objective and consistent theories *and* their empirical testing. Johnson-Laird and Wason are unusual, as they acknowledge, in privileging its non-empirical side.

To discuss appeals of this kind – to what researchers take to be "obvious" – I want to introduce another investigatory resource, one also introduced by Billig (1987: 138–9), but one, as I have mentioned before, that has always in fact been central to the whole rhetorical tradition: the idea of *topics*, the shared, two-sided *topoi* which, in being taken to be obvious, can serve both as the 'seeds' or 'roots' of argumentative formulations as well as a source of alternative formulations by others. 'Topics', already in existence in the background common sense of arguers, are what can hold an argument together as an intelligible social enterprise and give it its style, even when, as I have pointed out above, there is no possibility of being able to make sense of a term by placing it within a 'whole' or within a 'formal framework.' Thus it is that Johnson-Laird and Wason argue for the validity of AI in psychology – or at least, for it as an approach "worth trying" (1977: 10) – in the face of the claim in many other areas of psychology that it is experimentation that is crucial. For we all agree – don't we? – that unless theories are consistent and intuition-free, they cannot be unambiguously tested.

But what other common-sense norms (of science) do Johnson-Laird and Wason make use of in warranting *their* claims? And what else is accomplished here in their (implicit) appeals to them? To see what is going on here, it will be useful at this point to return to Billig who, it will be remembered, with Protagoras' maxim in mind, claims the cognitivist approach to be one-sided. In particular, Billig argues that what the one-sided image of the person excludes, with its emphasis in cognitivism upon categorization, is people's ability to particularize. Even the bureaucrat may "use wit and ingenuity to oppose routine categorization [to form a 'special case'] by particularization, and the same skills will be required should the special case be challenged by others" (Billig, 1987: 131). In fact, we could say that, if it is the commonplace understanding of human activity that it has both an objective and a subjective side, then it is the subjective side, the side to do with the particularity and uniqueness of an individual's point of view, that Johnson-Laird and Wason omit.

Indeed, science's omission of secondary (subjective) qualities, residing only (internally) in the consciousnesses of individuals, and its concern only with primary (objective) qualities existing in a common (external) world, goes back to Galileo and Locke. And it expresses itself now, as Bazeman (1988) notes, in the two norms influencing the formulation of accounts as a scientific field develops: the gradual elimination of the subjectivity and personal history of the investigators, and the gradual production of a description of nature in the ahistorical terms of form and structure. These are the norms Johnson-Laird and Wason emphasize, but in emphasizing them, they exclude once again the unique, subjective, historical or developmental side of people's make-up (a point I shall return to below).

I will not pursue these issues much further here, except to remark, as Potter and Wetherell (1987) and Prelli (1989, 1990) both show, that what in the past have been treated as the unequivocal norms held to be binding upon scientists, expressed in terms of prescriptions, proscriptions, preferences and permissions (Merton, 1938, quoted in Prelli, 1989), turn out when studied in practical contexts of their use – in arguments at conferences, in informal discussions in the lab, etc. – not to be normative at all. For each 'norm', it would seem, a 'counter-norm' can be identified which, at some point at least in verbal controversy, scientists also cite in their justification of their activities. For instance, as Potter and Wetherell (1987) report, transcripts of discussions (at a major international psychology conference) regarding the role of *testability* in recognizing theories as scientific theories, show that among the psychologists present, there was no consensus with respect to either the nature of testability or its importance. In other words, rather than with alleged norms or counter norms, we are dealing here with rhetorical *topoi*, with a set of taken-for-granted themes in the common sense of science, which can be used in persuading, justifying and criticizing. Thus, what it is *to be* a scientist is not in feeling oneself bound by one side or the other of such topoi, but (to refer back to MacIntyre's version of a tradition above) to appreciate that within a scientific tradition, these are the themes to which one must be responsive in warranting one's claims to knowledge. But are they sufficient when it comes to claims about people's psychological nature?

Institutional tests and the imaginary

Fundamental to a piece of narrative writing is that it can tell a story. Indeed, as mentioned above, a science fiction story can be so well crafted that it can work to 'manufacture', as it were, a strong sense of reality for the things of which it speaks, even things we feel utterly impossible – time travel, for instance. So, although such a piece of writing may seem to be *about* a reality already in existence somewhere, that cannot be. The 'things' apparently depicted in it, rather than *origins* or points of *reference* in an extralinguistic reality 'outside' the text somewhere, must be a *part* of it: such texts work to create the (imaginary) objects of which they speak. If this is so, if texts can be so powerful, how do scientific texts avoid being treated merely as fictions? Because, says Foucault (1972), scientific statements (and the texts which contain them) do not have their life in everyday settings. They have their being primarily within a professional arena, and gain their status from having satisfied various *institutional tests*, such as having been formed according to the rules of empirical confirmation or mathematical proof. It is, as we have seen in the section above, their method of institutional justification and criticism which confers upon statements in these arenas their claim to be knowledge.

Thus scientific texts, although they may have a dramatic, narrative quality – giving rise at least to the possibility of creating imaginary 'dragons' one feels motivated to quest for – they must contain, at various crucial points, *warrants* indicating that the appropriate institutional tests have been applied. For example, Boden justifies her claim – that if a psychological science is to be possible at all, then it must be a computational psychology specifiable in terms of "effective procedures" – by remarking that Turing (1936) has "*proved* that a language capable of defining 'effective procedures'[8] suffices, in principle, to solve any computable problem" (Boden, 1988: 259 emphasis in original).[9] Thus, we arrive at the situation in which, as long as the texts in question satisfy certain criteria – to do with their systematicity and various institutional tests – students (and *aficionados* alike) read them as texts in cognitive psychology, and as being accurately representative of an (as yet still not completely known) ideal reality behind appearances, that is, as genuine theoretical texts. And like the medieval search for dragons, we feel motivated by them to fill out the details of the knowledge they specify until we have a unified *system* of knowledge which, one day, will give us a one true answer to every one of our questions, with all the answers compatible with each other.

Thus it seems that, ahead of time, Turing's proof licenses a way of speaking in which, right from the start, certain terms have an unambiguous meaning, an unambiguous reference. But yet again, just as the rhetorical investigator cannot understand the precise meaning of theoretical terms hermeneutically, because he or she knows that neither a formal system nor a narrative whole has yet been produced by the researchers, so here also, the rhetorical investigator cannot accept the researchers' version of how they say their talk should be understood. For the investigator knows that no such actual unambiguous referents exist for such terms in an actual 'cognitive' realm – for, surprisingly, no one has yet succeeded in finding such a realm! Strictly, while meaningful in relation to the model or analogue, in relation to people's actual mental activities the terms within the text are meaningless; they lack (as yet) any clear referents. For the student and the researchers, what they take on in the text is not so much meaning as *intelligibility*, that is, they become capable of being grasped reflectively and intellectually. This results from the way in which fragmentary component parts – notions, say, to do with 'effective procedures' supplied by the approach's metaphor – are hermeneutically fashioned into a coherent whole *syntactically*.

It is the syntax of ordinary language which bridges the gaps and links possibly meaningful fragments into an apparent whole, a whole that *must* have the characteristics which such things in our way of talking about the world ought to have. For the order and coherence of a textualized way of speaking, a way of speaking disciplined or regimented by adherence to single metaphor, can create a sense of the reality for the things it 'depicts'. For instance, although no one has ever seen "our knowledge of language," it seems perfectly reasonable to treat it, as Chomsky has done, as "an abstract object," and to seek its "structure." Yet whence did this project emerge? It certainly did not emerge as an induction from a chaotic mass of linguistic data, nor from an intuition – for it is an organization imposed upon our linguistic intuitions, and not the only one possible by any means. Furthermore, many feel (Baker and Hacker, 1984; Harris, 1980, 1981) that the whole enterprise is utterly misconceived, carried forward in terms of what *must* be the case *syntactically*, on the basis of a metaphorical notion of language as a rule-governed calculus. The problem is created by 'carrying across' a legitimate way of talking into another sphere of life in which its legitimacy is unclear.[10]

It is precisely at this point, where syntax masquerades as meaning, that Wittgenstein's (1981: no. 446) warnings against the bewitchments of theoretical forms of language, and his recommendations to pay attention to situated, concrete phenomena, are particularly apposite:

> But don't think of understanding as a 'mental process' at all. – For *that* is a way of speaking that is confusing you. Rather ask yourself: in what kind of case, under what circumstances do we say "Now I can go on" . . . [A] way of speaking is what prevents us from seeing the facts without prejudice . . . *That* is how it can come about that the means of representation produces something *imaginary*, So let us not think we *must* find a specific mental process, because the verb "to understand" is there and because one says: Understanding is an activity of mind.

In other words, even though texts in psychology may satisfy all the criteria it was once thought proper scientific texts should satisfy, there is still something wrong with the criteria we apply in assessing their status.

What it is like to be a person?

They are not, as I have called it, *ontologically responsible* formulations: In failing to account reflexively for their own intelligible formulation, they do not allow us to see ourselves at work in their production; ethically, they do not respect what is involved in communicating with others – the opportunity for responsive speech and its responsive understanding. In assuming that the methods of the physical sciences enable one to 'see' into the hidden realities of the physical world, to 'see' into their inner workings, psychologists have dreamt of seeing into people's inner psychological workings in the same way. Thus it has been thought legitimate to formulate theories as potentially accurate representations of an underlying reality, and – as long as the theories were unambiguous (that is, one-sided), logical (that is, hierarchically structured as a unified system of dependencies), objective, consistent, and general – it was thought that the Darwinian winnowing process of empirical testing would lead us eventually to the right theory, and we would then have the 'insight' we desired. This has not happened. Why not? Because, I would claim, in lacking a proper respect for the being of our subject matter, we have not responsibly clarified for ourselves what it is like for us to be always *linguistically situated beings*, and it is to that task as it makes itself felt in academic psychology that I now want to turn.

As Nagel (1981) points out, all reductive and objectivist attempts to capture the character of people's 'inner life' fail because they are all logically compatible with its absence. The task cannot be solved by any laws, principles, propositions, or theories, that is, in Wittgenstein's terms, by 'saying' anything; it is not a matter of explaining. This is crucial: a proof cannot dispel the fog, as those such as Boden seem to think. As Wittgenstein realized, there are some things that we just cannot justify or explain to ourselves (although we might hold out the hope that one day we will) – not just like our ability to see colours (that Wittgenstein made a point of), but all our other abilities which, in their 'lower' forms, as Vygotsky would put it, we have in our biology – but we still get by perfectly well, none the less, without knowing how they work. Some things we do, on occasions, just 'see': for instance, the connection between words and their meanings in our everyday talk. We do not need after every sentence another to explain it. If we want to describe what is going on when we understand one another, a different way of talking altogether is required, one which 'shows' what understanding is like. Thus, we cannot discover what (our concept of) *understanding* 'is' for us by attempting to reflect upon it; we must study how 'it' necessarily 'shapes' those of our everyday communicative activities in which it is involved, *in practice*. Hence, what we require is an account which links together all our uses of the term in a revealing way.

But not just any kind of account of the results of such studies will do; an account of a special kind is required, one which reveals something about the form of our consciousnesses. Nagel points to its nature in making the claim that: "the fact that an organism has conscious experience *at all* means, basically, that there is something that it is like to *be* that organism" (quoted in Hofstadter and Dennett, 1981: 392)

– "something it is like *for* that organism," he adds. We require a way of talking which provides us with a way of seeing ourselves (or whatever organism is in question, for that matter) 'in' what is said. It must function as a "perspicuous presentation," an account which "produces just that understanding which consists in 'seeing connections'" (Wittgenstein, 1953: no. 122). Let us turn, then, to the task of describing what the 'inner' life of a 'linguistically situated person' in a socially constructed world is *like*.

Central to the social constructionist ontology I want to outline, is the view (shared, as I have already said, with Gergen, 1985; Harré, 1983, 1990) that the primary human reality is conversational or responsively relational, that one's "person–world" dimension of interaction or being exists within a whole mêlée of "self–other" relationships or dimensions of interaction. Above, I described these latter relationships in terms of "joint action" – where joint action, as we know, gives rise to a 'space' or 'situation' that seems both to 'contain' something and to be 'related to something other than or beyond itself', such that its inhabitants find themselves 'in' a *given* situation, but one that has a *horizon* and is 'open' to their action. In specifying the nature of such a situation further, we can say that those within them experience a need to be socially accountable. Social accountability has two major features. The situations generated in joint action, although not wholly unspecified, are always ongoing and open to yet further specification. Thus they 'afford' (to use the Gibsonian term) being 'given' or 'lent' a determinate specification within a medium of communication which their previously partial specification 'permits' or 'grounds'. This means that they can be further specified in different ways within different discourses. If, however, a dominant discourse is always used, they will be specified in a way which always leads to the survival (by its constant reproduction) of that discourse. Thus, what is allowed to count for us as our official reality is continually reconstituted for us in the ways in which we *must* talk in our attempts to account for ourselves and events within it – where the 'must' is a *moralistic* must in the sense that if we don't account for things in an acceptable manner, we shall be treated as in some way socially incompetent, or in fact 'bad', and be sanctioned accordingly.

Taking the two features of joint action and social accountability together means: first, that being involved in joint (conversational) action with others creates a continuously changing situation within which one's ontological 'position' in relation to those others – who one can or must *be*, for example, the 'looker', 'listener', 'speaker' – changes in a moment-by-moment way; second, that only those able to 'sense' how they are situated are socially competent to speak and act in relation to their position; and third, that while a way of talking can be said to give form to feeling, it lacks *authority* unless it is 'rooted' or 'grounded' in one's sense of one's position. Thus, although one may from within a conversation point to many other important spheres of human activity beyond it, conversation is the primary human reality in the following, judgemental sense: Given that human realities do not endure through the physical rigidity of their structures (it makes no sense even to talk of them in this crackbrained way), they are only sustained in existence by being continually remade in people's everyday social activities. In such processes, however, people mutually judge and correct each other as to the 'fittingness' of their actions to what they take their reality to be. And conversation is the ultimate sphere in which all such judging and evaluating takes place, and in which final assessments and shared agreements are reached. This is what gives it its priority – and, incidentally, its power to change otherwise unconsciously reproduced realities.

To the extent that the changing sea of enablements and constraints within which conversation takes place, is a changing sea of privileges and obligations, of entitlements and sanctions, the changes taking place are of a *moral* kind: people act with a respect both for their own and the being of the others around them. Thus, associated with each position is, we can say, a set of 'rights' and 'duties' to do with the care we must have for our being as persons: for instance, the rights and duties associated with us (as the Western individuals we are) being first-person speakers, second-person listeners, or third-person observers. As second persons, we are involved in and have duties to maintain an interaction in a way quite different from those of third person 'outsiders'; we do not have the right to step out of our personal involvement with a speaker and attend to aspects of their-person or performance to which they do not intend us to attend. This obligation does not extend, however, to third persons; hence our unease when, as first-person performers attempting a tricky interpersonal encounter, we find ourselves under the observation of uninvolved others. My point in making all these distinctions is to focus upon the fact that, for us, the conduct of our form of social life is based upon a right we assign to first persons to make 'non-observational self-ascriptions, to *tell* us about themselves and their experiences, by saying for example, "I'm frightened," or "I'm puzzled," or "I love you," and to have what they say taken seriously as meaning what they intend it to mean (Cavell, 1969) – as long as, that is, we also feel that they *already* have the social competencies required to sustain the society within which this right makes sense.

We feel justified in assigning people the right to speak like this, for what *their* world is like is unique to them. How might this uniqueness be characterized? One way is – to make use of some of the descriptive vocabulary introduced above – to say that we each (on particular occasions of joint action with others) construct for ourselves at those times, *from within* the conversation with them, so to speak, an "I–world" dimension of interaction, a set of interactional practices in which 'I' as a unique, first person, have a special status. For it does seem to us that we can investigate the character of *that* 'world' which is *external* to ourselves as individuals (while failing to notice that it is not external to us as a social group). Indeed, we can discriminate within it, that is, *sense*, at least the following three categories of activity: actions for which we personally are responsible (and must be able to justify to the others around us if challenged to do so); events which just happen, outside of our agency to control; and a whole, third set of activities (called "joint actions") in which we are uncertain as to whether they are enacted or caused. Thus, we can discover *from within* our present form of life that we cannot as individuals make just what we please occur; even aspects of our own bodily being are not under our own control. Thus, if I now ask myself in such a situation: 'What is it *like* to be me?' – thus to tell others should they ask me – as a unique first-person 'I' it is possible for me to answer by describing 'my external world', 'my situation'. I can describe it in terms of: the 'things' I perceive in it; the values I attach to them, how I perceive them, and the reactions I have towards them; the opportunities for action and understanding it 'affords' me; the nature of my rights, duties, privileges and obligations in relation to the others around me; and especially its 'horizon', that is, what is not actually at the moment 'visible' to me but what I can point to as being reasonable for me to expect in the future; and I can qualify all the above by remarking upon its precariousness, because they all depend upon my first-person right to speak and act, and have what I say or do taken seriously, and that is continually in contest.

This (to the extent that I am permitted to fill it out in detail) is my *identity*, who at this moment 'I' am. Indeed, my very use of the word 'I' – in such expressions as 'I think I may be able to see a solution', or 'I feel I have placed myself in difficulties here' – allows me to talk about what it is like, in my unique 'position' at the moment within different, changing, socially constructed situations, to be me. And it is this, my occupation of a unique trajectory of unique positions, which I alone occupy and can describe, which gives me a claim to have what I say for myself taken seriously, for no one else can occupy those positions and thus speak for me. They are all precarious and continually in contest though, because, associated with any position is an intrinsic scarcity and thus, an economics of exchange, a 'political economy': for, if I am to be someone else's listener, I cannot be the speaker; if I am to be someone else's reader, then inevitably I cannot at the same time be a writer; and I cannot simply assert my right to be a writer on my own, a writer is useless without readers. The view of the first person here, then – what it is like to be *me* – is of someone always in a seemingly 'given' but changing, socially constructed situation. Where the 'openings' to action in such a situation change as the course of one's action changes. This, I claim, is something of what the 'inner' life of a 'linguistically situated person' in a socially constructed world is like.

Conclusions

I have argued, then, that psychology fails if it cannot provide an account of what it is *like* to be one of us. For such an account is required if we are to give a proper account of a central feature of our social relationships: that they occur between people with distinctly unique *identities*, with unique positions and points of view. An 'information processing system' without an identity, without an understanding of who it is and how it is 'placed' in a social situation, could never play the part of a genuine person in everyday social life at large. Indeed, it could be argued that: the computer model fails to characterize the way in which people's everyday actions are always 'situated' or 'placed' within a *social* and *moral*, as well as a historically developed *political* order, actual or imagined; that the maintenance in good repair of that order is due to the social accountability of those 'within' it; that such accountability depends upon a first-person ability to distinguish eventualities for which one is oneself responsible, and those which lie outside one's own agency to control; and that one's motivation to be responsible in this way is sustained by the fact that one's *identity* is at stake in one's actions, for one is *oneself* morally committed in them (both to others and to oneself) to be who one 'claims'[11] oneself to be. Computers, lacking any sense of being individually and *personally* 'placed' in relation to those around them – to their 'parents', their 'friends', their other 'kith and kin', their 'mothers-in-law', their 'bosses' and 'subordinates', and indeed, to all the others both in and outside their community to whom they are morally bound in one way or another – would lack the kind of practical-moral knowledge required to act in a socially responsible and responsive manner. In being socially 'unplaced', computers are unable to relate their actions either to a self-known, situated 'I', nor to situated others. In short, they would be unable to be accountable in their conduct to others. And finally, they would have no sense at all, of course, of occupying a providential space of historically developed, ocassioned opportunities for action.

Why have we not appreciated all this before? Why have we been so uninterested in the rhetorical, responsive, and ethical nature of our activities in everyday social life? Why have we not appreciated the ineradicable nature of the first-person perspective? Because as professional academics, we have, I think, been doubly entrapped in a set of professional practices to do with the regimenting and systematizing our everyday social knowledge within a dominant, scientific form of talk which suggests, both that there *are* 'mental processes', and, that such processes work in terms of producing 'representations corresponding to reality'. In this double entrapment, we have not *felt* able to speak and act just as we please – and in a certain sense rightly so – for, at least, from within some spheres of our lives, such ways of acting and knowing have not only proved to be highly valuable, but to be in accord with our cultural identities. We have had to act 'into' an argumentative context of criticism and justification provided by our professional colleagues – but also more than that. Concerned to satisfy both 'the judge' and 'the witness' (recall Bakhtin above), we have felt various urges, cravings, longings, etc., provided in the 'providential space' we occupy. Thus, what is at issue here, clearly, is not a matter of whether what we say corresponds with the world in some way or not; it is a matter of warranting our voice (Gergen, 1989b), of finding a way to justify having our claims taken seriously.

It is also to do with the following struggle: whether, within the resources of our ordinary ways of making sense, we work to sustain the currency of dominant forms, those derived not from an image, but from a 'picture' of that image, that work to institute a certain, single social order; or, whether we find other resources within them, other ways of fashioning a more *ontologically responsible* form of talk, which although still working in terms of images, does not seek to literalize them into a picture. For, if what I have claimed here is correct, that is, is *just*, in the sense of more adequately respecting our being as the kind of things we are, then our dominant ways of talking are ways which render the ethical, social, cultural, political, historical, and the unique aspects of our being, rationally invisible to us, and, in particular, hide our historical possibilities from us, as a culture. The way of talking offered here, I claim, is one 'from within' which we might become more rationally visible to ourselves, one from within which we might be able to recognize ourselves at work.

NINE

What is a 'personal relationship'? Who can we be to each other?

> ... this is the love story, subjugated to the great narrative Other, to that
> general opinion which disparages any excessive force and wants the subject
> himself to reduce the great imaginary current, the orderless, endless stream
> which is passing through him, to a painful, morbid crisis of which he must
> be cured, which he must 'get over' ... the love story is the tribute the lover
> must pay to the world in order to be reconciled with it.
>
> (Barthes, 1983: 7)

Here, I want to continue the exploration of what, practically, is involved in thinking
about our personal relationships as occurring 'in' history, rather than 'within' an
intellectually coherent construction of some kind, that is, as occurring within an
everyday, living, providential space, rather than in an ordered space of supposed
empirical possibilities. How should we rethink our talk about our personal relationships? How might they be studied? Again, the tactic would seem to be to study
them at points of difficulty, at times when the people involved must draw upon
resources in the larger cultural environment around them in effecting repairs. Gergen
and Gergen (1987) take this approach, but discuss relationship difficulties within
the context of a discussion of "narratives of relationship." Thus for them, when talk
of a 'we' or an 'us' changes into talk of 'I' and 'you' – and instead of "*We* must think
about this," a couple begin to say, "*You* and *I* must talk about it" – such talk is seen
as a constituent in the "regressive narrative" (1987: 283) of a failing relationship.
What I want to do in this chapter is partially to agree – that such a change often
does indicate difficulties in an intimate relationship – but to explore other than
'narrative' reasons why this is so.

For, in line with my claims in previous chapters that we do not live 'in' theories,
what I want to claim here is that we do not live 'in' narratives either (or at least
not wholly so). We live within a culture with a history (but not a *historiography*) to
it. Thus the attempt to contain our lives within the purview of a narrative as a
cognitive instrument[1] exhibits once again exactly the trouble we had with theories:
for, as Mink (1978) points out, a narrative makes sense of history by representing

the regular movement of a single theme, discovered within it.[2] Indeed, this is the
point of the "grand narratives" of which Lyotard (1984) speaks: they legitimate (and
motivate) consistent work of a particular type to promote the unfolding of a certain
valued form of life – as if history itself has the character of an as-yet-untold story
simply awaiting discovery and accurate representation. Thus, once again we must
ask: whose story is it that is valued? Or, whose way of telling stories is it that is
valued? Who, in the cultural politics of our everyday lives, is the great narrative
Other of which Barthes speaks?

A theory of love?

The main aim in the investigation below is to explore the nature of the symbolic
resources we might draw upon in formulating an answer to the following questions.
What *is* a close or intimate personal relationship? What problems are raised (especially those of an ethical kind), not just for us as professional social scientists, but
for us as modern Westerners at large, in attempting to formulate an answer to this
question? The investigatory context I shall adopt is the one to do with *social
accountability* I introduced in the previous chapter. It consists in the two-fold claim
that: both our experience and our understanding of our *reality*, of the form of our
social *relationships*, and also of our *selves*, are constituted for us very largely in the
'basic' ordered ways of talking (see Chapter 7) which we *must* use if we are to be
accounted by the others around us as properly autonomous, socially competent
adults, able to account for ourselves and our own behaviour in our society; but that
this autonomy and competency is developed within essentially dialogical and thus
intrinsically unaccountable, and disorderly *joint* transactions with those others.
Thus again, aspects of Billig's (1987) *rhetorical* approach to social behaviour will
be relevant for us, in which, it will be recalled, he emphasizes the two-sided or
dilemmatic nature of the communicative resources provided by the 'dynamic
stabilities', the common 'stopping places' in the otherwise orderless, endless stream
of activity. Where it is these stabilities that enable members of a social group to
attribute a shared significance to shared feelings in shared circumstances, but which
can also import a degree of intrinsic argumentation and contest into the negotiation
of accounts of events, things and circumstances. I say 'can' here, because the other
side of the two-sided nature of such 'places' here – as we saw in Chapter 3 – is their
continual generation of novelty. And this is important in an intimate 'us' relation,
when the two fuse into one, so to speak.

In an earlier excursion into the sphere of close relationships research in psychology
(Shotter, 1987a), I investigated our ways of talking about that extraordinary phenomenon we call 'falling in (and out of) love'. Although, from a mundane point of
view, lovers are said to be 'blind' (to each other's imperfections), in another sense,
they are far from blind: they see new 'providential' possibilities in each other's lived
activities. The charity in their love allows them to 'see', within the vague, incomplete
responses they give each other, satisfying and gratifying, ideal ways in which they
might be completed. In their intense involvement with each other, they sense

possibilities, subtle 'motions', missed by those less attentive. Thus, as in other kinds of joint action, a 'hero' comes into existence, the judge of and the witness to what we do – the ideal image of who and what our loved one can become, what *in essence* they already are. Thus, fixated upon their ideal image, we see *through* what they actually do, to what they can become – as when mothers see their children's facial movements *as if* their child is smiling at them and they respond appropriately (Shotter, 1974a). Thus, we continually present our image ideal of our loved ones to themselves as if it should be *their* ideal, *their* project: to become fully what in fact they are only partially – as if, *ex post facto*, they must become what in fact they have been all along. I called it an illusion of passion.

Thus, in such a circumstance, in a special *private* zone of our lives – untouched by the great narrative Other who can call us to account – someone who was 'external' to us, a complete stranger, is 'internalized', and becomes such a needed part of ourselves that their loss is a loss we mourn. But in our highly individualistic culture, what happens in these ambiguous and uncertain moments of joint action, in which people do not act in a wholly individualistic or autonomous manner, is intrinsically *unaccountable*. Thus they are, in some sense, extraordinary, 'outside' of what is a normal part of everyday social life. Indeed, if it is the case that all of our personal modes of being are constructed in, and emerge out of, the general self–other dimension of interaction within which they are embedded, how in history might these special enclaves of privacy, in which people orientate towards each other, *not* in terms of their social positions, have been constructed? It is the construction of these both extraordinary and private, normally unaccountable regions of human conduct, which I wish to investigate below.

Duck (1990), a prominent worker in the field of close relationships research, has raised some of these same issues in precisely the same terms. He, too, sees the problem as to do with the degree to which something like a 'personal relationship' can be said to exist independently of what the people involved in it (and the people studying it) *say* about it. Especially when all this talk has the character, as Duck claims also under Billig's (1987) influence, of 'unfinished business' – for no personal relationship, once in existence, is ever over. But what Duck claims is that the dialectical, rhetorical, argumentative side of human life has been neglected in our *theorizing*, and that it is in our *theories* that we must try to capture personal relationships, as both constituted or mediated by talk, and as always in process, or in transition, and as still open to dialectical or argumentative change.

These suggestions of Duck, would be all very agreeable, if I could agree that our problem is of the kind he proposes: a problem of theory. But my claim here is, that this is not our problem. My claim in this chapter is that the unsatisfactory state *theory*, outlined by Duck (1990), as to what a personal relationship 'is', does *not* arise out of a continual failure yet to formulate 'the correct kind' of theory – as if one day we might finally hit upon a right formulation. The problem, I claim, arises out of another kind of difficulty altogether: a failure to grasp what 'theorizing' or 'theory' in a research area such as this should be like. It is still thought that proper theory in this area should copy natural scientific theory, as this is the only sort of theorizing which is respectable. Thus at present, because scientific theories in general are "free creations of the mind" (to quote Einstein), we feel free to formulate general theories in terms of any abstract principles which come to mind. But, as Duck (1990: 12–13) points out, this results in "descriptive impositions" becoming treated (often without warrant) as "real properties of relationships." However, if we accept that *normally* (and the normative nature of the issues in this sphere is something which has been crucially ignored) a relationship is constituted in the talk and other experiences of those who are involved in it, and cannot exist as something imposed upon them by outsiders, then our 'theorizing' must be of a very different kind. And my purpose below is to clarify its special nature and the degree to which it can only have its 'life', so to speak, within a tradition – a tradition of argumentation, in fact. And furthermore, a tradition which provides within it the resources required for the existence of such special enclaves of privacy.

Accountability and traditions of argumentation

My aim in taking the two themes of accountability, and the two-sided, rhetorically organized and 'topically rooted' nature of social behaviour, together, is to use them as resources in raising a number of interconnected issues to do with the nature of thought and talk within a *tradition*. Firstly, following Gauld and Shotter (1977), Shotter (1984), and MacIntyre (1981), we can note that human beings can only be held to account for that of which they are the authors – an 'action' is something for which it is *always* appropriate to ask the agent for an intelligible account. And people account for their actions by hermeneutically 'placing' them within a larger whole; the action is rendered intelligible in terms of the 'part' it plays within a possible sequence of other actions. However, because it is clearly possible to characterize a particular action under a large number of different possible descriptions (Menzel, 1978), we need to know in what way the persons *themselves* made sense of their actions. We need to know the 'basic preunderstandings' – the internalized or embodied form of life, with its associated *topoi*, into which the person has been socialized (Shotter, 1984; Wittgenstein, 1969) – in terms of which the person made sense of his or her own actions, such that, had these 'preunderstandings' been different, the person would not have acted as they did. In other words, we need to know the 'tradition' within which they make sense of what they take to be their 'primary intention(s)', that is, those for which they are prepared to be accountable.

This leads me to my second point. Following Bakhtin (1981, 1986), Bellah *et al.* (1985), Billig (1987), Billig *et al.* (1988) and MacIntyre (1981, 1988), we can note that the meaning of many important distinctions within Western life – such as those between public and private, personal and impersonal, the individual and the collective, the uniquely individual and the socially representative, intimate and merely personal relations, between public institutions and everyday life activities, between the stable and the changing, between the moral and the technical, and so on – are not in any sense fully predetermined, already decided distinctions. They are expressed or formulated in different ways in different, concrete circumstances, by the use of a certain set of historically developed (and to an extent, morally main-tained – see below) 'topological' *resources* within the Western tradition. Thus, what might be called a 'living tradition' does not give rise to a completely determined form of life, but to dilemmas, to different possibilities for living, among which one must choose.

Thus thirdly, a 'living tradition', in consisting in a set of shared two-sided 'topics', 'loci', 'themes' or 'commonplaces', gives rise to the possibility of formulating a whole 'ecology' of different and, indeed, unique 'positions' – each offering differ-ent possibilities for the 'best way' to continue and/or develop the tradition. Hence its characterization as a 'living' tradition, where, to repeat MacIntyre's (1981: 207) already quoted description: "A living tradition . . . is an historically extended, socially embodied argument, and an argument precisely in part about the goods which constitute that tradition." "Traditions, when vital, embody continuities of conflict" (1981: 206). Under the influence of modern individualism, which was meant to free us from restrictive traditions, we have tended to equate all traditions with hierarchically structured, *closed systems* of knowledge, which are supposed to provide members with ready-made solutions to problems, not with material for arguments. But, as Bellah *et al.* (1985: 140–1) have said: those who think of tradition in this way

> deeply misunderstand tradition even when they seek to embrace it. They defend not tradition but traditionalism, . . . whereas tradition is the living faith of the dead, traditionalism is the dead faith of the living. A living tradition is never a programme for automatic moral judgments. It is always in a continuous process of reinterpretation and reappropriation. Such a process assumes, however, that tradition has enough authority for the search for its present meaning to be publicly pursued as a common project.

If it does have that *authority* (and this is an issue to which we must return), then, although those with whom one argues may still find reasons to disagree, they will have to agree that one's arguments are 'grounded' in more than just one's personal feelings, preferences or opinions. They will have to agree that they do in fact relate to agreed common goods. So, although the 'grounding' of one's views or claims may not be sufficient to settle an argument – because your opponents may also, as you must also agree, have grounded their arguments in agreed goods – it does mean that you can reach the position of mutually respecting each other's views. The argument must then be resolved by, for instance, moving to a larger realm of considerations, in which more impersonal goods may play a part.

Thus fourthly, it is worth noting, as Billig (and his colleagues) have made clear, that whether it is in public, professional (and scientific), or private spheres of life, 'rooting' one's speech or thought in the 'topics' or 'themes' of a living tradition is a *necessity* if one is to be a proper participant in it, and to make genuine contribu-tions to debates about its problems: for such two-sided topics, as sources of novelty and difference, do not just channel and constrain thought, they both enable and motivate it. For instance, as we all now realize, we cannot avoid arguments about the nature of freedom: but what one person calls 'cultural hegemony' (the lack of public debate) another calls 'the right of individuals to decide their own lives'; what some call 'the road to serfdom' is what others say makes people 'free and equal'; what some call 'poverty and exploitation' government ministers call 'being less equal'; and so on. To such an extent, it is seemingly possible to characterize social groups, not only by the particular values or dimensions they prize most, but also by the intensity with which they adhere to one side, rather than the other, of a pair of antithetical values (Perelman and Olbrects-Tyteca, 1969). Indeed, as we saw in the previous chapter, all the main themes making up the scientific tradition can be used in a two-sided, rhetorical fashion by scientists, justifying their own theories and in criticizing those of their rivals. Where the answer to this is not somehow to be more clear about the criteria for 'good science', but, as Billig (1991: 208) puts it, to examine more deeply the nature of "those scientific arguments which deny their own rhetoric," thus to discover why they would rather hide than reveal the sources of their influence (this point will be expanded further below).

We must turn now to a fifth point to do with the nature of traditions, that MacIntyre (1981) raises in *After Virtue*: Central to his account of the concept of a tradition is his claim that we identify a particular action by placing the agent's intentions in doing it within both the individual's own history and the history of the setting or settings to which they belong.

> In doing this, in determining what causal efficacy the agent's intentions had in one or more directions, and how his short-term intentions succeeded or failed to be constitutive of long-term intentions, *we ourselves* write a further part of these histories. Narrative history of a certain kind turns out to be the basic and essential genre for the characterization of human actions.
>
> (1981: 194; emphasis added)

It is this, in MacIntyre's view, which allows *us* (as investigators) to establish a *true* identification of an action. For, just as in a court of law a witness's story can, if told appropriately, work to specify quite precisely the evidence required to corroborate or refute it, this is also the case with narratives generally: even in an area where no proofs are available as such, narratives can themselves function to establish the requirements in terms of which the reality they specify can be checked out – the true but as-yet-untold story.

But do ordinary people in the living of their everyday lives need to identify their own actions in this way, if they are to act accountably, that is, in a way which is routinely accountable? No, surely not. For, although we must act in a routinely accountable way in our everyday, practical living, we must also fit our own unique actions to our own unique circumstances. And we can do this as long as our actions are informed by the thematic or topical resources available to us in the tradition within which our actions play their part. Thus, although our actions may appear to outsiders as the "disjoined parts of some possible narrative," this does not mean, as MacIntyre (1981: 200) seems to suggest, that they do not have any meaning at all for us. They do: they have a practical meaning, in their own immediate context.

What they lack is a meaning that can be grasped reflectively and theoretically; thus it is not meaning they lack but *intelligibility*. And it is this, of course, that makes it impossible to pose and to investigate questions concerning their nature systematically and intellectually. Thus (*pace* MacIntyre), I think that to present human life in the form of a narrative – in order to render it reflectively intelligible – *is* to falsify it. The fact is, our life *is* lived as a sequence of disjoined parts, with each disjoined part gaining its local and immediate meaning from the context of its performance at the time of its performance – hence the importance of the 'primary intentions' condition mentioned above. Thus, the retrospective coherency of a narrative (and the resulting intelligibility of people's actions) is achieved at the expense of rendering the local and changing context of actual, individual actions 'rationally invisible'; the narrative's value, however (see, for instance, Freud), is in rendering the character of people's otherwise unaccountable actions 'visibly rational' for intellectual purposes – an oscillation between the local and particular, the overall and general, between the 'voice' of the individual and the 'voice' of an intellectual group.

The sixth point I want to raise in this section concerns personal (and social) identity. One thing that is crucial in a genuinely personal relationship with an other is being answerable for all that one has been *with him or her* in the past. Now MacIntyre (1981: 202) takes a rather stricter (and more general) view of one's moral duties here: "I am forever whatever I have been at any time for others – and I may at any time be called upon to answer for it – no matter how changed I may be now." He takes this view because, as he points out (quite rightly), there is no way of *founding* or *rooting* one's identity solely in one's feelings of psychological continuity; publicly criticizable criteria of continuity, he would say, are required.[3] Again, MacIntyre suggests that they are to be found within a twofold narrative concept of selfhood: that on the one hand, "I am what I am taken by others to be in the course of living out a story that runs from my birth to my death; I am the *subject* of a history that is my own and no one else's" (1981: 202). But on the other, "the narrative of any one life is part of an interlocking set of narratives . . . Asking what you did and why, saying what I did and why, pondering the differences between your account of what I did, and *vice versa*, these are essential constituents of all but the very simplest and barest of narratives" (1981: 203). But again we must ask, is all this necessary for an understanding of how ordinary persons can act in an accountable manner, as the unique persons they are? And perhaps of even more importance to us, interested as we are in private, intimate or love relationships: is all this emphasis upon *public* accountability of relevance in a relationship which, by its special nature, is extraordinary, 'outside' the larger schemes of mundane accountability? What MacIntyre sets out, I think, is a public ideal, and what we need to understand are the activities involved, not only in individual people doing the best they can practically, but also that very special form of 'morality' operating only *within a private relationship*, between an intimate couple – where the morality of the larger, public tradition to which they belong makes its appearance only upon the breakdown of their intimacy.

This leads me to the seventh and final issue I want to raise, to do with conversations. Having made the point about narratives above, it is only fair to add that

MacIntyre (1981: 196) himself considers the claim "that the supplying of a narrative is not necessary to make [an] act intelligible," that the placing of it in the context of a conversation may be sufficient. And about conversations he makes the following most important points:

> We allocate conversations to genres, just as we do literary narratives. Indeed, a conversation is a dramatic work, even if a very short one, in which the participants are not only the actors, but also the joint authors, working out in agreement or disagreement the mode of their production . . . Conversation, understood widely enough, is the form of human transactions in general.
>
> (1981: 196–7)

About this, I could not agree more, and in a moment I shall be turning in more detail to Bakhtin's (1986) work on speech genres, in an attempt to clarify the special nature of the speech genre making a private and intimate social life, as distinct from public life, possible. But when MacIntyre goes on to say that he is "presenting both conversations in particular . . . and human actions in general as enacted narratives" (1981: 197), then I must disagree, and reiterate the point I made above about the intrinsically, publicly unaccountable nature of joint action, of jointly authored activity (Shotter, 1980, 1984, 1987a): in many of our ordinary, everyday life activities, as we must interlace our actions in with those of others, their actions will determine our conduct just as much as anything within ourselves. The final outcomes of such exchanges cannot strictly be traced back to the intentions of any of the individuals concerned; they must be accounted *as if* 'external' to the participants concerned, *as if* a part of an 'independent reality'.

Thus MacIntyre ignores, I think, a number of issues. One is the special nature of private life as a distinct 'conversational' enclave within the public life of the world of Western individualism – and it is precisely its nature that we must investigate further below. Another is, I think, that it is a special feature of our tradition of individualism that it allows many different forms of life to go on within different regions and/or moments of everyday, social life at large, without them all having to form "an interlocking set of narratives" – the tradition of individualism gives rise, one might say, to an order of possible orders, or versions, of individualism, not just one. And establishing a 'private life' is one way in which we can act legitimately, precisely to avoid the necessity, felt by MacIntyre, to interlock our actions with those of others – hence, to appropriate to ourselves a degree of freedom at the expense of time spent contributing to one or another public order. The significance of this 'time out' from public life, of this 'haven in a heartless world', is what, I think, we must make sense of. Yet another important fact he fails to acknowledge, is the first-person right we assign to people to act freely, as long as their actions are routinely accountable, as long as they make sense (Shotter, 1984). But what he does not ignore, and what I think is of great importance to mention here, is the relation he introduces between our personal (or self-identity) and our social identity, for, as he sees it,

we all approach our own circumstances as bearers of a particular social identity. I am someone's son or daughter . . . I am a citizen of this or that
city . . . Hence what is good for me has to be good for one who inhabits these
roles. As such, I inherit from the past of my family, my city . . . a variety of
debts, inheritances, rightful expectations and obligations. These constitute
the given of my life, my moral starting point. This is in part what gives my
life its moral particularity.

(MacIntyre, 1981: 204–5)

This suggests that, as a version of individualism, we might propose the concept of
social individuality (Sampson, 1990; Shotter, 1990c), where social individuals are
known in terms of their relations to others. This would be in stark contrast to the
liberal concept of the possessive individual, who is known for those properties he
or she possesses solely within themselves, owing nothing to society for them
(Macpherson, 1962) – a kind of individual MacIntyre clearly does not like.

What has begun to emerge in this section, then, are a number of oscillations as
to where the *authority* in accounting for one's actions should be located: in one's
immediate local situation or in the larger tradition of one's community; in something essentially unsystematic or in something systematic; within something private or public; in the topological resources of a tradition or in an intellectually
produced narrative ordering of them; in the ordinary people or an intellectual elite?
But, as I have already hinted, all these oscillations are themselves located within a
living tradition, that of Western individualism and modernism, which contains the
seeds of all our arguments here. It contains the dilemmatic resources for the fashioning
of a whole range of different possible accounts as to both what the social and self
identities of individuals might be, and also, as to what a 'personal' relationship
between such individuals might be.

To look towards my conclusion for a moment, contrary to Gergen and Gergen's
(1987) claim that various narratives are involved 'in' sustaining a 'love' relationship,
I want to claim that to be 'in love', is to be involved in pure *joint action*, action which
because it is intrinsically unaccountable, *is* extraordinary; it takes place in regions
experienced as 'outside' those in normal, everyday life. Hence the point of the quote
from Barthes: the 'love story' is required to bring the extraordinary and creative
phenomenon of love within the bounds of the ordinary and the routine, to make
sense of it in mundane terms. Nevertheless, although experienced as 'outside' ordinary life, these private and extraordinary, normally unaccountable regions of human
conduct exist within the human *Umwelt* at large. To understand the fashioning of
these regions, it is to the communicative practices and commonplaces, the traditions
and the *speech genres* which embody them, that we must now turn.

Speech genres and styles: individuals and their identities

For Bakhtin (1981, 1984, 1986), as we have seen, the production of an *utterance* in
an actual everyday life setting, must be distinguished from the production of an

isolated, grammatical sentence: an utterance can in no way be regarded as a *completely free* combination of linguistic forms. It is always a link in an unbroken chain of communication, linked both to what precedes it and to what might follow it. And furthermore, it takes into account both the identity of the speaker and that of the addressee, and from the very beginning it is constructed, in part, in anticipation of certain possible responses. Thus *addressivity* – the quality of it being directed towards someone – is a constitutive feature of an utterance, without it the utterance as such does not exist; a part, then, of what it is that defines a *speech genre* is, that each sphere of speech communication has its own typical conception of its addressee, and of its addressee's speech:

> This addressee can be an immediate participant-interlocutor in an everyday dialogue, a differentiated collective of specialists in some particular area of cultural communication, a more or less differentiated public, ethnic group, contemporaries, like-minded people, opponents and enemies, a subordinate, a superior, someone who is lower, higher, familiar, foreign, and so forth. And it can also be an indefinite, unconcretized *other* . . . All these varieties and conceptions of the addressee are determined by that area of human activity and everyday life to which the given utterance is related.
>
> (Bakhtin, 1986: 95)

But also within a speech genre, we must note the speaker's *style*, this is, how both the 'voice' in which he or she speaks, and its 'tone', takes into account both the interlocutor's position and an expectation of how he or she might respond: with trust, doubt, surprise, concern, earnest search for deep meaning, the acceptance of shared conventions, etc.

Indeed, the 'voice' of the other whom one is addressing is always present in one's own utterance. In this sense, as Bakhtin (1981: 279–80) points out, even individual words are "internally dialogized."

> The word is born in a dialogue as a living rejoinder with it; the word is shaped in dialogic interaction with an alien word that is already in the object. A word forms a concept of its own object in a dialogic way. But this does not exhaust the internal dialogism of the word. It encounters an alien word not only in the object itself: every word is directed toward an *answer* and cannot escape the profound influence of the answering word that it anticipates.

And sometimes the other's voice is present to such an extent that within many speech genres – in the giving of a paper at an academic conference, for instance, in which the voice of the great professional Other is also present – it is not difficult at all for one's own 'personal voice' to be almost absent. There is, thus, an "internal politics of style" (Bakhtin, 1981: 284) at work, a politics which influences the degree to which, in "the combat zone of the word" (Holquist), one feels able to speak with one's own voice – in the face of demands by the others, or Other.

But, in everything I say, I also make a claim – to sincerity, justice, truthfulness, beauty, etc. – a claim which will occasion a response. Thus, if I am to speak in my own voice, to realize myself (at least to some degree) as the author of my own actions, then I must express my own relation to what I say. To answer in my own voice – and not just in the voice of science, claiming that what I say must be true because I have observed certain conventional procedures in warranting it – I must *myself* be able to account it. Thus my *answerability* for my claims is the other side of addressivity: hence, besides speaking with an actively responsive understanding of what I am saying, with an anticipation of my interlocutor's response, I must not only know how this interlocator is 'placed', but also how I am myself 'placed' in relation to what I am saying. Thus even within a speech genre, people's different ways of talking issue from and are indicative of their different points of view within it.

The different forms of addressivity and answerability contribute, then, to the different forms of responsivity and internal dialogization constitutive of a speech genre – where, my interest here, is the degree to which one can, or cannot, speak in one's own voice. Typical speech genres might be in business, science, bureaucracies, education, philosophy, everyday life, families, and so on. In these speech genres, not only the addressee's social position, rank and importance are reflected in the speaker's utterances, but also, to the extent that such genres constitute orderly institutions, an institutional judge and witness Other. Finer nuances of style and intonation are determined by the nature and degree of personal proximity of the addressee to the speaker. We have here, then, a way of characterizing the style or the form of a person's consciousness, both of him or herself, and of the providential time-space in which he or she lives. And what Bakhtin has done in his studies is to trace the different chronotopes (the different providential time-spaces) – and hence the different forms of consciousness and self-consciousness – made available by the invention of different speech genres in Western literature – and in particular, those genres that make the formulation of intimate, 'private', relationships possible. Formulations that make it possible *not* to have to take all kinds of things to do with the mundane nature of everyday social life into account.

Now, in studying Bakhtin's proposals in this sphere, it is necessary to say that he does not pretend to completeness or precision in his formulations and definitions. How could he? As in Vico's poetic history, Bakhtin's task is not that of the analytic historian, i.e., that of discovering the true facts. However, although the facts of history may 'permit' or 'afford' a large number of different formulations, not just 'anything' goes. Thus, like Wittgenstein, his method is that of comparisons, the exploration of differences between actual speech genres, in an effort *to create* possible dimensions of relation between them. His accounts, then, must be seen as prosthetic images, as tools or devices enabling us to 'see' how it was possible for certain kinds of speech genres to have given rise to the forms of identity and modes of interpersonal relations we talk of as appropriate to an intimate 'love' relationship – a mode of relationship that seems to be almost the opposite of the world of everyday life which, if Dostoevsky's novels are in anyway indicative of it, is "a plurality of unmerged voices and consciousnesses, a genuine polyphony of fully valid voices" (Bakhtin, 1984: 6).

Turning first to the broad distinctions between public and private speech genres, Bakhtin (1986: 97) begins by making a fundamental distinction: "With all the immense differences among familiar and intimate speech genres (and consequently styles)," he says, "they perceive their addressees in exactly the same way: more or less outside the framework of the social hierarchy and social conventions, 'without rank', as it were." Thus in speaking in an *intimate* speech genre (as opposed to a *public* one), in trying to anticipate the responses of their addressees, people do not take into account either their own or their addressee's title, class, rank, wealth, social importance, age, but address those to whom they speak almost as if, says Bakhtin, they had merged completely. Returning now to the problems of personal (and social) identity raised by MacIntyre above, we can see that one aspect of the task – of accounting for oneself now in terms of a sequence of relations between what had happened to one in the past – involves the development and use of an appropriate speech genre. In the notes Bakhtin offers towards the development of what he calls a *historical poetics* for the expression of genres, he begins with the so-called 'Greek romance' and ends with the Rabelaisian novel. To give the flavour of his description, I shall draw from the third period he discusses, what he calls the *biographical novel*.

Whereas in earlier Greek writing, events took place in "an alien world of adventure-time," such that they lay outside the biographical time of the heroes involved, and changed nothing in their lives – in a time that accumulated no traces – in later novels, they took place in a mixture of adventure-time with everyday time. In this chronotope, the transformational events occurring in the novel – for example, Lucius' metamorphosis into an ass – provided a method for portraying the whole of an individual's life in its more important moments of *crisis*: for showing *how an individual becomes other than he was* – these are times in which events do leave accumulating traces. In comparing the different kinds of identity generated by these two genres, Bakhtin (1981) has this to say: first, in contrast to all classical genres of ancient literature, the image of human beings in these novels is of people as *individuals*, as *private persons*. They are not parts of a social whole. This gives rise to problems. For this private and isolated person in the Greek romance

> often behaves, on the surface, like a public man, and precisely the public man of the rhetorical and historical genres. He delivers long speeches that are rhetorically structured and in which he seeks to enlighten us with the private and intimate details of his love life, his exploits and adventure – but all in the form of a *public accounting*.
>
> (Bakhtin, 1981: 108–9)

Thus, in this chronotopic representation, the unity of the human being is characterized precisely by what is *rhetorical* and juridical in it.

But if we now turn to the second genre – in which Lucius as an ass has the chance to spy upon the inner, intimate details of much of Greek life – Bakhtin (1981: 122–3) points out that:

The everyday life that Lucius observes and studies is an *exclusively personal and private life*. By its very nature there can be nothing *public* about it. All its events are the personal affairs of isolated people . . . By its very nature this private life does not create a place for the contemplative man, for that 'third person' who might be in a position to mediate upon this life, to judge and evaluate it . . . Public life adopts the most varied means for making itself public and accounting for itself (as does its literature). Therefore, the particular positioning of a person (a 'third person') presents no special problem . . . But when the private individual and private life enter literature (in the Hellenistic era) these problems inevitably were bound to arise. *A contradiction developed between the public nature of the literary form and the private nature of its content* . . . The quintessentially private life that entered the novel at this time was, by its very nature as opposed to public life, *closed*. In essence one could only *spy* and *eavesdrop* on it.

The *biographical novel* is the genre which, to an extent, solved this problem.

Biographical-time allows for the fashioning of a form of individuality that can be sensed as a unitary movement through the course of a whole life (but see Chapter 10 for an account of how the unity in biographical genres might be changing in these postmodern times). As the development of this genre is much more multiform than the other two, I will limit my comments to just one of its many versions, what Bakhtin calls the *rhetorical* autobiography – typified in the *encomium*, the civic funeral or memorial speech. It is in such forms as these, suggests Bakhtin, in which people gave a public account either of others or themselves, that the self-consciousness of the Greek individual originated. Here, there was at first

no internal man, no 'man for himself' (I for myself), nor any individualized approach to one's own self. An individual's unity and his self-consciousness were exclusively public. Man was completely *on the surface*, in the most literal sense of the word.

(1981: 133)

The concept of silent thought first only appeared with the mystics, and this concept had its roots in the Orient; even in Plato, the process of thought – conceived of as a 'conversation with oneself' – did not entail any special relationship with oneself, says Bakhtin (1981: 134), "conversation with one's own self turns directly into conversation with someone else, without a hint of boundaries between the two." So: what was the origin of what one might call an 'internal' self-consciousness?

This begins, suggests Bakhtin, with two further developments. One is the directing of the encomium towards an account of an idealized image of a particular life type, a specific profession – that of military commander, ruler, political figure – thus to import into it a *normative* character. Another was (with a degree of breakdown in the Greek image of the person as a wholly public being) the rise of the Roman patrician family. Here, self-consciousness begins to organize itself around the particularized memory of a clan and ancestors. The traditions of the family had

to be passed down from father to son. And an account of a person's works is thus
written, not for a general 'someone', but rather for a specific circle of readers. But,
because older forms for autobiographical expression were adapted to this new task
– that of evaluating the unity of a single person's life – the available public and
rhetorical forms became stilted; they were unable to realize the nuances of the
unique life.

> Moreover, the available public and rhetorical forms could not by their very
> nature provide for the expression of life that was private, a life of activity that
> was increasingly expanding in width and depth and retreating more and more
> into itself. Under such conditions the forms of *drawing-room rhetoric* acquired
> increasing importance, and the most significant form was the *familiar letter*.
> In this intimate and familiar atmosphere . . . a new private sense of self, suited
> to the drawing room, began to emerge. A whole series of categories involving
> self-consciousness and the shaping of a life into a biography – success, hap-
> piness, merit – began to lose their public and state significance and passed
> over into the private and personal plane . . . Other categories as well undergo
> analogous transformations in this new little private drawing-room world.
> Numerous petty details of private life begin to take on an importance; in
> them, the individual feels 'at home', his private sense of self begins to take
> its bearings from these petty details. The human begins to shift to a space
> that is closed and private, the space of private rooms where something
> approaching intimacy is possible, where it loses its monumental formedness
> and exclusively public exteriority.
>
>   (1981: 143–4)

Here, then, suggests Bakhtin, we can begin to find the origins of intimacy, of
intimate speech genres, which have their currency within these 'private' enclaves,
away from public life at large.

These are genres in which people account for their lives, not just to anyone in
general, publicly, but to a limited group of others located in a familiar (family)
setting. This, of course, raises problems for us, as academics, as scientists or as
writers in the humanities, facing the task of accounting for close relationships in
general, publicly agreed terms. And it is to these that I now turn.

Two kinds of 'theory'

If we take Bakhtin's comments about the origins and nature of speech genres
seriously, the possibility of our being able to use language in the sphere of research
into personal relationships, in the same way as it is used in the natural sciences –
with each term having a discreet, unambiguous meaning – is remote. For, if we
recollect what Bakhtin (1986: 293–4) says about the nature of language in general,
that,

> prior to [the] moment of [its] appropriation [for one's own use], the word
> does not exist in a neutral and impersonal language (it is not, after all, out

of a dictionary that the speaker gets his words!), but rather it exists in other people's mouths, in other people's contexts, serving other people's intentions: it is from there that one must take the word, and make it one's own.

Thus we find that someone who wants to speak to someone else intimately, but tries to do it in the *scientific* language of personal relationship research, finds himself, as Bakhtin points out, literally unable to speak in his own words, unable properly to express his own 'authentic inner self'. Besides his own intentions, his talk has hidden in it other intentions, and this is bound to raise all the kind of conflicts in his relations that Billig *et al.* (1988) formulated as the dilemmas inherent in a 'lived ideology', that is, unavoidable dilemmas in the very practices of both everyday life, and our professional lives.

Indeed, for those of us who, as professional psychologists, want to do empirical research on the nature of intimate relationships, the consequences are especially problematic. For if we use in our talk about our research into people's intimate, personal relations the kind of specially invented, abstract terms we usually feel free to use in our theorizing in psychology, then, we end by putting *their* words into *our* terms, inviting an 'ideological dilemma' of a very particular kind: for our words work to 'colonize', so to speak, the modes of being of those we study.

If we are critically to describe and illuminate the nature of the transactions in intimate personal relations (and perhaps to explain them), then we must, I think, as in our everyday communicative practices, oscillate not only among and between both sides of a number of different dilemmatic topics, but also between the general and the particular (Billig, 1985). We must realize that while relationship dilemmas – those to do with, for instance, autonomy–connection; openness–closedness; and predictability–novelty (Baxter, 1988, 1990) – *can be* argued over in general theoretical, political and ethical debates in society at large, they must also be faced and resolved in their own different particular and practical ways, in different particular sites or situations. In such circumstances, whatever 'theory' we have to offer does not function as a set of laws or principles giving us as professionals analytic access to a reality which is otherwise hidden from us, thus easily to manipulate it – we all must now accept, surely, that 'theory' has never worked for us in the human sciences like this. And now, even if the invitation still exists to use it in this way, should we do so: for that is to silence the 'voices' to be heard at all the different particular sites where problems are being faced and resolved, in different ways and in different circumstances.

As Said (1985: 40, 33, 67) says about the West's colonization of the 'Orient':

> what gave the Oriental's world its intelligibility and identity was not the result of his own efforts but rather the whole complex series of knowledgeable manipulations by which the Orient was identified by the West . . . [Thus] it does not occur to Balfour [lecturing the House of Commons in 1910 about Egypt] to let the Egyptian speak for himself, since presumably any Egyptian who would speak is more likely to be 'the agitator [who] wishes to raise difficulties' than the good native who overlooks the 'difficulties' of foreign

domination . . . [Hence] truth becomes a matter of learned judgment, not of the material itself, which in time seems to owe even its existence to the Orientalist . . . [who receives] these cultures not as they are but as, for the benefit of the receiver, they ought to be.

And this could be said of any field in which a group of academic experts speak on behalf of those they study: the characterization of a supposed "subject matter" is influenced just as much, if not more, by matters of professional selection and judgement, by matters in the providential space of the profession, as by anything in the actual character of what is being studied.

At present, however, it *is* still felt that proper theory in psychology, and thus also in the psychological investigation of personal relationships, should copy natural scientific theory, as this is the only sort of theorizing thought respectable in our scientistic culture. And this, as I have already mentioned, allows us to formulate general theories in terms of any abstract principles or laws (or rational models) we please – as long as we subsequently attempt to prove them true, to prove that they correspond with reality in some way. We can do this by selecting a number of 'sites' for their test – (at best one or two, say, marital or non-marital relations, same-or different-sex relations, etc.) and, if our theory holds up, then we can publish it with the suggestion that such laws or principles can be generalized, and used to control and predict what is the case elsewhere in social life. This, however, is a recipe which not only leads to what Duck (1990) politely calls the field's "subtly changing *Zeitgeist*" – the fact that theories come and go like comets, with a slowly fading tail research which disappears almost completely when another comet appears on the scene. It also blinds us to the very real complexities in the nature of personal relationships themselves (and in particular to the nature of genuinely 'private' relationships).

But, perhaps even more importantly, it blinds us to the nature of our relations with/to those we study. And in particular, it obscures from us the fact that we share with them a traditional set of ideological dilemmas, and a common set of topical, symbolic resources in terms of which we *must necessarily* make sense, if we are to be seen by them as contributing to *their* dilemmas in our investigations. In failing to notice this fact, we run two interconnected risks. We run the very risk which science was supposed to avoid, of accepting as literally true what is merely a cultural convention, an opinion of the day (that the only 'real knowledge' is scientific knowledge), and in refusing to open our position to argumentation and debate, of closing off new avenues of thought – just what was said to be the defect of the older religious traditions science struggled to replace. We also, to the extent to which scientific traditions of thought are to do with prediction, in the service of manipulation and control, run the risk of being accused of seeking knowledge only in the name of 'mastery' and 'domination'.

These risks can be avoided, I think, only if we give up the attempt to form explanatory theoretical orders ahead of time, thus to attempt to impose a particular social order; and if we accept Billig's (1987; Billig *et al.*, 1988) claims about the argumentative, dilemmatic nature of our actual everyday thought. Then, if we want to understand why we have the kind of arguments we do, and feel them 'in our bones' to be significant and to matter, we must attempt to describe the two-sided topics in which our culture is 'variously rooted' (Wittgenstein), and which give it its 'style'. As I see it, our arguments then will recursively oscillate between the general and the specific, the finished and the unfinished, the individual and the collective, the public and the private, first-person autonomy and social dependence, authority and equality, between what 'is' (already existing in space) and what 'might be' (possibilities in time), and between what 'is' (the sciences and the study of 'the facts') and what 'should be' (the humanities and the study of practical-moral knowledge), as well as many other such two-sided topics besides, all of which exist as symbolic *resources* in the common sense of our culture.

If we apply this kind of approach reflexively to our own thinking about personal relationships, as well as to our own conduct and reporting of our investigations, then we can perhaps see that 'theory' in the understanding and study of personal relationships, and theory in the natural sciences *must differ* in a number of fundamental ways. Thus in this chapter, I want to give two sets of conclusions: the first to do with the nature of our personal relations now; the second to do with the nature of 'theory' in relation to such topics.

Conclusions

For personal relationships

What I have argued above, then, is that on certain, extraordinary occasions, people can relate themselves to one another within special (non-argumentatively structured) speech genres, but that these have been formed historically as a common but unusual resource within a whole Western tradition of accountability and argumentation. Indeed, the forms of personal relationship within the different regions of our modern (and postmodern) societies are clearly many and varied. Thus, to return to our point of departure, we can now begin to see the complexity of the claim that personal relationships are both constituted and mediated by talk. Society seems to contain a whole 'ecology' of different interdependent regions and moments, containing different forms of social life sustained by different speech genres, constituting different forms of social and personal relationship. But there do seem to be some common features of all the genres used in 'personal' or 'intimate' relationships. Rather than being public discourses – in which one feels oneself accountable to the discourse's Other – they can all have a 'conversational' character, that is, the participants's have no sense of having a 'position' in public life to sustain in the responsive nature of their exchanges. Indeed, as Bakhtin notes, the speech genres created for use in genuinely intimate exchanges not only operate in a 'private' sphere, removed from public life, but also 'open up' a special 'inner', self-conscious aspect of life, separate and different from the genres used in public life.

But these two realms – the private and the public – are related to one another, and people can 'move' from the intimate interpersonal realm into the realm of public affairs in a (careless) instant. The 'move' occurs when the interpersonal flow of activity between them breaks down to such an extent that they feel they must *account* for (that is, justify) their conduct to one another as properly socially competent individuals – instead of finding the resources required from within their relationship. Thus, instead of saying "Oops, there *we* go again. *We've* got overtired again. Let's talk about it in the morning when *we're* not so tired," they lapse into saying "*You* always do that when *I* try to be helpful," or similar such things accountable from with a more public domain. For it is when such resources are, or seem to be, lacking that appeals to larger, more public schemes of accountability become apparent. We can see now why it is that within an intimate, personal (love) relationship that, irrespective of whether the participants have been able to establish an appropriate narrative or not, the transition from an 'us' to a 'you'-and-'I' way of talking indicates a fading of intimacy. From having been merged in their love (in pure joint action) into an 'us', the participants re-emerge into their separate individualities, into still a personal relationship, but now one of a more publicly accountable kind.

For relationships research

My claim in this chapter, then, is that the unsatisfactory state of 'theory' in the understanding of what a personal relationship 'is', does not arise out of a continual failure yet to formulate 'the correct' theory, but that it arises out of a failure to understand what 'theory' in this area should be like. It is still thought that it should copy natural scientific theory, as this is the only sort which is respectable. Whereas, if we apply Billig's (1987) proposals – to do with the rhetorical, argumentative, two-sided nature of thought, as well as with the oscillation between the general and the particular, the decontexted and the contexted – reflexively to our thinking about personal relationships, then we can perhaps see that theory in the natural sciences and theory in the understanding and study of personal relationships must differ fundamentally. For if we are to be of any assistance at all in helping people to discover their own 'way about' inside their own knowledge of personal relationships, then it is not a theoretical science but a practical science we need – where a practical science is to do with creating/discovering aids to living with indeterminacy *in practice*. What might such aids be?

In science, our task is to reason *from* 'grounds' (empirically warranted, theoretical premises) to conclusions, in order to *explain* people's behaviour. Thus, what we want from our theories (at least) is explicitness, abstractness (generality), systematicity, and the power of predicting – thus to enable us to control – what is *in fact* the case. Is this what we want here in the sphere of personal relationships research? In politics and ethics in everyday life, our task is to reason from people's (and our own) actions *to* their 'grounds', in order to *justify* their (or our) behaviour – a movement in the opposite direction to scientific reasoning. Thus, what we want from our 'theoretical resources', is not so much explicitness as open-texturedness (adaptability to a specific context), not abstractness but specifiability (of their significance in the context), not systematicity but a perspicuousness, for we do not want to predict behaviour but to see the 'connections' between things, thus to understand what in the circumstances we *ought* to do. In science, we are already in touch with the grounds of our reasoning and we wish to extend its scope. In politics and ethics, we know what we would like to do, but we are not in immediate touch (or have lost touch) with the 'grounds' of our reasoning – we are unsure as to how our actions should be evaluated, we are puzzled as to their *normative accountability*. This, I think, is the kind of puzzle we face in trying to understand what the nature of a personal relationship 'is'.

For, in practice, it is not the case that we must choose between already existing but *incommensurate* moral premises, nor even that of acting (within a discourse) in terms of an already determined good, because one does not have to choose *in general, ahead of time*. In practice, one must make different, particular choices in particular, local circumstances – and if one is 'rooted' in one's circumstances and has 'grounds' at the time for one's choice – there is always a 'best' choice in the circumstances, one which one can justify to others, and feel to have manifested some honour and virtue in having so chosen. Indeed, as MacIntyre points out, this is why the manifestation of a virtue in the solution of a *moral* problem is not at all like the practice of a *professional* skill, making use of the techniques of the productive sciences – in which one can be judged against the standards of the profession. Thus, just like the blind person's stick, we need an appropriate 'tool' through which we can make contact with the 'grounds' of choice available to us. This, once again, would seem to be the form of 'theory' we need.

TEN

The politics of identity and belonging

This land is your land, this land is my land . . .

(Woody Guthrie)

. . . stay in the process . . .

(Anon)

Turning, in this last chapter, to the present moment, what can we say about the cultural politics of everyday social life now? What are people's concerns now? What are the resources available to people these days for them to draw upon in their attempts to be someone of worth? What part might academics play in debates about how to answer questions such as these? Although this is not the final answer I shall offer, we can, as an initial strategy, make a number of comparisons between proposed solutions to these questions now, and in the late 1960s and early 1970s, for between then and now clear changes have taken place. I shall begin by examining the speech genres used in those semi-popular, sociological and psychological texts from which we sometimes draw resources in currently making sense of our lives,[1] to see if anything has changed in them: are we making a different kind of sense of ourselves now than in the 1960s and 1970s? Then, I shall examine the talk of social critics, to see whether the issues worrying them now are also issues of a kind different from those in the 1960s and 1970s, and go on to ask what talk of 'identity' and 'belonging' means compared with our 1960s and 1970s talk about 'persons'.

Again, we will encounter precisely the issue I formulated at the outset: to do with whether we locate our political struggles within structures of 'already spoken words' or in 'words in their speaking'. For the question we shall face, in our attempts to contest and realize our political claims in mutually intelligible terms, is from within *whose* 'shaping container', so to speak, we should formulate those claims. If we are all agreed that ahistorical, hierarchical systems of (supposedly logical) dependencies, that is, theories, are unsatisfactory, could it be that, as MacIntyre (1981, 1988) proposes, a *narrative* tradition is what we require? I shall disagree, and suggest instead, that what is required is continuous debate over certain topics that resist by their very nature any final coherent formulations in *somebody's* terms – topics that I will call *imaginary* topics. And I shall suggest that it is talk and debate upon the topics of citizenship and belonging that can generate just that continuous tradition of argumentation required to constitute a 'providential space', that is, a civil society, *our* civil society, as the 'container' from within which we can all draw the mutually intelligible resources we require in making sense of the rest of our lives.

From the 'life cycle' to 'blurred' genres

Between the late 1960s and now, the 1990s, times seem to have changed. The narrative resources available to people in making sense of their lives now seem more extensive, thus changing the genres available. A best selling book of the 1970s was Gail Sheehy's (1976) *Passages*, a popularized report on scientific research claiming to solve the mysteries of the 'life cycle'. Now, we have Mary Catherine Bateson's (1990) *Composing a Life* – a "blurred genre" (Geertz, 1983) – part autobiography, part biography, reflexively illuminated by many of the literary and social scientific commonplaces or *topoi* currently shared among college-educated people.[2] In it, the idea that the proper living of a life involves the following of a 'cycle' has disappeared, and one's task has become instead "an improvisatory art" – where "adjusting to discontinuity is not an idiosyncratic problem of my own," Bateson (1990: 14) says, "but the emerging problem of our time." Giddens (1991: 14), too, suggests that, instead of a 'sense of place'[3] – a place in which one was surrounded by traces of the past and intimations of the future, and in which the idea of 'stages' in a life thus made sense – "self-identity for us forms a *trajectory* across the different institutional settings of modernity over the *durée* of what used to be called the 'life cycle'". Currently, as Gergen (1991) has described in detail, due to developments in our technologies of communication and travel, there has been a quantum leap in our exposure to each other; we have become 'saturated' with the voices of others. We have become embroiled not only in cultural pluralisms in our immediate contexts, but also in what Giddens (1991) calls a dialectic of the local and the global: events distant from us in both space *and time*, transmitted to us through communication media, play an intimate part in who we feel we want or ought to be.

No wonder that, at least for some of us – according to the speech and behavioural genres we play a part in – 'identity' has become the watchword of the times, for it provides the much needed vocabulary in terms of which we now define our loyalties and our commitments. How should we relate ourselves to each other and to our worlds? Should we have shown our solidarity with the students in Tiananmen Square? How should we stand in relation to the Serbs and Croats – or the Kurds? Ought we to grieve over Gorbachev's being deposed and replaced by Yeltsin? Applaud Bush's 'environmental presidency', and Quale's concern with 'family values'? How do these mesh with larger concerns? What about taking a new job away from one's home town – but will that promote the return to community values one fears are being lost? Perhaps one should return to school to retrain as a doctor, the genetic engineering one found enthralling when young having lost its charm in these polluted times? How might (yet another) New Left constitute itself in the face of the New Right? What about the current nationalisms – is there anything I can or should be doing? Worries over global issues feed into more local concerns. Times have changed. If life has become an improvisatory art, and adjusting to discontinuity is not an idiosyncratic problem of one's own, but the emerging problem of our time, what is involved in becoming the authors of our own lives? What are our sources of self?

While Gergen (1991) talks of vocabularies and Taylor (1989) talks of sources, both are clear that the two major unitary sources of self in the past – the romantic and the modern – either separately or together, are no longer adequate to our needs. While romanticism provided much of the vocabulary of the person, and fostered a belief in the deep interior and the dynamics of personality, modernism provided the mechanistic, instrumental vocabulary required for coping with the external world – thus, as Gergen points out, we have found ourselves suspended between two clearly opposing discourses, with the modernist view more at the centre and the romantic on the margins. Although neither was adequate within itself, in conditions of social stability and constancy, it was perhaps possible not to notice their inadequacies, to devise stable strategies or rituals for coping with any sense of inadequacy, or feelings of lack, they engendered. Surely, a properly modern, scientific psychology will explain to us once again the 'inner mechanisms' of human behaviour that the displaced romantic vocabulary used to explain in terms of personality dynamics? – as we might thus reassure ourselves. But the stable conditions changed. We became more immersed in communicational activities that exposed us more and more to the opinions, values and lifestyles of others. And, says Gergen (1991: 49):

> It is my central thesis that this immersion is propelling us toward a new self-conscious: the postmodern. The emerging commonplaces of communication . . . [those he cites to do with our continuous involvement in now global networks] are critical to understanding the passing of both the romantic and modern views of self. What I call *technologies of social saturation* are central to the contemporary erasure of individual self . . . There is a populating of the self, reflecting the infusion of partial identities through social saturation. And there is the onset of a *multiphrenic* condition, in which one begins to experience the vertigo of unlimited multiplicity.

The romantic vocabulary gave way to the modern, which in turn gives way to the postmodern. But how shall we understand the consequences of such a change in our ways of talking?

If we turn to examine the nature of the verbal processes involved in the practical authorship of oneself, we can again remind ourselves of Bakhtin's claim: that authorship involves an inner dialogue in which one must use words responsively, and that the words one uses are always also another's words; we both shape and are shaped by them. Thus (to use Bakhtin's words!):

> The author (speaker) has his own inalienable right to the word, but the
> listener has his rights, and those whose voices are heard in the word before
> the author comes upon it also have their rights (after all, there are no words
> that belong to no one).
>
> (Bakhtin, 1986: 121–2)

Previously, in quoting this passage from Bakhtin, I focused upon the freedom a
speaker (an author) has to use a word to create within a new, living context, a new,
living sense. Here, however, I would like to focus on the opposite pole: to raise
questions about the degree to which speakers (authors) are limited in the degree of
new sense they can make by the 'taste'[4] of a word's past usages, to raise questions,
in particular, about its embedding in well-formed narrative traditions. For we find
feelings within ourselves, urges, desires, longings, compulsions – that we must
have, do, be, etc., this or that – that arise in our inner dialogic use of words that
we 'inherit', so to speak, from such traditions.

To understand the import of this for the nature of the ideological context within
which our authorship of ourselves has functioned recently, we might turn, for
instance, to the different traditions of individualism studied by Bellah *et al.* (1985),
and the different resources these traditions provide for what it is deemed sensible
(and legitimate) to say about how people ought to be. For me, one aspect of the
ideology of self-contained individualism is best captured in expressions of what I
would call "the John DeLorean complex": when accused in the early 1980s of drug
dealing, his wife, in defending him in court, said, "John has done nothing wrong.
He has always believed in the American dream, that you can be anyone you want
to be, if you want to be it *enough*." In other words, much of our self-authorship in
recent times has emerged within a context in which individuals have felt themselves
to be wholly responsible for what they become, and that their lives and those of
others are freely chosen. It is also within this context that the idea of the lifespan
as being made up of a distinct set of stages has flourished, for although the 'impulses'
toward each stage of change were always meant to come from within a person's
"deep interior" (Gergen, 1991), the causes of people's (predictable – Sheehy, 1974)
identity crises were to be found in their failure properly to 'manage' crucial events
in their surrounding circumstances.

However, in fostering a belief in rational control and autonomy, even in those
situations in which it is impossible, the ideology of individualism is now, it would
seem, in trouble. Times have changed; its constituency has withered; not only do
people no longer seem to be having 'mid-life crises', but their mood has changed.
A "culture of [me-first] narcissism" (Lasch, 1979) has given way to a "culture of
survivalism" (Lasch, 1985), in which respect is sought for a 'minimalist' or a 'privatized' self, in a set of extremely restricted circumstances. Those who still embody
the ideology of individualism feel beleaguered and embattled, for, as Giddens (1991)
points out, the world of modernity has turned out to be much riskier than was at
first hoped or imagined. Instead of occurrences falling neatly into the categories of
actions ('I' can control) or events (naturally caused), we have become more enmeshed

in joint action, in ongoings outside the power of individuals to control ahead of time; *fortuna*, as it was called in medieval times, Giddens (1991) points out, seems to have reclaimed a central position for itself in human affairs.[5] But what has happened also – which, incidently, it seems to me, Giddens (1991) fails properly to analyse – is that those 'othered' and 'silenced' in modernity have, in this postmodern, postcolonial age, begun to benefit from its pervasive reflexive awareness. They have begun to find their 'voices', and to talk back.

From 'personhood' and 'authenticity' to 'identity' and 'belonging'

If we turn to the background, taken-for-granted *themes* and *images*, in terms of which debates to do with the culture of everyday social life in the late 1960s and early 1970s were conducted, we find a number of changes. Then, the debate was about personhood – now, as we shall see, at least in some quarters, it is about identity and belonging. An image that sticks in my memory from those times is of a newspaper picture of a young person in a protest march wrapped in a cardboard cylinder the shape of a punched card – punched cards at that time used to have DO NOT FOLD, SPINDLE OR MUTILATE printed on them – and upon *his* card-costume the young man had written "Do not fold, spindle or mutilate, I am a person." Those who still remember the struggles in those Vietnam times, will recall that we then thought the crisis in human beings was a struggle against the inhuman, mechanical conditions of life, conditions which did not allow the 'natural' human selves hidden within us to blossom out. "Humanity is estranged from its authentic possibilities", said R.D. Laing (1967: 11). "We are . . . strangers to our true selves" (1967: 12). And we thought one way to be more human, more authentic, was to relate to each other in more *personal* terms – and of course we still retain some of the terminology of those times in the new *person*-words we introduced then.

The motifs governing the critical thought of this time were: similarities rather than differences; harmony and agreement rather than conflict and discord; homogeneity rather than heterogeneity; order rather than chaos; structures and products rather than formations and processes; unity and stability rather than plurality and instability; finding and discovering rather than inventing and making; already shared foundations rather than living *in medias res*; already existing forms and frameworks rather than formative processes or resources; explanations rather than descriptions; logic and mathematics rather than rhetoric and poetry. In short, there was the assumption that, in fact, we all already lived in a common world, if only we could discover what it was. Thus all the first terms played a privileged part in our discourses, while all the second terms were left unvoiced.

But the inadequacies inherent in that project are, I think, now becoming very clear to us. Central among them, I think, is the implicit framework of "possessive individualism" (Macpherson, 1962) within which they were all formulated, placed as it then was within the classical world picture, a world supposed to be the same for us all: the picture of a universe consisting of atomic particles in motion according to an absent God's pre-established laws. It was such images as these which allowed us to believe that human beings are born 'naturally' as already-formed individuals, possessing (also 'naturally') within themselves the 'potential' for an authentic inner self, a potential which in itself owes nothing to society.[6] And that if only our nasty, inhuman environment was changed, that potential would flower out into an *authentic* self of its own accord. Thus such images suggested to us that our task was to discover the universal nature of the 'atomic' human being (individuals), and the general 'laws' governing their motions. But quite suddenly, this view – which seems to have been the received view, more or less, for the last three hundred years or so – began to change. What was responsible for this change?

Many possibilities have already been mentioned. But here I want to pursue further the theme of what is happening with those who previously were our 'subject matter', who were 'subjected' by us in our investigations or other activities, who were 'silenced', and have now begun to 'talk back' – "In the world of the southern black community I grew up in," says Hooks (1989: 5), "'back talk' and 'talking back' meant speaking as an equal to an authority figure. It meant daring to disagree and sometimes it just meant having an opinion." – As Hall and Held (1989) point out, in recent times there has been an expansion of claims to rights in a whole host of new areas: not only among feminists, black and other ethnic groups, but also among those groups acting on behalf of other species, or on behalf of nature itself, as well as those concerned with other vulnerable minorities like children; we are now seeing nationalist movements emerging both in (what was) the Communist world and in other regions victims of 'external' hegemonies (Anderson, 1983); but also problems raised in a genuine recognition of the importance of differences rather than similarities. Colonialism is all but over. So, as Hall and Held see it, these new claims to rights have arisen out of a complex interplay between identity and selfhood: between 'who' one is or can be, and one's feelings about one's 'position' in society; and from the differentiated ways in which people participate in a modern, pluralistic, multi-ethnic, multi-ontological (varied life-style) society. In other words, the demand to 'belong' as a unique, distinctive individual in a genuine community is beginning to emerge, as dissatisfaction with the role of an indistinguishable, atomistic individual within a liberal individualist or a socialist state increases.

But: "Who belongs and what does *belonging* mean in practice?" (Hall and Held, 1989: 175). In this new politics, what seems to be at stake is not the possession of material property as such, but access to opportunities to give shape and form to one's own life, that is, access to, what earlier I called "a political economy of developmental opportunities" that limits who or what we can become. For we cannot just position ourselves as we please; we face differential invitations and barriers to all the 'movements' (actions and utterances) we try to make in relation to the others around us. It is thus, they suggest, that such a politics can be formulated as an 'identity politics' or 'politics of citizenship', as distinct from the old 'politics of class'.

But what is involved in 'belonging'? What does it *feel* like, to belong, not to belong? What I want to argue below is that if one is to grow up and to qualify as a self-determining, autonomous person with one's own identity – to feel that one has grown up to be 'someone' who 'counts' in one's society – then although one must grow up as a human being within that society, that in itself is not enough. For even as a participating member of it, one can still remain either dependent upon other members of it in some way, or under their domination in some other way. To be a person and to qualify for certain rights as a free, autonomous individual, one must also be able to show in one's actions certain social competencies, that is, to fulfil certain duties and to be *accountable* to others in the sense of being able to justify one's actions to them, when challenged, in relation to the 'social reality' of the society of which one is a member. Being someone in this sense is a rhetorical achievement.

But this is still not enough to provide one with a 'sense of belonging', with a sense of 'being at home' in the reality which one's actions help to reproduce. For, to live within a community which one *senses* as being one's own, a community for which one feels able to be answerable, one must be more than just a routine reproducer of it; one must in a real sense also play a part in its creative reproduction and sustenance as a 'living' tradition – where, as we have found before, with reference to both Billig (1987) and MacIntyre (1981), a living tradition can be thought of as a historically extended, socially embodied argument, containing what one might call reflexive arguments, that is, arguments about what should be argued about, and why. Thus, to participate in the reproduction of the tradition, one must be able to participate in such arguments.

To do this, and to be able to feel that in doing so one is contributing to one's own world, one must be able to participate in the argument, interpersonally, in interaction with others, as well as intrapersonally, in one's 'thinking', in one's own 'inner speech'. But what if the words one uses in one's talk to oneself make this impossible? For, to repeat, "prior to [the] moment of appropriation, the word does not exist in a neutral and impersonal language" (Bakhtin, 1981: 293–4). What if the very words one uses in participating in the arguments reproducing the tradition, make one feel that one does not belong? Are there any kinds of words which might do this? The answer is in the affirmative. But before being able to answer in detail, I must assemble a number of resources for use in it.

First, we can note that Bakhtin (1981) makes a distinction between whether the words one uses come from an *authoritative discourse* or an *internally persuasive* one. Of the former he says:

> the authoritative word demands that we acknowledge it, that we make it our own; it binds us quite independently of any power to persuade us internally; we encounter it with its authority fused to it. The authoritative word is located in a distanced zone, organically connected with a past that is felt to be hierarchically higher.
>
> (1981: 342)

And of the latter:

> the internally persuasive word is half-ours and half-someone else's. Its creativity and productiveness consists precisely in the fact that such a word awakens

new and independent words, that it organizes masses of our words from within, and does not remain in an isolated and static condition.

(1981: 345)

Next, I must go back to MacIntyre (1981), for it is at this point that I must now modify what I appropriated from him earlier, and note that he sees a living tradition as not just being an argument containing reflexive arguments, but also as having a specific *constitutive focus*. What the argumentation is constitutive of is a tradition with a particular narrative *order* to it. Such traditions "have to sustain relationships to the past – and to the future – as well as in the present," he claims (1981: 206).

And finally, we must also note that, implicit in the ideology of possessive individualism, as Macpherson (1962) remarks, is the idea that our 'natural powers' only become our own 'personal powers' if we work to master them.[7] Thus, if this is the case, people are only deserving of respect to the extent that it is so; and the index of that is their success in general. Thus, the lesson of this historic fly in the ointment is that respect is a *reward* rather than a *right*. And the stage is now set for all the ontological insecurities possessive individualism generates within us today.

It is in these terms – of authoritative words, narrative traditions, and the ideology of possessive individualism – that, I think, we can now begin to grasp what a *sense* or *feeling* of 'not belonging' is like. For, perhaps those who feel they do not belong question themselves, in their inner dialogues with themselves, and respond (feelingly) to themselves, along the following (crazy?) lines: "How is it, if we are all equal, and we all begin with the same inner powers as each other, that many of the others around me are respected and have authority over me, while no one listens to me? What I say doesn't seem to count. If, as an ordinary person, I was born with the powers of rational thought within me, just like all those above me whose orders I must carry out, how do I explain their power over me? Perhaps it is because I am inferior to them? Perhaps there is something wrong with me? Perhaps it is because they have developed their powers more than me, perhaps they worked harder? How else can I make sense of the inequality and the indignities? A belief in an innate human dignity doesn't help. Indeed, the opposite is the case: there is a secret self-accusation in me for even thinking us unequal when I know we are all born equal. I wish I didn't feel so bad about myself!"[8]

If we *first* have to qualify for membership, *before* we can receive respect, it is corrosive of our confidence in ourselves. For, due to the intrinsic uncertainty of all human action, one can always fail in one's actions in the most unexpected ways. Yet, all the same, one notices others for whom failures do not seem to matter. They seem to have a kind of unconditional membership in the society; they can expect unconditional support from those around them, even when they fail. For those of us with only 'conditional' membership, however, such failures are a proof of our lack of qualification. 'We do not belong'. Such people as these, as Sennett and Cobb (1972: 33–4) put it, live with a certain anxiety for which they hold themselves responsible:

This fear of being summoned before some hidden bar of judgment and being found inadequate infects the lives of [many] people who are coping perfectly well from day to day; it is a matter of a hidden weight, a hidden anxiety, in the *quality* of experience, a matter of feeling inadequately in control where an observer making material calculations would conclude the [person] had adequate control.

It is in the very narrative structure of the speech genre, within which those in the tradition of liberal, possessive individualism *must* make sense of their lives, that such a feeling is constructed. It is the discursive Other – the judge and witness – the third entity in the discourse that many of those participating in the discourse find themselves both 'in' and having 'within' them (Bakhtin, 1986: 137). It judges them harshly: somehow, it is in their very nature that whatever they do, they *feel* not quite up to requirements: 'they do not belong'.

To live within a narrative *order* not one's own is to live in a world not one's own. But what alternatives are there? Is it a question of a stand-off: your narrative order or mine? Is there a way to hold the arguments of a social group together without them all being 'contained', so to speak, within the same, already determined, intelligible order? To repeat the claim I made above: no prior ordering is required, only a tradition of argumentation 'rooted' in an appropriate common *topic*, for, if it is a topic of an appropriate kind, then, the very activity of arguing about its various instantiations will work to establish patterns of relation between people that will be its instantiation: that topic, I think, is citizenship, when considered, as above, as concerned with a sense of belonging.

Narrative entrapment

However, to see why a narrative tradition is not required, we must first examine some of the discursive urges, desires, longings, etc., that have given rise to it. In the Bakhtinian/Vygotskian/Wittgensteinian view being canvassed here, all the 'links' or 'hook-ups' between not only us and our surroundings, but also every phase of our own perceptions, actions, speakings, thinkings, and valuings, must be fashioned by us. We must link ourselves to our past and to our future (and death), to each other, to nature, to our parents and our children, and to, seemingly, something beyond ourselves, a horizon of ideals. All these great spheres of uncertainty and insecurity require at one time or another an intelligible response from us, and we feel we would like to be prepared, ahead of time, with just such a ready response. And in one of its forms at least, explanation seems to afford us the clear foresight we seek.

As I emphasized in the Introduction, the Enlightenment concern with explanation was realized in terms of analysis – where one point of such a form of analytic explanation was to be able to predict and control. Thus one dream was that explanation of this kind can be achieved by a special analytical form of observation that grasped the 'underlying' reality behind appearances. This involved the reconstructing of events such that they could be *represented* within a certain *order* and thus be *rationally* manipulated. Thus, one of the urges motivating the search for explanation was to penetrate into the mysterious, hidden, underlying *essence* (note the patriarchal undertones in many of these terms) of things. This – or at least, so it is said – is clearly, an urge for "mastery and possession" (Descartes). But the urge is not 'in' the individual as such, the individual is 'in' it. It is one of the judge and witness, third-entity Others (Bakhtin, 1986: 137) of the Enlightenment discourse.

Besides mastery and possession, though, there was another explanatory dream. As MacIntyre (1988) points out, it was also one of the great dreams of the Enlightenment to provide, for debate in public realms, standards or principles in terms of which rational debate could be conducted, such that alternative plans of action could be adjudicated as just or unjust, rational or irrational, etc., ahead of time. Thus, it was hoped that reason would replace authority and tradition. For "rational justification was to appeal to principles undeniable by any rational person and therefore independent of all those social and cultural particularities which the Enlightenment thinkers took to be mere accidental clothing of reason in particular times and places" (1988: 6). They would be undeniable once their basis had been explained. Unfortunately, no such undeniable principles could be found. The judge and witness, third-entity Other of the discourse here, would seem to be the urge for uniformity, for all to be in the same world in the same way as each other.

MacIntyre (1981) clearly still feels the 'tug' of yet another judge and witness, third-entity Other of the Enlightenment discourse – Kant's dream, I quoted in the Introduction to this book. For, in the face of philosophy's failure to find an ahistorical 'container' for rational argumentation, any agreed foundational principles, he still seeks a 'container' for rational argumentation, but now where the Enlightenment (for good reasons of its own at the time) refused to look – in traditions. And I, too, I hasten to add, have responded to this urge in a similar manner, to the degree of suggesting that a tradition of argumentation can carry culture's style and its history 'in' its argumentative activities – including the arguments it has over its recorded histories and historiographies, etc., to do with its supposed narratives of itself. My differences here with MacIntyre are to do with his urge still for an *orderly*, narrative container for its conduct.

But, to bring out these differences, we must examine his arguments for the supposed necessity of a narrative structure. First, we can note that his concept of people as authors does not allow for the possibility of responsive acting or understanding, that is, for dialogic, joint action, in one's authoring. His is a very isolated, autonomous notion of authoring.

> Human beings can be held to account for that of which they are the authors . . . It is therefore to understand an action as something for which someone is accountable, about which it is always appropriate to ask the agent for an *intelligible* account.
>
> (MacIntyre, 1981: 195; emphasis added)

Next, we might note that when he gives a practical example, it is of a young man in a bus queue saying a single, at first unintelligible sentence, which only "becomes *intelligible* by finding its place in a narrative" (1981: 196; emphasis added). We can also notice that his argument against Mink's (1970) claim – that narrative is very different from life and that to present human life in the form of a narrative is to falsify it – hinges again upon what is involved in rendering people's actions *intelligible*, that is, capable of being grasped, reflectively and intellectually, as meaningful within an order of things.

These comments are, I think, sufficient to see what it is that MacIntyre is after. He wants to place people's actions within a narrative structure, because he still sees his task as that of making their actions reflectively intelligible; he needs himself to be able to 'picture' that aspect of them that enables him to understand how *they* 'hang together' in *his* terms. He makes no allowance for the possibility of only being able responsively to understand another in a practical context. Indeed, to put it in Bakhtin's (1984: 292–3) terms, MacIntyre's stance here is a monologic one, in the sense that

> monologism, at its extreme, denies the existence outside itself of another
> consciousness with equal rights and equal responsibilities, another *I* with equal
> rights (thou). With a monologic approach (in its extreme or pure form)
> *another person* remains wholly and merely an *object* of consciousness. Monologue
> is finalized and deaf to the other's response, does not expect it and does not
> acknowledge in it any *decisive* force.

And this, of course, is still the traditional analytic view of things: we treat what we are studying as something which, as individuals, we can entertain as an object of thought, in order to form order or coherent *theoretical* schemes representing it, to guide our further, deliberate actions, as individuals, in relation to it. But as Wittgenstein said about the non-orderly character of everyday life, and MacIntyre quotes Mink as saying also: if you complete it (into a pattern), you falsify it.

A short conversation between an Enlightenment Mind (EM) and a Postmodern Mind (PM):

> EM: But the lack of an orderly, surveyable, inner mental representation of
> things, the lack of a theory or coherent narrative structure, makes me
> feel uncomfortable; I lack confidence in my knowledge to act in-
> dependently, autonomously; without a rational scheme, I feel I'm un-
> able to account for my actions verbally if challenged to do so . . . I don't
> know what I'm doing . . . I feel vulnerable to criticisms I can't rebut;
> not knowing how to argue for my position, I feel my position unjust-
> ified; I don't quite know where I stand; where I should 'see' order, I 'see'
> only disorder; I want to offer in my studies plans of action, ready-made
> to the public, thus I feel I must have an orderly account of my 'subject
> matter' ahead of time; I need something 'in my head' to put what I am
> studying 'into'.
>
> PM: But disorder, variability, difference is what you must make 'sense' of,
> and not sooner or later, either, but on the spot, now.

EM: But you must have an 'idea' of the order hidden in it first.

PM: But that's impossible, the order doesn't exist yet, it's only on its way into existence. One day, perhaps, you might have an 'idea' of it 'in your head'. But to begin with, you have to use your common sense!

EM: To study what doesn't exist yet is crazy. Why can't I have an idea of it now? And anyway, common sense is just a disorderly distraction. It's not proper knowledge.

PM: Well, can I remind you of Foucault's (1972: 49) claim, that our task "consists of not – of no longer – treating discourses as groups of signs (signifying elements referring to contents or representations) but as practices that systematically form the objects of which they speak." What we talk about, at first, only exists, or 'subsists', in the activities between us.

EM: Yes, I know about Foucault, but I didn't understand it when you said it the first time. And as for what goes on between us, I don't get anything out of it at all.

PM: Oh!? Well, what follows will be even worse; I want to talk about the *imaginary*.

EM: Oh dear!

The imaginary

The Bakhtin/Volosinov claim that uttered words in a context are actively understood *responsively* amounts to this: that the listener does not *first* have to recognize the form used in order to understand its meaning. For, to the extent that a word's use strikes into a dynamic unity of intellectual and affective factors, what is involved in 'making sense' amounts, says Volosinov (1973: 68), "to understanding [a word's] novelty and not to recognizing its identity." What matters, practically, is the difference it makes to people's lives in the context in which it is uttered; how it 'moves' people. But this realization – of words as being only a *means* of communication and of them as not having an already determined meaning, and the fact that any 'hook-up' between our words and our circumstances is created between us, in the circumstances of their use – has many devastating consequences: not only to do with a rethinking of many of the basic topics of our research, but also to do with our understanding of our inescapable situatedness – the fact that we faced at the outset: that everything we do and say and . . . make sense of from 'out of' and 'into' a certain 'background'. It is in relation to this background that I want to explore the necessity for talk of *the imaginary*, of its *uses* in social theory, especially of the part it can play in issues to do with the nature of the cultural politics of identity and belonging.

Let us first turn to the nature of our research topics. As I mentioned in Chapter 2, it is still too easy for us to think that when we argue about such things as 'society', 'the individual', 'the person', 'identity', 'the citizen', 'civil society', 'thought', 'speech', 'language', 'desire', 'perception', 'motivation', etc., and plan a research project upon any one of them, we all know perfectly well what 'it' is that is represented by the concepts we use in our arguments, and what 'it' is that we are researching into. We find it difficult to accept that 'objects' such as these are not already 'out there' in the world in some primordial naturalistic sense. The idea that they are "essentially contested" concepts (Gallie, 1962); that they only 'make sense' as they are developed within a discourse; that such entities either have an imaginary component to them or are wholly or radically imaginary; that they are 'entities' (hidden) within the movement of a process, which do not at first have a distinctive existence as such at all, but which, in the continued 'movement' of the process, emerge as an identifiable part of it, all that is radically alien to us.

But, for example, consider these cases in which past activities 'accumulate' themselves, so to speak, in the present: the *parting* of a space into two becomes *a part* of the space so parted (historically); a *speaking*, which is a *means* of further specifying one's position in a situation, becomes a part of what one's position 'is'; a *hearing* produces something heard; a seeing some thing seen; and so on. Where what must be counted as 'the heard', 'the seen', and – to return to our concern with discourses – 'the said', is incomplete and ambiguous until the hearing, seeing and speaking is over (and even then, to the extent that they are all open to further specification, ambiguity and contest is still possible).

In the light of these comments, let us return to the claim made above: that we need talk of "the imaginary," because discourses work to produce rather than simply to reflect the 'objects' to which the words uttered within them seem to refer; we need a way of talking about (indicating) their transitional status, their only as yet partial existence, and the possibilities they contain for their own further realization. But to say this, we now realize, is itself to say something ambiguous, to make a claim with an unclear meaning. Do we mean something that can be *imagined*, or do we mean by the *imaginary* something much more fundamental?

What is the nature of something that can be imagined? Well, most often, we talk about it in terms, so to speak, of having a 'picture in our heads'. As we have already seen, this is not so much an image, as an image 'literalized' into a 'picture' which shows how everything hangs together in a single, orderly way. To say, then, that the imaginary represents something with a single order to it leaves us in a difficult position: for we want to say that no single image as such is adequate to our needs. Thus, we need to move from the imagined to the realm of the imaginary.

The point in *talking* of the imaginary is that we need a way of talking about entities which have the following properties:

1 They are incomplete, ongoing, on the way to being other than what they are – in short, they are unimaginable and extraordinary.
2 They are non-locatable, either in space or time, but which can none the less have 'real' attributes in the sense of functioning in people's actions in enabling them to achieve *reproducible results* by the use of socially sharable procedures.
3 They 'subsist' only in people's practices, in the 'gaps', 'zones', or 'boundaries' between people.

4 To this extent, we must talk of them as 'negotiated', 'political', 'contestable', or 'prospective' (Myhill, 1952) entities, ones which exist 'in' the world only to the extent that they can play a part in people's discourses – in short, their function is to make a way of human being, a form of life possible.[9]

5 Such entities are the *means* of its formation.

6 However, their 'structure' can never be made wholly rationally visible; indeed, it makes no sense to talk of them as having a 'spatially surveyable, complete structure', that is, their partial structuring can only be revealed in 'grammatical' investigations.

7 In short, such entities – like words themselves (cf. Volosinov above) – are sources of continuous, unforeseeable creativity and novelty. As such, they provide the 'thematics' in terms of which novel statements, perceptions, and actions are lent their intelligibility.

A typical imaginary entity is, of course, $\sqrt{(-1)}$, which indeed is now called an imaginary number,[10] although it used to be called an 'impossible' number. On consideration, imaginary numbers will be found to have all the properties mentioned above, except perhaps the lack of a *contested* nature – they are certainly a current source of mathematical novelty. And although they cannot exist as mathematical objects, they none the less play a 'real' part in mathematical procedures; not in the sense of correspondence with reality, but in the sense of achieving *reproducible results* by the use of socially sharable (mathematical) procedures. They can function as an originary source in mathematical research; in bridging 'gaps' (as between positive and negative in electrical engineering) they are a focus of tension, conflict and oscillation.

The new 'politics of identity'

How is all of this of relevance to us with our interest in identity and belonging? In his book, *Imagined Communities*,[11] Benedict Anderson (1983) sets out three two-sided dilemmatic themes (paradoxes) that seem to characterize nationalism and nationalisms: their objective modernity to historians versus their subjective antiquity to nationalists; its formal universality as a concept versus the irredeemable particularity of its concrete manifestations; and their political power versus their philosophical poverty and even incoherence. He adds further, that in trying to grasp nationalism as an object of thought fails. "Like Gertrude Stein in the face of Oakland, one can rather quickly conclude there is 'no there there'" (1983: 5). Nevertheless, there is a mistaken tendency to hypostatize its existence, and then to misclassify 'it' as *an* ideology. I want to suggest that it is, in fact, best thought of as a tradition of argumentation, a way of people continually arguing with each other over who or what they are. For, as we have already grasped, given the poetic, rhetorical and 'reality-creating' nature of talk (speech), it is possible for dialogue, for argument, *to produce* the very object which the talk in the argument is supposed to be about. Anderson (1983: 6) comes very close to just such a formulation:

With a certain ferocity Gellner makes a comparable point when he rules that "Nationalism is not nations coming to self-consciousness; it *invents* nations where they do not exist". The drawback of this formulation, however, is that Gellner is so anxious to show that nationalism masquerades under false pretenses that he assimilates "invention" to "fabrication" and "falsity", rather than to "imaging" and "creation". In this way he implies that "true" communities exist which can be advantageously juxtaposed to nations. In fact, all communities larger than primordial villages of face-to-face contact (and perhaps even these) are imagined.

In other words, compared with the cultural systems preceding it – religious communities and dynastic realms – nationalism is a new way for a people to argue about who or what they are, or might be. And the very fact of their arguing about it sustains their form of nationalism in existence.

Given this, given that the appropriate tradition of argumentation could function as a 'container' within which everyone could find a place, and 'belong in the argument', one of the tasks in the new 'politics of citizenship' is to articulate a new critical descriptive vocabulary of terms, a new set of formative-relational commonplaces (*topoi*), that all the new and diverse groups within civil society can use in expressing their (ontological) needs – their feelings of anger and despair, their dreams and expectations, their need for respect and for civil relations with others, if one is to be one's own self while still 'belonging', along with others, to one's society – while still participating in the debate, while still playing their own part *in the invention of 'our' form of citizenship*. For at the moment, we have something of a stand-off: those with a respect for the being of others fear claiming solidarity with them; they fear claiming to recognize and understand *their* 'position'. For, within a referential theory of meaning, any difference, any lack of correspondence between what their circumstances are said to be and what they themselves feel them to be, means: "You don't understand; I'm not like you say I am!" Within a rhetorical-responsive perspective, however, solidarity with others does not mean everyone thinking and feeling the same. It simply means that, in realizing the degree to which one relies upon one's responsive relations with others in being oneself, one cares about establishing a common ground with them *when required*. Without a common set of terms in which to share disagreements and criticisms openly, as Mercer (1990) points out, the improvising of alliances and coalitions with others, when required, is inhibited – people are paralysed by the fear of being seen as insensitive, as not 'politically correct' or as not 'ideologically right on'.

Lacking the required arena of collective or public creativity, debates about freedom and democracy are currently carried on in the language of 'the market'. For the market, as Milton Friedman (1962: 200) has described it, "is one of the strongest most creative forces known to man – the attempt by millions of individuals to promote their own interests." But it is clear that the existing social conditions of the market do not 'afford' the conditions of possibility required for the invention of citizenship. Indeed, in assigning us all to the role of producers or consumers, it would seem to reproduce those very forms of exclusion and closure (classes) – that particular lack of a sense of belonging – that the idea of citizenship was originally concerned to address. As a genre, market economics is inadequate to our tasks. A new, yet-to-be-fashioned genre is required. Thus the politics of citizenship is not something to be instituted in society at large through a top-down system of power relations. It cannot be passed down, once the concept of citizenship has been first clarified, and an appropriate genre for its discussion has been fashioned, by a philo-sophical and social scientific vanguard. The Party in that sense is over.

This is where those of us concerned with the 'politics of personhood' in the 1960s failed: then, we did not grasp the *formative* and *relational* power of language – its "social function of co-ordinating diverse social actions" (Mills, 1940: 439). Oper-ating within a hierarchical model of power, we thought the emancipatory task was one of protest, of making those in power see the wrong of their mechanistic, inhuman ways. We did not realize then the power of our talk, the 'political' nature of genres Laing used in his writings, the fact that new ways of talking, new forms of debate, work to produce, to invent, rather than simply to reflect the entities we talked about. Thus now we realize that if everyone is to participate in that process of invention, citizenship cannot simply be instituted as a new ideology in a top-down power-play by an elite group. It must emerge as a 'living ideology', a new 'tradition of argumentation', consisting in a whole diversity of interdependent arenas in which, and between which, argument over "precisely . . . the goods which constitute that tradition" (to repeat MacIntyre's formulation) can take place. In this view, common sense is a great repository of culturally developed resources, not a 'marketplace' of possibilities put forward by already ontologically well-developed individuals in com-petition with one another for personal profit, but a great 'carnival' (Bahktin, 1968) of different ways of socially constituting *being* in which everyone can have a 'voice' – in which they can play a part in the shaping and reshaping of their lives. It is these forces, operating in civil society in the 'providential spaces' in between people, not the forces of the market which are 'the strongest and most creative forces known to man', for they provide the resources out of which other cultural products, including the market, are shaped.

Critical 'tool-making'

Human choice, by its very nature most uncertain, is made certain by the common sense of men with respect to human needs or utilities, which are the two sources of the natural law of the gentes . . . Common sense is judgment without reflection, shared by an entire class, an entire people, an entire nation, or the entire human race.

. . . as much as the poets had first sensed in the way of vulgar wisdom, the philosophers later understood in the way of esoteric wisdom; so the former may be said to have been the sense and the latter the intellect of the human race.

(Vico, 1968: paras 141–2 and 363)

(Were I a braver man, I might render Vico's *'unomo ingegnoso'* as 'civil engineer'!)

(Mooney, 1985: 135)

It pleases me to have been able to begin this book and to end it with a reference to 'engineering'. Indeed, it has often seemed to me that I have a 'car mechanic's' attitude to language: I want to know how the saying of something 'works'; how, practically, an utterance 'goes', what 'drives' it, what it 'does.' It pleases me also to be able to end it by returning to Vico again. He has been a great 'textual friend'[1] in my inner dialogues – along with all the others – and to find Mooney all but calling Vico's 'hero' an engineer especially pleases me: a prodigious builder of 'bridges', a 'maker of connections' indeed!

I began this book with a distinction between 'already spoken words', and 'words in their speaking', and said that it was 'from within' the activity of speaking that I was going to attempt to conduct my investigations. And in fact, what essentially we have been discussing in this book is the 'bridging' of 'gaps' between different regions and moments in our activities, by humanly invented and constructed devices – themselves 'made' out of aspects of our own activities, so to speak – 'from within' those self same activities. What I have sought to show is that, central to all the writers I have drawn upon is a sensitivity to the fact that sensuous activity, that is, 'living movement', is basic to everything human. Hence, whenever two people are together, there is a flux of 'living movement' between them, undifferentiated as to 'whose' movement it is. And the great puzzle people have faced throughout history is to find ways of gradually differentiating out 'from within' that flux its sources. Thus "doctrines must take their beginning from the matters of which they treat," suggests Vico (1968: para. 314). But this is not so easy. We have lives to live in the meantime. Thus it's no wonder that philosophers "have neglected the study of the world of nations, or civil world" (para. 331). "This aberration was a consequence of that infirmity of the human mind by which, immersed and buried in the body, it naturally takes notice of bodily things, and finds the effort to attend to itself too laborious; just as the bodily eye sees all objects outside itself but needs a mirror to see itself" (para. 331).

Indeed, as Rorty (1980: 239) says, but in a rather different context, "if the body had been easier to understand, nobody would have thought that we had a mind." And certainly, within social constructionism, the *mythic* nature of 'the mind' – in the sense of it failing 'to speak' its own origins – is becoming increasingly apparent. "The bastard! He doesn't exist!" says Hamm of God, in Samuel Beckett's *Endgame*.

So although, within the continuous, oscillating flow of activity in the self–other dimension of interaction between us, there is no problem of detecting the activity of 'mind', the problem is, 'whose mind is it?' The task has been (and still is) that of differentiating the activity due to oneself, that due to others, and that due to neither – and devising (making) ways of finding in what is continuous and irreversible something that is none the less stable and reproducible. But, unless we can stabilize the 'movements' between ourselves, between 'us', we cannot stabilize those between what is 'us' and what is 'not us' – what I have called the person–world dimension of interaction. Hence the importance of those moments, 'common places', when shared feelings, in shared circumstances, could be given a shared significance, and re-membered, or re-called. Quite literally, the human task seems to have been that of 'making out' 'from within'. And mirrors *have* been important to us in all of this: they have reflected back to us what we have 'done'. And we have 'penetrated' by 'analysis' into the fine structure of those 'done things' – and we have learnt a lot about them, including ways to 'picture' them, thus to make more things like them. We could not, however, 'recognize ourselves in them'.

But what Vico did was to invent a method, of not so much reflection as differential refraction, that is to say (to stay with luminal metaphors for the moment), he discovered that by comparing the different 'distortions' we ourselves introduced at different times into our own 'doings', he could *detect* (but not completely 'see') the workings – "within the modifications of our own human mind" (Vico, 1968: para. 331) – of the different 'instruments' we were using to produce those distortions or modifications.

> [T]he proper and continual proof here adduced will consist in comparing and reflecting whether our human mind, in the series of possibilities it is permitted to understand, and so far as it is permitted to do so, can conceive more

or fewer or different causes than those from which issue the effects of this civil world.

(para. 345)

And his great discovery by use of it was

that the first gentile people, by a demonstrated necessity of nature, were poets who spoke in poetic characters. This discovery, which is the master key of this Science, has cost us the persistent research of almost all our literary life, because with our civilized natures we [moderns] cannot at all imagine and can understand only with great toil the poetic nature of these first men.

(para. 34)

He could not actually 'see' clearly what they were. But, as "it is a property of the human mind that whenever men can form no idea of distant unknown things, they judge them by what is familiar and at hand" (para. 122), he took what was familiar and near to hand for him as *his* instrument: namely, the metaphor, the device for giving intelligible form to feeling. And *through* metaphors, he 'saw' in the 'distortions' he had detected, something very like 'metaphors' at work. But what were these original metaphors like? They were bodily metaphors, mute metaphors, bodily activities with a *shared* sense: he called them 'sensory topics', 'places' that could be used for re-membering, for re-calling one's relations with others.

Thus, his new science must begin with a

vulgar metaphysics, such as we shall find the theology of the [first] poets to have been, and seek by its [i.e., his 'method of refractions'] aid that frightful thought of some divinity which imposed form and measure on the bestial passions of these lost men and thus transformed them into human passions.

(Vico, 1968: para. 340)

For something seems to be at work in the activities between people. The activities are not just repetitive, they 'grow', they 'develop', they are 'creative', they 'make history'; they also take on a form, families, then cities, then nations appear, laws are formulated, action regulated. A 'double divinity' seems to be hidden in our joint actions: a 'creator' and a 'judge' that resides in the group's *sensus communis*, that is, 'in' its shared ways of 'seeing sense' and 'making sense'.

This is amazing! "Divine providence" is his greatest discovery.

But why had no one 'seen' this before? Because, instead of seeing *through* our own instruments, instead of sensing in their use the 'movements' due to 'us' and those due to 'not us', we just looked 'at' the results we could produce using them. "One thinks that one is tracing the outline of a thing's nature over and over again, and one is merely tracing round the frame through which we look at it" (Wittgenstein, 1953: no. 114). We fall victim to certain conceits, or *borie*, we become entrapped in certain 'pictures' of our own making that we repeat to ourselves in our language to ourselves. How could the use of metaphors prevent this? For in no way did the metaphors he knew of be made truly to *correspond* in any one-to-one way with the *sensuous movements* he wanted to talk about – after all, they *were* 'movements'. If he could not form a representation of them, how could he speak 'truly' of them at all? Speak of them in such a way that in his own speakings he did not 'distort' their nature? For he needed to communicate their 'sense' somehow. Here again, he realized, he himself could use metaphors; his science would be a poetic science.

How can metaphors work to communicate the results of his discoveries? For metaphors can only arouse a certain sense of 'this' and a certain sense of 'that' in an audience. From what he knew of rhetoric, and the *ars topica*, it would clearly involve a kind of 'civil engineering', a 'making' of the appropriate devices required for arousing the right kind of sense in the audience. And it would have to rely upon the audience not only to 'sense' the connections, the 'movement' between them, but also to assign a shared significance to that movement. It would depend upon a *sensus communis*. Thus, poetic 'scientists' would not offer 'pictures', 'plans' or representations. They would only offer "poetic wisdom or metaphysics," where a poetic metaphysics "is not rational and abstract like that of learned men now, but felt and imagined as that of these first men must have been, who, without power of ratiocination, were all robust sense and vigorous imagination" (Vico, 1968: para. 375). But of what use on earth is that! For after all, conceits or not, we have to make our way in the world. And what Vico has to say is not to do with plans for action, with 'analyses' of what is external to us, with reaching for the moon. Why should we even care about the workings of such things as "sensory topics," "divine providence," "*borie*," "poetic wisdom," and the like?

Because, he says, "things do not settle or endure out of their natural state" (para. 134). Because, who we 'are' between 'us', determines who and what we are to 'our world', and (who) and what 'our world' is to us. If to an extent 'we' fall apart, 'our world' to an extent does, too. And who we are to each other is up to us to care about. That is why it matters. And your common-sense "judgment without reflection" (para. 142) that these things do not matter is just that, *your* common sense, "made certain" (para. 141) by *your* needs and *your* utilities, not mine. We must talk about this.

So what is it so far that Vico has done for us? Let me first just list what seem to me to be his main topics, or *topoi*: sense; his method of refractions; conceits (*borie*); sensory topics; imaginative universals, plus metaphors generally; *sensus communis*, and, above all, divine providence. Six metaphors, six very useful 'tools' *through* which to 'see sense' in things. In large engineering concerns, in which they want to reproduce the same product over and over again, the ones who produce the means for doing that are called 'tool-makers'. They are very special engineers. 'Tool-making' is a central aspect of Vico's 'civil engineering'. But he does not provide just any old tools that might just possibly, one day, be useful. They are tools which have been arrived at through "exasperating difficulties which have cost us the research of a good twenty years" (para. 338), in which the task has been to differentiate the sense at work in things *not due* to the operations of one's own instruments of investigation. His 'tool-making' is thus a 'critical tool-making'. And so far, we have a tool-box of six critically useful tools, useful, for understanding what it is that makes us an 'us', makes us as individuals into an 'us' that is a community.

Besides their critical nature, though, notice that I have called them topics (I could equally have well called them 'imaginary entities'). As such, they can be thought of as new 'places' within our common sense, as devices for possible use by us all. While it is true that in their natures they are vague, ambiguous and incompletely characterized – and thus, of course, contestable, such that a tradition of argumentation could form around each[2] – they are nonetheless flexible and negotiable in use, and can thus be used variously (as are all common-sense resources – see Chapter 7). But like all tools, their use requires a bit of getting used to. Are they really for use by anybody?

At this point I would now like to turn to the substantive concern in this book – the politics of everyday social life – and to explore briefly our place as academics in all of this. I raised problems with explanatory theories, with narratives, and indeed, with any discursive 'containers' in which other voices were more dominant than one's own. And a critic might suggest here that the same difficulty arises: isn't this *my* text? Well, yes, indeed, and perhaps I could add to Vico's list of tools a few of those *I* have introduced – like the 'providential space' of 'joint action', 'prosthetic devices', the category of the 'imaginary', and so on – for, although not perhaps for twenty exasperating years, I have worked hard on this text. Yes, it is mine alright. But, on the other hand (there is always another side to the question), it is not mine at all. First, it is utterly soaked in the voices of my 'textual friends'. But that is not enough to prevent it being mine, after all, I am very selective of my friends. What importantly prevents it being just mine, I want to claim, is that all the 'tools' offered are *topics*, that is, they are at least two-sided in a number of ways. Besides their main investigatory function, as prosthetic devices for seeing connections, and as rhetorical devices for making connections, they are also providential sources in which other people may find many other uses.

Some people might still want to say that what I have called "critical 'tool-making'" is simply what they would call "theory," and want to know why I have invented a cranky term. Because another of my 'textual friends' (Ludwig Wittgenstein) convinced me that there was no getting away from the implicit 'taste' of the supposed *orderliness, completeness* and *'picturableness'* of things that goes along with all talk of *theory* these days. Those who argue about theory are, more often than not, arguing about one or another social *order*. I like the tool-box analogy because there is no order to the tools in the box. Indeed, my tools are hardly ever in the box, but are spread about everywhere, and thus not always accessible to me when I need them. But that, I think, it just as it is in the politics of everyday life.

References

Allport, D.A. (1980) Patterns and actions. In G. Claxton (ed.), *Cognitive Psychology*. London: Routledge and Kegan Paul.

Anderson, B. (1983) *Imagined Communities: Reflections on the Origins and Spread of Nationalism*. London: Verso.

Arendt, H. (1964) *Eichman in Jerusalem*. New York: Viking Press.

Argyle, M. (1969) *Social Interaction*. London: Methuen.

Argyle, M. (1990) An empirical interpretation of ethogenics. In R. Bhaskar (ed.), *Harré and His Critics: Essays in Honour of Rom Harré with His Commentary on Them*. Oxford: Blackwell.

Aristotle (1991) *The Art of Rhetoric*. Translated with an introduction by H.C. Lawson-Tancred. London: Penguin Books.

Austin, J. (1970) *Philosophical Papers*. London: Oxford University Press.

Averill, J. (1980) A constructivist view of emotion. In R. Plutick and H. Kellerman (eds), *Theories of Emotion*. New York: Academic Press.

.Bacon, F. (1858) *Of the Dignity and Advancement of Learning (1605)*. London: Longman.

Baker, G.P. and Hacker, P.M.S. (1984) *Language, Sense and Nonsense*. Oxford: Blackwell.

Bakhtin, M.M. (1965) *Rabelais and his World*, trans. H. Iswolsky. Cambridge, MA: MIT Press.

Bakhtin, M.M. (1981) *The Dialogical Imagination*. Edited by M. Holquist, trans. by C. Emerson and M. Holquist. Austin: University of Texas Press.

Bakhtin, M.M. (1984) *Problems of Dostoevsky's Poetics*. Edited and trans. by Caryl Emerson. Minneapolis: University of Minnesota Press.

Bakhtin, M.M. (1986) *Speech Genres and Other Late Essays*. Trans. by Vern W. McGee. Austin: University of Texas Press.

Bakhtin, M. (1990) *Art and Answerability: Early Philosophical Essays by M.M. Bakhtin*. Edited by Micheal Holquist and Vadim Liapunov. Translation and Notes by Vadin Liapunov. Austin: University of Texas Press.

Barnes, B. (1982) *T.S. Kuhn and Social Science*. London: Macmillan.

Baron, R.A. and Byrne, D. (1984) *Social Psychology: Understanding Human Interaction*. Boston: Allyn and Bacon.

Barthes, R. (1983) *A Lover's Discourse*. New York: Hill and Wang.

Bartlett, Sir Frederic C. (1932) *Remembering: A Study in Experimental Psychology*. London: Cambridge University Press.

Bateson, M.C. (1990) *Composing a Life*. New York: (Plume) Penguin Books.

Bauman, Z. (1987) *Intellectuals: Legislators or Interpreters*. Oxford: Polity Press.

Bauman, Z. (1989) *Modernity and the Holocaust*. Ithaca, NY: Cornell University Press.

Baumgarten, M. (1982) *City Scriptures: Modern Jewish Writings*. Cambridge, MA: Harvard University Press.

Baxter, L.A. (1988) A dialectical perspective on communicational strategies in relationship development. In S.W. Duck, D.F. Day, S.E. Hobfall, W. Iches and B. Montgomery (eds), *Handbook of Personal Relationships*. London: Wiley.

Baxter, L.A. (1990) Dialectical contradictions in relationship development. *Journal of Social and Personal Relations*, 7, 69–88.

Bazeman, C. (1988) *Shaping Written Knowledge: The Genre and Activity of the Experimental Article in Science*. Madison: University of Wisconsin Press.

Bellah, R.N., Madsen, R., Sullivan, W.M., Swidler, A. and Tipton, S.M. (1985) *Habits of the Heart: Individualism and Commitment in American Life*. Berkeley: University of California Press.

Berlin, I. (1976) *Vico and Herder*. London: The Hogarth Press.

Bernstein, R.J. (1983) *Beyond Objectivism and Relativism*. Oxford: Blackwell.

Bernstein, R.J. (1992) *The New Constellation: The Ethical-Political Horizons of Modernity/ Postmodernity*. Cambridge, MA: MIT Press.

Best, J.B. (1986) *Cognitive Psychology*. New York: West Publishing Company.

Bhaskar, R. (1989) *Reclaiming Reality: A Critical Introduction to Contemporary Philosophy*. London: Verso.

Bhaskar, R. (ed.) (1990) *Harré and His Critics: Essays in Honour of Rom Harré with His Commentary on Them*. Oxford: Blackwell.

Billig, M. (1985) Prejudice, categorization and particularization: from a perceptual to a rhetorical approach. *European Journal of Social Psychology*, 15, 79–103.

Billig, M. (1986) Thinking and arguing: an inaugural lecture. Loughborough: University of Loughborough.

Billig, M. (1987) *Arguing and Thinking: A Rhetorical Approach to Social Psychology*. Cambridge: Cambridge University Press.

Billig, M. (1991) *Ideology, Rhetoric and Opinions*. London: Sage.

Billig, M., Condor, S., Edwards, D., Gane, M., Middleton, D. and Radley, R. (1988) *Ideological Dilemmas*. London: Sage Publications.

Bloor, D. (1975) *Knowledge and Social Imagery*. London: Routledge and Kegan Paul.

Boden, M. (1982) Formalism and fancy. *New Universities Quarterly*, 36, 217–24.

Boden, M. (1989) *Computer Models of Mind: Computational Approaches in Theoretical Psychology*. Cambridge: Cambridge University Press.

Boden, M. (ed.) (1990) *The Philosophy of Artificial Intelligence*. Oxford: Oxford University Press.

Bohm, D. (1965) Appendix: physics and perception. In *The Special Theory of Relativity*. New York: Benjamin.

Bohm, D. (1980) *Wholeness and the Implicate Order*. London: Routledge and Kegan Paul.

Bowers, J. (1990) All hail the great abstraction. In I. Parker and J. Shotter (eds), *Deconstructing Social Psychology*. London: Routledge.

Bransford, J.D., Franks, J.J., McCarrell, N.S. and Nitsch, K.E. (1977) Toward unexplaining memory. In R. Shaw and J. Bransford (eds), *Perceiving, Acting, and Knowing: Toward an Ecological Psychology*. Hillsdale, NY: Erlbaum.

Broadbent, D.E. (1961) *Behaviourism*. London: Methuen.

Broadbent, D.E. (1970) In defence of empirical psychology. *Bull. Brit. Psychol. Soc.*, 23, 87–96.

Broadbent, D.E. (1973) *In Defence of Empirical Psychology*. London: Methuen.

Cassirer, E. (1951) *The Philosophy of the Enlightenment*. Trans by Fritz C.A. Koelln and James P. Pettegrove. Princeton, NJ: Princeton University Press.

Cavell, S. (1969) *Must We Mean What We Say?*. London: Cambridge University Press.

Chomsky, N. (1957) *Syntactic Structures*. The Hague: Mouton.

Chomsky, N. (1965) *Aspects of the Theory of Syntax*. Cambridge, MA: MIT Press.

Code, L. (1987) *Epistemic Responsibility*. Hanover and London: University Press of New England.

Cole, M. (1990) Cultural psychology: a once and future discipline? In J.J. Berman (ed.), *Nebraska Symposium of Motivation, 1989: Cross Cultural Perspectives*, vol. 37. Lincoln: University of Nebraska Press.

Coulter, J. (1979) *The Social Construction of Mind*. London and Basingstoke: Macmillan.

Coulter, J. (1983) *Rethinking Cognive Psychology*. London and Basingstoke: Macmillan.

Coulter, J. (1989) *Mind in Action*. London and Basingstoke: Macmillan.

Clark, K. and Holquist, M. (1984) *Mikhail Bakhtin*. Cambridge, MA: Harvard University Press.

Craik, K.J.W. (1943) *The Nature of Explanation*. Cambridge: Cambridge University Press.

Davis, P.J. and Hersh, R. (1983) *The Mathematical Experience*. Harmondsworth: Penguin.

Dawkins, R. (1978) *The Selfish Gene*. St Albans: Paladin Books.

Derrida, J. (1976) *Of Grammatology*. Baltimore, MD: Johns Hopkins University Press.

Descartes, R. (1968) *Discourse on Method and the Meditations*. Harmondsworth: Penguin Books.

Descartes, R. (1986) *Meditations on First Philosophy: with Selections from Objections and Replies*. Translated by J. Cottingham, with an introduction by B. Williams. Cambridge: Cambridge University Press.

Dewey, J. (1944) The concept of the reflex arc in psychology. In W. Dennis (ed.), *Readings in the History of Psychology*. New York: Appleton-Century-Croft, 1944. Originally published in *Psychological Review*, 3, 13–32.

Duck, S.W. (1990) Relationships as unfinished business: out of the frying pan and into the 1990s. *Journal of Social and Personal Relationships*, 7, 5–28.

Eagleton, T. (1986) *Against the Grain: Essays 1975–1985*. London: Verso.

Eagleton, T. (1989) *The Significance of Theory*. Oxford: Blackwell.

Eagleton, T. (1991) *Ideology: An Introduction*. London: Verso.

Edwards, D. and Potter, J. (1992) *Discursive Psychology*. London: Sage.

Edwards, J.C. (1982) *Ethics without Philosophy: Wittgenstein and the Moral Life*. Tampa: University Presses of Florida.

Einstein, A. (1979) On the method of theoretical physics. In A.P. French (ed.), *Einstein: A Centenary Volume*. London: Heinemann.

Feyerabend, P. (1975) *Against Method*. London: New Left Books.

Feyerabend, P. (1978) *Science in a Free Society*. London: New Left Books, Verso Editions.

Fish, S. (1989) Anti-professionalism. In *Doing What Comes Naturally: Change, Rhetoric, and the Practice of Theory in Literary and Legal Studies*. Durham and London: Duke University Press.

Fleck, L. (1979) *The Genesis and Development of a Scientific Fact*. Chicago: Chicago University Press.

Foucault, M. (1970) *The Order of Things: An Archaeology of the Human Sciences*. London: Tavistock Publications.

Foucault, M. (1972) *The Archaeology of Knowledge*. Trans. A.M. Sheridan. London: Tavistock.

Foucault, M. (1979) *Discipline and Punishment: the Birth of the Prison*. Trans. A.M. Sheridan. Harmondsworth: Penguin Books.

Gadamer, H.-G. (1975) *Truth and Method*. London: Sheed and Ward.

Gallie, W.B. (1962) Essentially contested concepts. In M. Black (ed.), *The Importance of Language*. Englewood Cliffs, NJ: Prentice Hall.

Garfinkel, H. (1956) Conditions for successful degradation ceremonies. *American Journal of Sociology*, 61, 101–5.

Garfinkel, H. (1967) *Studies in Ethnomethodology*. Englewood Cliffs, NJ: Prentice Hall.

Gauld, A.O. and Shotter, J. (1977) *Human Action and its Psychological Investigation*. London: Routledge and Kegan Paul.

Geertz, C. (1983) *Local Knowledge: Further Essays in Interpretative Anthropology*. New York: Basic Books.

Gergen, K.J. (1985) The social constructionist movement in modern psychology. *American Psychologist*, 40, 266–75.

Gergen, K.J. (1989a) Social psychology and the wrong revolution. *European Journal of Social Psychology*, 19, 463–84.

Gergen, K.J. (1989b) Warranting voice and the elaboration of self. In J. Shotter and K.J. Gergen (eds), *Texts of Identity*. London: Sage.

Gergen, K.J. (1990a) Social understanding and the inscription of self. In J.W. Stigler, R.A. Shweder, and G. Herdt (eds), *Cultural Psychology: Essays on Comparative Human Development*. Cambridge: Cambridge University Press.

Gergen, K.J. (1990b) If persons are texts. In S.B. Messer, L.A. Sass and R.L. Woolfolk (eds), *Hermeneutics and Psychological Theory*. New Brunswick: Rutgers University Press.

Gergen, K.J. (1991) *The Saturated Self: Dilemmas of Identity in Contemporary Life*. New York: Basic Books.

Gergen, K.J. and Morowski, J.G. (1980) An alternative metatheory for social psychology. In L. Wheeler (ed.), *Review of Personality and Social Psychology*. Beverley Hills, CA: Sage.

Gergen, K.J. and Gergen, M. (1987) Narratives of relationship. In R. Burnett, P. McGee and D. Clarke (eds), *Accounting for Personal Relationships: Social Representations of Interpersonal Links*. London: Methuen.

Gibson, J.J. (1979) *The Ecological Approach to Visual Perception*. London: Houghton Mifflin.

Giddens, A. (1979) *Central Problems in Social Theory: Action, Structure and Contradiction in Social Analysis*. London: Macmillan.

Giddens, A. (1984) *The Constitution of Society*. Cambridge: Polity Press.

Giddens, A. (1991) *Modernity and Self-Identiy: Self and Society in the Late Modern Age*. Stanford, CA: Stanford University Press.

Goffman, E. (1959) The presentation of self. *The Presentation of Self in Everyday Life*. New York: Doubleday.

Goody, J. (1977) *The Domestication of the Savage Mind*. Cambridge: Cambridge University Press.

Grassi, E. (1980) *Rhetoric as Philosophy*. University Park and London: Pennsylvannia State University Press.

Greenwood, J. (1992) Realism, empiricism, and social constructionism: psychological theory and the social dimensions of mind and action. *Theory and Psychology*, 2, 131–58.

Habermas, J. (1979) *Communication and the Evolution of Society*. Boston: Beacon Press.

Habermas, J. (1984) *The Theory of Communicative Action, I: Reason and Rationalization of Society*. Boston: Beacon Press.

Hall, S. and Held, D. (1989) Citizens and citizenship. In S. Hall and M. Jacques (eds), *New Times: the Changing Face of Politics in the 1990s*. London: Lawrence and Wishart.

Harré, R. (1970a) *The Principles of Scientific Thinking*. London: Macmillan.

Harré, R. (1970b) Powers. *Brit. J. Philos. Sci.*, 21, 81–101.

Harré, R. (1972) *Philosophies of Science*. Oxford: Oxford University Press.

Harré, R. (1979) *Social Being: A Theory for Social Psychology*. Oxford: Blackwell.

Harré, R. (1983) *Personal Being: A Theory for Individual Psychology*. Oxford: Blackwell.

Harré, R. (1986a) The step to social constructionism. In M.P.M. Richards and P. Light (eds), *Children of Social Worlds*. Oxford: Polity Press.

Harré, R. (1986b) *Varieties of Realism*. Oxford: Blackwell.

Harré, R. (1986c) Social sources of mental content and order. In J. Margolis, P.T. Manicas, R. Harré and P.F. Secord (eds), *Psychology: Designing the Discipline*. Oxford: Blackwell.

Harré, R. (1986d) The social construction of selves. In K. Yardley and T. Honess (eds), *Self and Identity*. Chichester: John Wiley.

Harré, R. (1986e) An outline of the social constructionist viewpoint. In R. Harré (ed.), *The Social Construction of Emotions*. Oxford: Blackwell.

Harré, R. (1990) Exploring the human Umwelt. In R. Bhaskar (ed.), *Harré and His Critics: Essays in Honour of Rom Harré with His Commentary on Them*. Oxford: Blackwell.

Harré, R. and Secord, P.F. (1972) *The Explanation of Social Behaviour*. Oxford: Blackwell.

Harré, R. and Madden, E.H. (1975) *Causal Powers: A Theory of Natural Necessity*. Oxford: Blackwell.

Harré, R., Clarke, D. and De Carlo, N. (1985) *Motives and Mechanisms: An Introduction to the Psychology of Action*. London: Methuen.

Harris, R. (1980) *Language-Makers*. London: Duckworth.

Harris, R. (1981) *The Language Myth*. London: Duckworth.

Heidegger, M. (1967) *Being and Time*. Oxford: Blackwell.

Heider, F. (1958) *The Psychology of Interpersonal Relations*. New York: Wiley.

Heller, J. (1975) *Something Happened*. London: Corgi.

Hempel, C.G. (1963) The theoreticians's dilemma: a study in the logic of theory construction. In *Minnesota Studies in the Philosophy of Science*, Vol. 2. Minneapolis: University of Minnesota Press.

Hertz, H.H. (1954) *The Principles of Mechanics*. New York: Dover. First published in German in 1894.

Holquist, M. (1983) Answering as authoring: Mikhail Bakhtin's trans-linguistics. *Critical Inquiry*, 10, 307–19.

Hooks, B. (1984) *Feminist Theory: From Margin to Center*. Boston, MA: South End Press.

Hooks, B. (1989) *Talking Back: Thinking Feminist, Thinking Black*. Boston, MA: South End Press.

Hooks, B. (1990) Choosing the margin as a space of radical openness. In *Yearning: Race, Gender, and Cultural Politics*. Boston, MA: South End Press.

Hull, J.M. (1991) *Touching the Rock: An Experience of Blindness*. New York: Pantheon.

Ingold, T. (1990) An anthropologist looks at biology. *Man (n.s.)*, 25, 208–29.

Jacoby, R. (1975) *Social Amnesia: A Critique of Conformist Psychology from Adler to R.D. Laing*. Hassocks: Harvester Press.

James, W. (1890) *Principles of Psychology*, vols 1 and 2. London: Macmillan.

Janik, A. and Toulmin, S. (1973) *Wittgenstein's Vienna*. New York: Simon & Schuster.

Johnson-Laird, P.N. (1983) *Mental Models*. Cambridge: Cambridge University Press.

Johnson-Laird, P.N. and Wason, P.C. (1977) *Thinking: Readings in Cognitive Science*. London: Cambridge University Press.

Kant, I. (1965) What is Enlightenment? In F.E. Manuel (ed.), *The Enlightenment*. Englewood Cliffs, NJ: Prentice Hall.

Kimble, G.A. (1989) Psychology from the standpoint of a generalist. *American Psychologist*, 44, 491–9.

Kline, M. (1980) *Mathematics: The Loss of Certainty*. Oxford: Oxford University Press.

Koch, S. (1964) Psychology and emerging conceptions of knowledge as unitary. In T.W. Wann (ed.), *Behaviorism and Phenomenology*. Chicago: University of Chicago Press.

Kuhn, T.S. (1962) *The Structure of Scientific Revolutions*. Chicago: University of Chicago Press.

Laing, R.D. (1967) *The Politics of Experience and the Bird of Paradise*. Harmondsworth: Penguin Books.

Lasch, C. (1979) *The Culture of Narcissism: American Life in an Age of Diminishing Expectations*. New York: Norton.

Lasch, C. (1985) *The Minimalist Self*. New York: Norton.

Lazarus, N. (1991) Doubting the new world order: Marxism, Realism, and the claims of postmodernist social theory. *Differences*, 3, 94–138.

Lopez, L.L. (1991) The rhetoric of irrationality. *Theory and Psychology*, 1, 65–82.

Luria, A.R. (1974) *Cognitive Development: Its Cultural and Social Origins*. Cambridge, MA: Harvard University Press.

Lyotard, J.-F. (1984) *The Postmodern Condition: A Report on Knowledge*. Manchester: University of Manchester Press.

MacIntyre, A. (1981) *After Virtue*. London: Duckworth.

MacIntyre, A. (1988) *Whose Justice? Which Rationality?* London: Duckworth.

Macmurray, J. (1957) *The Self as Agent*. London: Faber and Faber.

Macmurray, J. (1961) *Persons in Relation*. London: Faber and Faber.

Macpherson, C.B. (1962) *The Political Theory of Possessive Individualism: Hobbes to Locke*. Oxford: Oxford University Press.

Manicas, P. (1990) Modest realism, experience and evolution. In R. Bhaskar (ed.), *Harré and His Critics: Essays in Honour of Rom Harré with His Commentary on Them*. Oxford: Blackwell.

Manicas, P.T. and Secord, P.F. (1983) Implications for psychology of the new philosophy of science. *American Psychologist*, 38, 399–413.

Manuel, F.E. (ed.) (1965) *The Enlightenment*. Englewoods Cliffs, NJ: Prentice Hall.

Marx, K. and Engels, F. (1970) *The German Ideology*. London: Lawrence and Wishart.

McCloskey, D.M. (1983) The rhetoric of economics. *Journal of Economic Literature*, 21, 481–516.

McGuire, W.J. (1973) The yin and yang of progress in social psychology. *J. Pers. and Soc. Psychol.*, 26, 446–56.

Meacham, J.A. (1977) A transactional model of remembering. In N. Datan and H.W. Reese (eds), *Life-span Developmental Psychology: Perspectives of Experimental Research*. New York: Academic Press.

Mead, G.H. (1934) *Mind, Self and Society*. Chicago: University of Chicago Press.

Menzel, H. (1978) Meaning – who needs it? In M. Brenner, P. Marsh and M. Brenner (eds), *The Social Contexts of Method*. London: Croom Helm.

Mercer, K. (1990) Welcome to the jungle: identity and diversity in postmodern politics. In J. Rutherford (ed.), *Identity: Community, Culture, Difference*. London: Lawrence and Wishart.

Merleau-Ponty, M. (1962) *Phenomenology of Perception*. London: Routledge and Kegan Paul.

Merton, R.K. (1938) Science and the social order. *Philosophy of Science*, 5, 321–37.

Meyrowitz, J. (1985) *No Sense of Place: the Impact of Electronic Media on Social Behavior*. New York: Oxford University Press.

Middleton, D. and Edwards, D. (1990) *Collective Remembering*. London: Sage Publications.

Mills, C.W. (1940) Situated actions and vocabularies of motive. *American Sociological Review*, 5, 904–13.

Mink, L.O. (1970) History and fiction as modes of comprehension. *New Literary History*, 1, 541–58.

Mink, L.O. (1978) Narrative form as a cognitive instrument. In R.H. Canary and H. Kozicki, (eds), *The Writing of History: Literary Form and Historical Understanding*. Madison: University of Wisconsin Press.

Monk, R. (1990) *Ludwig Wittgenstein: the Duty of Genius*. New York: Free Press.

Mooney, M. (1985) *Vico and the Tradition of Rhetoric*. Princeton, NJ: Princeton University Press.

Morson, G.S. and Emerson, C. (1990) *Mikhail Bakhtin: Creation of a Prosaics*. Stanford, CA: Stanford University Press.

Mulkay, M. (1985) *The Word and the World*. London: George Allen & Unwin.

Myhill, J. (1952) Some philosophical implications of mathematical logic. *Review of Metaphysics*, 6, 156–98.

Nagel, T. (1981) What is like to be a bat? In D.R. Hofstadter and D.C. Dennett, *The Mind's I*. New York: Basic Books. First published in *The Philosophical Review*, October 1974.

Nelson, J.S. and Megill, A. (1986) Rhetoric of inquiry: projects and problems. *Quarterly Journal of Speech*, 72, 20–37.

Norris, C. (1990) *What's Wrong with Postmodernism: Critical Theory and Ends of Philosophy*. Baltimore, MD: Johns Hopkins University Press.

Norris, C. (1992) *Uncritical Theory: Postmodernism, Intellectuals, and the Gulf War*. London: Lawrence and Wishart.

Ong, W.J. (1978) *Orality and Literacy: The Technologizing of the Word*. London: Methuen.

Ossorio, P.G. (1981) Ex post facto: the source of intractable origin problems and their resolution. Boulder, Colorado: Linguistic Research Institute report no. 28.

Parker, I. (1992) *Discourse Dynamics: Critical Analysis for Social and Individual Psychology*. London: Routledge.

Pearce, W.B. and Cronen, V. (1980) *Communication, Action and Meaning*. New York: Praeger.

Perelman, C. and Olbrechts-Tyteca, L. (1969) *The New Rhetoric: A Treatise on Argumentation*. Trans. by J. Wilkinson and P. Weaver. Notre Dame, ID: University of Notre Dame Press.

Peters, R.S. (1958) *The Concept of Motivation*. London: Routledge and Kegan Paul.

Polanyi, M. (1958) *Personal Knowledge: Towards a Post-Critical Philosophy*. London: Routledge and Kegan Paul.

Pollner, M. (1974) Mudane reasoning. *Philosophy of the Social Sciences*, 4, 35–54.

Pollner, M. (1975) 'The very coinage of your brain': the anatomy of reality junctures. *Philosophy of the Social Sciences*, 5, 411–30.

Potter, J. and Wetherell, M. (1987) *Discourse and Social Psychology: Beyond Attitudes and Behaviour*. London: Sage.

Prelli, L.J. (1989) The rhetorical construction of scientific ethos. In H. Simons (ed.), *Rhetoric in the Human Sciences*. London: Sage Publications.

Prelli, L. (1990) *A Rhetoric of Science: Inventing Scientific Discourse*. Columbia: University of South Carolina Press.

Prigogine, I. (1980) *From Being to Becoming: Time and Complexity in the Physical Sciences*. San Francisco: Freeman.

Prigogine, I. and Stengers, I. (1984) *Order out of Chaos: Man's New Dialogue with Nature*. New York: Bantam Books.

Quine, W.V. (1953) Two dogmas of empiricism. In *From a Logical Point of View*. Cambridge, MA: Harvard University Press.

Rommetveit, R. (1985) Language acquisition as increasing linguistic structuring of experience and symbolic behaviour control. In J.V. Wertsch (ed.), *Culture, Communication and Cognition: Vygotskian Perspectives*. London: Cambridge University Press.

Rorty, R. (1980) *Philosophy and the Mirror of Nature*. Oxford: Blackwell.

Rorty, R. (1982) *The Consequences of Pragmatism*. Minneapolis: University of Minnesota Press.

Rorty, R. (1989) *Contingency, Irony and Solidarity*. Cambridge: Cambridge University Press.

Ryle, G. (1949) *The Concept of Mind*. London: Methuen.

Said, E. (1985) *Orientalism*. Harmondsworth: Penguin Books.

Sampson, E.E. (1985) The decentralization of identity: toward a revised concept of personal and social order. *American Psychologist*, 40, 1203–11.

Sampson, E.E. (1988) The debate on individualism: indigenous psychologies of the individual and their role in personal and societal functioning. *American Psychologist*, 43, 1203–11.

Sampson, E.E. (1990) Social psychology and social control. In I. Parker and J. Shotter (eds), *Deconstructing Social Psychology*. London: Routledge.

Saussure, F. de (1960) *Course in General Linguistics*. Edited by C. Bally and A. Sechehaye. London: Peter Owen.

Schaeffer, J.D. (1990) *Sensus Communis: Vico, Rhetoric, and the Limits of Relativism*. Durham, NC: Duke University Press.

Scharff, R.C. (1992) Rorty and analytic Heideggerian epistemology – and Heidegger. *Man and World*, 25, 483–504.

Schutz, A. (1964) *Collected Papers II: Studies in Social Theory*. The Hague: Martinus Nijhoff.

Sennett, R. and Cobb, J. (1972) *The Hidden Injuries of Class*. Cambridge: Cambridge University Press.

Sheehy, G. (1976) *Passages: Predictable Crises of Adult Life*. New York: Dutton.

Shotter, J. (1969) A note on a machine that 'learns' rules. *British Journal of Psychology*, 59, 173–7.

Shotter, J. (1970) Men, the man-makers: George Kelly and the psychology of personal constructs. In D. Bannister (ed.), *Perspectives in Personal Construct Theory*. London and New York: Academic Press.

Shotter, J. (1973a) The transformation of natural into personal powers. *J. Theory Soc. Behav.*, 3, 141–56.

Shotter, J. (1973b) Prolegoma to an understanding of play. *J. Theory Soc. Behav.*, 3 47–89.

Shotter, J. (1974a) The development of personal powers. In M.P.M. Richards (ed.), *The Integration of a Child into a Social World*. Cambridge: Cambridge University Press.

Shotter, J. (1974b) What is it to be human? In N. Armistead (ed.), *Reconstructing Social Psychology*. Harmondsworth: Penguin Books.

Shotter, J. (1975) *Images of Man in Psychological Research*. London: Methuen.

Shotter, J. (1980) Action, joint action, and intentionality. In M. Brenner (ed.), *The Structure of Action*. Oxford: Blackwell.

Shotter, J. (1984) *Social Accountability and Selfhood*. Oxford: Blackwell.

Shotter, J. (1986a) Realism and relativism; rules and intentionality; theories and accounts: a reply to Morss. *New Ideas in Psychology*, 4, 71–84.

Shotter, J. (1986b) A sense of place: Vico and the social production of social identities. *British Journal of Social Psychology*, 25, 199–211.

Shotter, J. (1987a) The social construction of an 'us': problems accountability and narratology. In R. Burnett, P. McGee and D. Clarke (eds), *Accounting for Personal Relationships: Social Representations of Interpersonal Links*. London: Methuen.

Shotter, J. (1987b) The rhetoric of theory in psychology. In W.J. Baker, M.E. Hyland, H.V. Rappard and A.W. Staats (eds), *Current Issues in Theoretical Psychology*. Proceedings of the first International Conference of the Society for Theoretical Psychology. Amsterdam: North Holland.

Shotter, J. (1989a) Vygotsky's psychology: joint activity in a developmental zone. *New Ideas in Psychology*, 7, 185–204.

Shotter, J. (1989b) Rhetoric and the recovery of civil society. *Economy and Society*, 18, 149–66.

Shotter, J. (1989c) The social construction of 'you'. In J. Shotter and K.J. Gergen (eds), *Texts of Identity*. London: Sage Publications.

Shotter, J. (1990a) Underlabourers for science, or toolmakers for society. Review essay on R. Bhaskar, *Reclaiming Reality: A Critical Introduction to Contemporary Philosophy, 1989. History of the Human Sciences*, 3, 443–57.

Shotter, J. (1990b) Wittgenstein and psychology: on our 'hook up' to reality. In A. Phillips-Griffiths (ed.), *The Wittgenstein Centenary Lectures*. Cambridge: Cambridge University Press.

Shotter, J. (1990c) Social individuality versus possessive individualism: the sounds of silence. In I. Parker and J. Shotter (eds), *Deconstructing Social Psychology*. London: Routledge.

Shotter, J. (1991) A poetics of relational forms: the sociality of everyday social life. Special issue on "Evolutionary models in the Social Sciences," edited by T. Ingold. *Cultural Dynamics*, 4, 379–96.

Shotter, J. (1992) Is Bhaskar's realism only a theoretical realism? Review essay on R. Bhaskar, *Philosophy and the Idea of Freedom*, 1991. *History of the Human Sciences*, 5, 175–82.

Shotter, J. and Gergen, K.J. (1989) *Texts of Identity*. London: Sage.

Simons, H. (1989) *Rhetoric in the Human Sciences*. London: Sage.

Simons, H.W. and Billig, M. (eds) (in press) *Ideology Critique and Beyond: Possibilities for Practice in Postmodern Times*. London: Sage.

Smedslund, J. (1980) Analysing the primary code. In D. Olson (ed.), *The Social Foundations of Language: Essays in Honour of J.S. Bruner*. New York: Norton.

Stolzenberg, G. (1978) Can an inquiry into the foundations of mathematics tell us anything interesting about mind? In G.A. Miller and E. Lenneberg (eds), *Psychology and Biology of Language and Thought: Essays in Honour of Eric Lenneberg*. New York: Academic Press.

Takatori, K. (1992) Voices of the Mind. Review of J.V. Wertsch. *Human Development*, 35, 60–3.

Taylor, C. (1971) Interpretation and the sciences of man. *Review of Metaphysics*, 34, 1–51.

Taylor, C. (1984) Philosophy and its history. In R. Rorty, J.B. Schneewind and Q. Skinner (eds), *Philosophy in History: Essays in the Historiography of Philosophy*. Cambridge: Cambridge University Press.

Taylor, C. (1987) Overcoming epistemology. In K. Baynes, J. Bohman and T. McCarthy (eds), *After Philosophy: End or Transformation?* Cambridge, MA: MIT Press.

Taylor, C. (1989) *Sources of the Self: the Making of the Modern Identity*. Cambridge, MA: Harvard University Press.

Toulmin, S. (1979) The inwardness of mental life. *Critical Inquiry*, 6, 1–16.

Toulmin, S. (1982) The construal of reality: criticism in modern and postmodern science. *Critical Inquiry*, 9, 93–111.

Turing, A.M. (1936) On computable numbers, with an application to the Entscheidungsproblem. *Proc. London Mathematical Society*, series 2, 42, 230–65.

Turing, A.M. (1950) Computing machinery and intelligence. *Mind*, n.s., 59, 433–60.

Uexküll, J. (1957) A stroll through the world of animals and men. In C.H. Schiller (ed.), *Instinctive Behaviour*. London: Methuen.

Valsiner, J. (1988) *Culture and Human Development*. Lexington, MA: D.C. Heath and Co.

Verene, D.P. (1981) *Vico's Science of the Imagination*. Ithaca, NY and London: Cornell University Press.

Vico, G. (1944) *The Autobiography of Giambattista Vico*. Translated by M.H. Fisch and T.G. Bergin. Ithaca, NY: Cornell University Press.

Vico, G. (1965) *On the Study Methods of Our Time*. Translated by Elio Gianturco. New York: Bobbs-Merrill.

Vico, G. (1968) *The New Science of Giambattista Vico*. Edited and translated by T.G. Bergin and M.H. Fisch. Ithaca, NY: Cornell University Press.

Vico, G. (1988) *On the Most Ancient Wisdom of the Italians*. Translated by Lucina Palmer. Ithaca, NY: Cornell University Press.

Volosinov, V.N. (1973) *Marxism and the Philosophy of Language*. Translated by L. Matejka and I.R. Titunik. Cambridge, MA: Harvard University Press.

Volosinov, V.N. (1976) *Freudianism: A Critical Sketch*. Bloomington and Indianapolis: Indiana University Press.

Vygotsky, L.S. (1962) *Thought and Language*. Edited and translated by E. Hanfman and G. Vakar. Cambridge, MA: MIT Press.

Vygotsky, L.S. (1966) Development of the higher mental functions. In A.N. Leont'ev, A.R. Luria and A. Smirnov (eds), *Psychological Research in the USSR*. Moscow: Progress Publishers.

Vygotsky, L.S. (1978) *Mind in Society: The Development of Higher Psychological Processes*. Edited by M. Cole, V. John-Steiner, S. Scribner, and E. Souberman. Cambridge, MA: Harvard University Press.

Vygotsky, L.S. (1986) *Thought and Language*. Translation newly revised by Alex Kozulin. Cambridge, MA: MIT Press.

Vygotsky, L.S. (1987) *Thinking and Speech*. In *The Collected Works of L.S. Vygotsky: Vol. 1*. Edited by R.W. Rieber and A.S. Carton, and translated by N. Minick. New York: Plenum Press.

Wallerstein, J. and Blakeslee, S. (1989) *Second Chances*. London: Bantam.

Wertsch, J.V. (1991) *Voices of the Mind: A Sociocultural Approach to Mediated Action*. Hemel Hempstead: Harvester Wheatsheaf.

Whorf, B.L. (1956) *Language, Thought and Reality: Selected Writings of Benjamin Lee Whorf*. Edited by J.B. Carroll. Cambridge, MA: MIT Press.

Winch, P. (1958) *The Idea of a Social Science and its Relations to Philosophy*. London: Routledge and Kegan Paul.

Wittgenstein, L. (1922) *Tractatus-Logico-Philosophicus*. London: Routledge and Kegan Paul.

Wittgenstein, L. (1953) *Philosophical Investigations*. Oxford: Blackwell.

Wittgenstein, L. (1965) *The Blue and the Brown Books*. New York: Harper Torch Books.

Wittgenstein, L. (1969) *On Certainty*. Oxford: Blackwell.

Wittgenstein, L. (1980a) *Remarks on the Philosophy of Psychology*, vols 1 and 2. Oxford: Blackwell.

Wittgenstein, L. (1980b) *Culture and Value*. Introduction by G. Von Wright and translated by P. Winch. Oxford: Blackwell.

Wittgenstein, L. (1981) *Zettel* (2nd edn). Edited by G.E.M. Anscombe and G.H.V. Wright. Oxford: Blackwell.

Notes

Introduction

1. As Foucault (1970: 387) argues, the idea of man, as a sovereign subject, possessing within himself all the capacities required to understand himself as an objective entity, "is an invention of recent date. And one perhaps nearing its end."
2. See Geertz (1983).
3. Wittgenstein (1953: 227) discussed the nature of the problem here as involving the making of "correct judgments." "There are . . . rules, but they do not form a system, and only experienced people can apply them right. Unlike calculating-rules.
   What is difficult here is to put all this indefiniteness, correctly and unfalsified, into words."
4. Here, we are on contested territory; what quite *is* ethically proper or not is something about which we must endlessly argue. The concepts involved are "essentially contested concepts" (Gallie, 1962). This does not mean to say, however, that it is therefore pointless to argue about them. For, given my thesis in this book, it is the *terms* within which argument about them is conducted that are an important determinant of our social relations together.
5. The central political theme of the Enlightenment – the worry over the degree to which one is able to be self-determining in one's life – is still my central worry here.
6. Where here, and for the next couple of paragraphs, I shall use the now beginning to be abrasive Enlightenment terms, Man or man. The degree to which this usage grates (or not) upon one's sensibilities, is clearly a partial measure of how far one has moved away from the humanism, and patriarchy, of the Enlightenment.
7. Thus growing up as children of the Enlightenment, we find embodied within ourselves, as Wittgenstein (1965: 18) terms it, a "craving for generality." Thus: "Philosophers constantly see the method of science before their eyes, and are irresistibly tempted to ask and answer questions in the way science does. This tendency is the real source of metaphysics, and leads the philosopher into complete darkness."
8. To quote the subtitle of his *Discourse on Method* of 1637.
9. It is no accident, it seems to me, in these times of changing social relations, that Giddens (1979) now finds it necessary to talk about "time-space" as a container of social action. For, although the spatialization of time as a fourth dimension of space allows theorists to constitute action as a structure that can be visualized, such a structure precludes change, especially 'developmental' change. Rather than the spatialization of time, it is the temporalization (or historicizing) of space that is required, in which spaces become non-neutral containers only of actions with a Viconian, historical continuity to them.

Bakhtin (1981), as we shall see (Chapter 9), uses the term "chronotope" for the same reasons.

10. To talk like this is, of course, to oversimplify, for these two polarities play into each other and borrow from each other to such an extent that all theories in the 'human sciences' (psychology included) contain aspects of both tendencies.

11. Here I have in mind Marx's first thesis on Feuerbach, that "the chief defect of all hitherto-existing materialism (that of Feuerbach included) is that the thing, reality, sensuousness, is conceived only in the form of the *object of contemplation*, but not as *sensuous human activity*, *practice*, not subjectively . . ." (Marx and Engels, 1970: 121).

12. Indeed, not only Norris, but also Eagleton, Lazarus, and Parker all feel that the ills inherent in postmodernist, post structuralist 'theories' of discourse can be cured by a dose of Bhaskar's (1989) realism. I cannot agree (Shotter, 1990a, 1992).

13. Until recently, it has been customary to treat Volosinov as a 'voice' through which Bakhtin spoke, or ventriloquated. Morson and Emerson (1990) give good reasons for not taking this view. I shall still 'recruit' certain statements of Volosinov's, however, to Bakhtin's cause.

14. Both Harré (1990) and I (Shotter, 1984) have used the term *Umwelt*, in the sense of Uexkull (1957), to describe the nature of that part of the material world that is available as a living space to the members of species. Where, from within it, the task of knowledge is both to expand that *Umwelt*, and to make everything already existing within it self-consciously known. The realism involved here could be termed a *situated realism*.

15. And clearly, it is in the unbridgeable 'gap' between this reality and its representation, opened up both in recent philosophy and poststructuralist literary criticism, that 'the unending free play of signifiers' occurs. This, however, it seems to me, is only possible as a state of affairs 'in theory', that is, within a theoretical system unaware of its own social conditions of possibility (intelligibility). In practice, the dilemmatic themes intrinsic to our ways of talking and knowing *are* resolved; that its what the practical politics of everyday life is about.

16. Here, I am appropriating a term of Garfinkel's (1967). He talks of ethnomethodology as analysing people's everyday activities in a reflexive attempt to render rationally visible "members' methods for making those same activities visibly-rational-and-reportable-for-all-practical-purposes, i.e., "accountable', as organizations of commonplace everyday activities" (1967: vii). What is rationally visible is amenable to rational discussion and debate.

Chapter 1

1. As an example of this, Hull (1991) talks as a recently blind person, of his discovery of the value of rain. Steadily falling rain creates a continuity of acoustic experience. Instead of an intermittent and fragmented acoustic world, the rain gives a sense of perspective, the fullness of an entire situation all at once.

2. Wittgenstein discusses the disregarding of *possibilities* in the formulation of a concept. He asks whether, if this is done, it gives rise to a different concept, and replies: "if the indefiniteness were missing we should not have 'the same thing meant'. The picture we employ symbolizes the indefiniteness" (1980: II, no. 640).

3. Indeed, as Wittgenstein (1953: no. 129) reminds us, the real foundations of our inquiries often remain 'invisible' to us: "The aspects of things that are most important for us are hidden because of their simplicity and familiarity. (One is unable to notice something

– because it is always before one's eyes.) The real foundations of his enquiry do not strike a man at all. Unless *that* fact has at some time struck him. – And this means: we fail to be struck by what, once seen, is most striking and powerful."

4. Unlike in Shotter (1990a), I now feel that our different ways of knowing can be seen as arising out of our different ways of being, that is, epistemology depends upon ontology. My change of mind has been occasioned by the recent opportunities afforded me to critique Bhaskar's work more closely (Shotter, 1992).

5. See Chapter 4 also, in which I argue that to be descriptive in the Wittgensteinian sense, is to be *critically* descriptive. Eagleton's (1989: 34) claim that the Wittgensteinian reply to a child's question 'Where does capitalism come from, mummy?' is 'This is just the way we do things, dear' is slick and unworthy of him. Wittgenstein's (1980: I, no. 548) point is that a 'wrong description' is not one "that does not accord with established usage," but one "that does not accord with the practice of the person giving the description." The idea that Wittgensteinian description is merely description that conforms with the dominant ideology of the day, is a travesty.

Chapter 2

1. Here, I have inverted Garfinkel's (1967) term. The very 'methods' that make aspects of our everyday activities "visibly-rational . . . [and] 'accountable', as organizations of commonplace everyday activities" (1967: vii), render these non-individualistic, dialogical moments rationally-*in*visible to us as academics. To us, in not being normatively accountable, they are extraordinary.

2. To contrast with a systematic (or scientific), objective realism, that is, with what some call "entity realism" (Harré, 1986b).

3. Indeed, the kibitzing, debunking, 'nothing but' *tone* of his writing, that is to say, the relational form of the conversational response it 'invites', tends to provoke mere acceptance or rejection of his views, rather than their further reasoned development, to close off rather than to open up a more communally extensive programme of conversational politics.

4. The discovery of the 'pictures' and 'metaphors' implicit 'in' our talk is achieved not by reflecting upon the supposed contents of our minds when we talk, but by studying their influence in 'shaping' those of our everyday communicative activities in which they are involved, *in practice*; an influence which is only revealed in the 'grammar' of such activities. Hence Wittgenstein's (1953: no. 373) claim that: "Grammar tells us what kind of object anything is."

5. Here, I am indebted to Scharff (1992).

6. We shall find a discussion of just such a sensuous form of solidarity in Chapter 3 on Vico.

7. We see now that the situated realism mentioned above is a realism only to those *within the situation*. To those outside, it looks like a relativism. But we are never not in a situation, of one kind or another.

8. "Society is both the ever-present *condition* and the continually reproduced *outcome* of human agency: this is the duality of structure. And human agency is both work (generically conceived), that is (normally conscious) *production*, and (normally unconscious) *reproduction* of the conditions of production, including society: this is the duality of praxis. Thus agents reproduce, *non-teleologically* and *non-recursively*, in their substantive motivated productions, the unmotivated conditions necessary for – as a means of – those productions; and society is both the medium and the result of this activity" (Bhaskar, 1989: 92–3).

9. For instance, Baron and Byrne (1984: 4) say of the "informal knowledge" provided by "poets, philosophers, playwrights and novelists," that while it is "brilliant and insightful . . . [and] often quite impressive," it "seems both confusing and inconsistent." They then go on to say that while common sense may be a rich source of suggestions" for further study, it cannot "by itself, . . . provide an adequate basis for understanding the complex nature of social relations." Thus, they ask (rhetorically), "how aside from speculation, insight and intuition, can this important task be accomplished?" Well, they say, "social psychologists contend that we *can* come to understand the complex nature of social behaviour provided we are willing to study it in an essentially scientific manner" (1984: 5).

10. This moves us yet further away from Rorty's stance, that words acquire their meaning from their place within conventionalized systems of meanings.

Chapter 3

1. Ingold quotes Dawkins (1986: 288) as assuring us that "Darwinian theory is in principle capable of explaining life. No other theory that has ever been suggested is in principle capable of explaining life."

2. We will not follow Saussure's theory of language. For, as I hope will become clear, his theory of language as a system of differences is parasitic upon *written* language in which 'visual images' of (formally defined) linguistic constituents of *sentences* replace the sensuous effects of *utterances* – he fails to observe Vico's maxim (see below).

3. Where by the term *sensibly distinct*, I mean that each aspect is not perceived as a distinct, momentary whole, but that each aspect is none the less distinguishable from every other to the extent that its coming into existence can be sensed, that is, its emergence makes a sensuous difference.

4. A critic of my previous work, noting my interest in *divine* providence, suggested that I had found the world of politics somewhat too bleak, and that I had as a consequence spiralled off into mystical realms. This is far from the case.

5. Para. 134 again.

6. This is a central concern of Vico's. For he sees the attempt to place a society's *sensus communis* by a 'philosophy' as dangerous, for as "as the popular states became corrupt so did the philosophies. They descended into skepticism" (Vico, 1968: para. 1102). The upshot of this is to produce a second "barbarism of reflection," in which "peoples, like wild beasts, have fallen into the custom of each man thinking for himself only of his own private interests and have reached the extreme of delicacy, or better of pride, in which like wild animals they bristle and lash out at the slightest displeasure. Thus no matter how great the throng and press of their bodies, they live like wild beasts in a deep solitude of spirit and will, scarcely any two being able to agree since each follows his own pleasure or caprice" (1968: para. 1106).

7. As Merleau-Ponty (1962: 416) put it, "Our future is not made up exclusively of guesswork and daydreams. Ahead of what I can see and perceive, it is true, nothing more actually visible, but my world is carried forward by lines of intentionality which trace out in advance at least the style of what is to come."

8. See Billig *et al.* (1988) for a discussion of such 'topics' as sources of discussion and argument.

Chapter 4

1. In the chapter I shall oscillate between talk of 'reality' and talk of 'surroundings' or 'circumstances'. While in the *Tractatus* Wittgenstein thought of 'reality' as grounding our talk, in the *Remarks on the Philosophy of Psychology*, and in *On Certainty*, he came to talk of it as grounded in its 'surroundings', in 'our acting'. Again, I suggest, what we might call a *situated realism* is in operation here, a realism that reveals itself as a limitation upon the possibilities available in a situation.

2. Even before Wittgenstein, others began to express a degree of unease about the nature of scientific theories, and to grant that the mathematically expressed axioms and theories of physics were not necessarily truths about the physical world. One such is Einstein. Indeed, about such propositions, he said: "Insofar as the propositions of mathematics give an account of reality they are not certain; and insofar as they are certain they do not describe reality . . ." (quoted in Kline, 1980: 97). A theory is, he said, a "free invention of the mind." "It is a work of pure reason; the empirical contents and their mutual relations must find their representation in the *conclusions* of the theory" (Einstein, 1979: 311). It is *not*, as classical empiricist philosophers claimed (and many empiricist psychologists still claim), deduced from experience 'by abstraction'. Indeed, "a clear recognition of the erroneousness of [the classical empiricist view] really only came", says Einstein (1979: 312), "with the general theory of relativity, which showed that one could take account of a wider range of empirical facts . . . on a foundation quite different from the Newtonian one." So: although both views may be "permissible" – as Hertz (1954: 2) put it – "two permissible and correct models of the same external objects may yet differ in respect of appropriateness."

3. The crucial assumption of the uniformity of Nature in the natural sciences is just that, an assumption. As Wittgenstein (1969: no. 213) wrote, "our 'empirical propositions' do' not form a homogenous mass."

4. Garfinkel (1967: 31) takes a similar view: "Not *a* method of understanding, but the immensely various methods of understanding are the professional sociologist's proper and hitherto unstudies and critical phenomena. Their multitude is indicated in the endless list of ways that persons speak. Some indication of their character and their differences occurs in the socially available glosses of a multitude of sign functions as when we take note of marking, labeling, symbolizing, emblemizing, cryptograms, analogies, anagrams, indicating, minaturizing, imitiating, mocking-up, simulating – in short, in recognizing, using, and producing the orderly ways of cultural settings from 'within' those settings."

5. Cf. the discussion of grammatical illusions, entrapment, and the *ex post facto* fact fallacy, in Chapter 1.

6. 'Idiots savants', as we know, say that they instantly 'just see' the solution to the most complex of arithmetic problems, leaving us totally puzzled as to the 'processes' involved.

7. Indeed, as we have seen, it is its immethodicalness which gives our everyday common-sense knowledge its accessibleness. And the fact that it is *common* knowledge ought to mean that we do not require a (conceptual) 'container' to render it common between us; we already have such a container: our bodies.

8. Also: "We move through conventional thought patterns, automatically perform transitions from one thought to another according to the forms we have learned. And then finally we must sort through what we have said. We have made quite a few useless, even counter-productive motions and now we must clarify our movements of thought

philosophically" (Wittgenstein, 1980: II, no. 155). Further, Wittgenstein (1980: I, no. 219) also makes a passing reference to James in this connection in discussing what purpose there is in saying to someone 'At first I thought you meant . . . ': "One might (of course", he says, "call the report of such a conception the report of a *tendency* (James)" (see note 9 below).

9. This is not a prelinguistic intuition, but a sense (an intuition?), a "feeling of tendency," a "sign of direction in thought," from within a flow of inner speech (James, 1890: 249–260).

10. Rorty (1989), as we have seen, seems to have no other vision of significant linguistic communication than that which takes place from the interior of a language game.

11. Here Wittgenstein makes contact with his views about language in the *Tractatus* (Wittgenstein, 1922), where he sees propositions as determining a place in a space of possibilities. For instance: "The picture represents reality by representing a possibility of the existence and non-existence of atomic facts" (1922: 2.201); "The picture represents a possible state of affairs in logical space" (1922: 2.202). See also Janik and Toulmin (1973: 142–4) for an account of Hertz's and Boltzman's influence here.

12. "A philosophical problem has the form: 'I don't know my way about' " (Wittgenstein: no. 123).

13. As Wittgenstein (1953: no. 308) comments: "How does the philosophical problem about mental processes and states and about behaviourism arise? – We talk of processes and states and leave their nature undecided. Sometime perhaps we shall know more about them – we think. But that is just what commits us to a particular way of looking at the matter. For we have a definite concept of what it means to learn to know a process better. (The decisive movement in the conjuring trick has been made, and it was the very one we thought quite innocent.) – And now the analogy which was to make us understand our thought falls to pieces. So we have to deny the yet uncomprehended process in the yet unexplored medium. And it now looks as if we had denied mental processes. And naturally we don't want to deny them." "We have only rejected the grammar which tried to force itself upon here." We want only to say that whatever their nature is, it is indeterminate.

14. For instance, Broadbent (1961: 9) says: "It is a cliché nowadays to say that our mastery of the material world is outstripping our ability to control ourselves . . . It is urgent that our behaviour should be brought up to the standard of our knowledge . . . [P]erhaps the most hopeful road is to apply to behaviour itself the method of attack which has proved so useful in dealing with the material world . . ." See also Argyle (1969) for an identical view.

15. A very important paper in this respect is Gallie (1962) on 'essentially contested concepts'. See also my own paper on rhetoric and the recovery of civil society (Shotter, 1989b). It was because of the possibility of interminable arguments in ethics and morals, of course, that Leibnitz sought his *Characteristica Universalis*, which if we had it, would enable us when confronted with such problems to say: 'Let us take our slates and calculate.' Indeed, Broadbent (1961: 11) justifies the natural scientific approach along these lines, too.

Chapter 5

1. See Eagleton (1986, 1989), Lazarus (1991), Norris (1990, 1992), and Parker (1992).

2. Indeed, I spent the first six years of my own academic life in the 1960s living on money from various (unclassified) military contracts to do with research into aspects of speech

and visual recognition – for a while, at least, I argued that its unclassified nature made it 'pure' knowledge available to all. This is a view I now repudiate. It is, of course, Arendt's (1964) *Eichman in Jerusalem* that displays at its most blatant the total amorality of the instrumental rationality rife in the natural sciences – 'I was only doing my job'. See also Bauman (1989).

3. Here, we can see some of the parallels between Vico's large-scale historical processes, and Vygotsky's small-scale developmental ones.

4. Then, he clearly sought an "entity-realism" which many seem to me still to espouse; see, for example, Bhaskar (1989) and Greenwood (1992). To the extent that they are concerned with describing structures, now existing independently of human action (which may, in the past, have been humanly constructed), they are concerned with empirical or factual possibilities, but not with historical ones, that is, they are concerned with an already existing order of possibilities, rather than a possible order of possibilities, only providentially available. I will pursue this issue again later in the chapter.

5. To be somewhat redundant, as if there could be a non-relational ethics! By this term, I mean an ethics that does not exist ahead of time in a set of principles or laws, but only comes into existence 'in' the relations in which its influence operates, that is, what is often called the relationship's *ethos*.

6. "A simile that has been absorbed into the forms of our language produces a false appearance, and this disquiets us. 'But *this* isn't how it is!' – we say. 'Yet *this* is how it has to *be*!'" (Wittgenstein, 1953: no. 112).

7. Notice what is claimed in its fuller version (see note 13, Chapter 4). It is not that reality is denied; just the opposite. It is an inadequacy in the 'grammar' of representations that is involved.

8. Indeed, it is precisely in this respect that Manicas (1990) criticizes the attempt to ground a realism in Gibson's (1979) ecological theory of direct perception. He quotes Harré (1986) as saying: "without some basis in veridical perception scientific realism, whether it be based on 'truth' [which Harré rejects] or upon 'reference' [which Harré affirms] must founder in a mess of relativism," and goes on correctly to point out that such a theory could not give us *concepts*, still less *veridical* concepts, true of the world which exists independently of us (Manicas, 1990: 35).

9. I shall discuss 'basic' ways of talking further in Chapter 7. But also see Shotter (1984).

10. But to judge by his attempts, still, to arrive at a definitive realism (see Harré, 1986b, 1990), he continues to feel the urge to come up with an in-principle solution.

11. What elsewhere (Shotter, 1984) I have called "practical-theory," due to its help in giving rise to a practice.

12. In that sense, I still have a use for the word "truth".

Chapter 6

1. I say *new* themes, but in fact, the presentation of psychology as a *moral* science of action rather than as a natural science of behaviour, concerned with things people themselves do rather than with things which merely happen to them, now dates back some time (see Harré, 1983; Shotter, 1974a,b, 1975). Originally, both Harré and I drew our inspiration from Vygotsky's claims about the origins of deliberate, self-controlled actions by individuals being in the spontaneous activities occurring between people. What *is* much more recent, is the emphasis in social theory upon the argumentative, responsive, conflictful nature of social interaction introduced by Billig (1987; Simons, 1989), but even here we

might note Vygotsky's (1966: 41) comment that "reflection is the transfer of argumentation within . . .".

2. This, as we shall discover, is the wrong term, if 'express' is taken to mean representing in an order of words the supposed order of one's thoughts (the 'picture theory'). "Experience teaches us that thought does not express itself in words, but rather realizes itself in them" (Vygotsky, 1986: 251).

3. Vygotsky (1986: 245), like Wittgenstein, distinguishes between words as in a dictionary (which have a *meaning*) and words in use in a context (which have a *sense*): "A word acquires its sense from the context in which it appears; in different contexts, it changes its sense. Meaning remains stable throughout the changes of sense. The dictionary meaning of a word is no more than a stone in the edifice of sense, no more than a potentiality that finds diversified realization in speech."

4. Embodied agencies voice their utterances in a creative or forming 'movement' that displays in that movement – its intonation – their response to their circumstances, a response influenced not only by an evaluative orientation to whom they are addressing, but in particular to their own position. As Volosinov (1973: 87) says, regarding one's own apprehension of one's hunger, say, "one can apprehend one's hunger apologetically, irritably, angrily, indignantly, etc.," and thus, among other things, influence the style of one's addressee's response, their relation to one. I will pursue these issues further in the next chapter.

5. Here, we make contact with Bakhtin's (1990) and Volosinov's (1976) concept of the *hero*. While one side, so to speak, of an author's voice is turned towards the listener – the second person in the situation – another side is turned towards a mysterious third person, the hero, the 'entity' both first and second person are 'in'. Such is the nature of all creative experiences, says Bakhtin (1990: 6–7), that authors "experience their object and experience themselves *in* their object."

6. "The idea of the *conventionality, the arbitrariness of language*, is a typical one for rationalism as a whole, and no less typical is the *comparison of language to the system of mathematical signs*. What interests the mathematically minded rationalist is not the relationship of the sign to the actual reality it reflects nor to the individual who is its originator, but the *relationship of sign to sign within a closed system* already accepted and authorized. In other words, they are interested only in the *inner logic of the system of signs itself*, taken, as in algebra, completely independently of the ideological meanings that give the signs their content" (Volosinov, 1973: 57–8). See also Wittgenstein (1953: no. 81).

7. Here I shall remain neutral on the controversy over whether Volosinov's texts were authored by Bakhtin or not, and will reference quotations separately.

8. The contrast, as we shall see, is with an *ontological* process where merely cognitive processes affect the content of people's 'minds', while ontological ones affect people in their ethical being, that is, they determine the kind of world to which people are responsive.

9. Rather than marking this distinction in terms of the comparison between 'unconsciously' and 'consciously', I shall talk in terms of the child coming to act *self*-consciously – the reasons for this will become apparent later.

10. What the child learns, of course, are written 'grammatical forms', hence Vygotsky's (1986: 181–2) claim that: "In learning to write, the child must disengage himself from the sensory aspect of speech and replace words by images of words . . . In written speech, we are obliged to create the situation, to represent it to ourselves. This demands detachment from the actual situation." It is this which makes it possible, of course, to think about linguistic forms divorced from their (socio-ethical) functions.

11. We might say, biology and cultural history are interwoven, all the way down and all the way back.

12. Bakhtin (1981: 84–258) gives the name *Chronotopes* (literally 'time-spaces') to the different structuring structures which are developed – as organized, non-linearly connected series of interacting moments in time, of simultaneously interactive activities in space – within different forms of literature and discourse. Here, I have called them 'providential spaces'.

13. For example, Fish (1989: 244–6) discusses the need for antiprofessionalism in the middle of professionalism, because professionals are so totally constituted (socially determined) by the society in which they are placed, that they are utterly unable themselves, as professionals, to 'see through' the cultural and historical forces that have conditioned them. "That is the one thing a historically conditioned consciousness cannot do – scrutinize its own beliefs, conduct a rational examination of its own convictions; for in order to begin such a scrutiny, it would have to escape the grounds of its own possibility and it could only do that if it were not historically conditioned and were instead a contextual or unsituated entity that is rendered unavailable by the first principle of the interpretivist or conventionalist view," Fish holds. On the view I am urging in this book, this is not the case. To be a professional, one does not just follow rules or conventions, one must be able to *sense* certain 'movements' in one's professional circumstances and make judgements in one's response to them.

14. The point made by Wittgenstein (1922: 2.171) in the *Tractatus*: "The picture, however, cannot represent its form of representation; it shows it forth."

15. The utterance is never defined, as such. For of course, we all know what utterances are, don't we? Well, like St Augustine with time, we do until we have to make it clear to someone else. In this sense, it is not so much a theory of the utterance Bakhtin supplies, as an image, a 'providential space' of possibilities.

16. The concept of 'voice' lies at the heart of Bakhtin's non-referential – that is, *responsive* – theory of language. It plays the same part in his philosophical anthropology of embodied thought as the concept of 'mind' plays in more disembodied Enlightenment philosophies. As Emerson (in Bakhtin, 1984) puts it: "Bakhtin *visualizes* voices, he senses their proximity and interaction as bodies. A voice, Bakhtin everywhere tells us, is not just words or ideas strung together: it is a 'semantic position', a point of view on the world, it is one personality orienting itself among other personalities within a limited field. How a voice sounds is a function of where it is and what it can 'see', and, one might add, how the person feels."

17. Although it may seem undeniable that words are in fact used referentially, a Bakhtinian would say they are so only from within a form of social life *already constituted* by the speech genres within which such words are first used responsively – see below for an account of speech genres.

18. Recall that he says: "each word tastes of the context and contexts in which it has lived its socially charged life" (Bakhtin, 1981: 293, quoted in Chapter 2).

19. Recall his claim mentioned in Chapter 2, that "a word (or in general any sign) is interindividual" (Bakhtin, 1986: 121–2).

Chapter 7

1. Descartes's dream was, that by the use of his method, we could "thereby make ourselves, as it were, masters and possessions of nature" (Descartes, 1968: 78).

2. The working-class child is 'enabled' here, too: "I give myself verbal shape from another's point of view, ultimately from the point of view of the community to which I belong" (Volosinov, 1973: 86).

3. Representations are not grounded in yet further representations, but in the knowledgeable grasp we have of the world as socially competent agents within it. If we need some vocabulary for the discussion of its status in relation to our other forms of knowledge – of already existing, *real* things, or of non-existing, *fictitious* things – we might claim it relates to a third *imaginary* realm of only partially existing entities, entities on the way to coming into existence (Shotter, 1991).

4. Where, of course, the 'pictures' in a discourse can function like Bakhtin's and Volosinov's 'heroes' in a text: they are both 'in' us while we are 'in' them.

5. In Foucault's (1972: 49) terms, discourses are "practices that systematically form the objects of which they speak", that is, form them as objects of rational contemplation and debate.

6. The quote concerned appears in Cole's preface (Vygotsky, 1978: 8) and is from unpublished notebooks.

7. I take the phrase from Barthes (1983: 34).

8. Whose proper title, as Kozulin (in Vygotsky, 1986: lvii) points out, should be *Thought and Speech*.

9. Here we might also talk of *architectonic tendencies* . . . a bit of extra vocabulary is always useful.

10. That is, the complex affective and communicational intentionalities in actual acts of speaking, intentionalities which change and 'temporally develop' as an utterance is executed, must be replaced by something merely imaginable: an already completed, spatialized image.

11. In this view, the emergence of "representation" is due to the fact that, as linguistic competency increases, one becomes more adept in constructing a network of *references* to function as a context into which to direct one's utterances. In other words, there is a move away from a reliance upon the sense of one's speech, that is, a reliance upon a referent in the immediate, shared context, and a move towards a reliance upon meaning and syntax, that is, upon links within what has already been or with what might be said. In essence, this is a decrease of reference to what 'is' with a consequent increase of reference to what 'might be', an increased reference to a hermeneutically constructed imaginary (or theoretical) world.

   As a result, what is said requires less and less grounding in an extralinguistic context – for it can find its supports almost wholly within a new, intralinguistically constructed context. Thus one can tell people about (represent to them or give them an account of) situations not actually at the moment present. Such a consequence requires, however, the development of methods for *warranting* in the course of one's talk (that is, giving support to) one's claims about what 'might be' as what being what 'is' – one must learn to say, for instance, when making a claim about a state of affairs, that others saw it that way, too, and so on. By the use of such methods and procedures, adults can construct their statements as factual statements, and adult forms of speech can thus come to function with a large degree of independence from their immediate context.

12. Although, here, too, Bakhtin (1986: 121–2) points out that other 'voices' are at work: "The word cannot be assigned to a single speaker. The author (speaker) has his own inalienable right to the word, but the listener has his rights, and those whose voices are heard in the word before the author comes upon it also have their rights (after all, there are no words that belong to no one)."

13. In the past, I have talked of these 'dialogical moments' in terms of "joint action" (Shotter, 1984). I now feel Bakhtin's designation of them as dialogical is to be preferred.

14. Indeed, the talk of a single person may exhibit what Bakhtin calls "hidden dialogicality," that is, "although only one person is speaking . . . [each] uttered word responds and reacts with its every fiber to [an] invisible speaker, points to something outside itself, beyond its own limits, to the unspoken words of another person" (Bakhtin, 1984: 197).

15. "On this 'jointly seen' (snowflakes outside the window), 'jointly known' (the time of the year – May) and 'unanimously evaluated' (winter wearied of, spring looked forward to) – on all this the utterance *directly depends*, all this is seized in its actual, living import – is its very sustenance. And yet all this remains without verbal specification or articulation" (Volosinov, 1976: 99).

16. We will see the connection to Wittgenstein in a moment.

17. Rorty (1989: 19) approves of "the Davidson claim that metaphors do not have meanings," and takes it as implying that we cannot therefore *argue* for new ways of talking, for meanings as such, he claims, can only come "from the interior of a language game" (1989: 47). Thus all we can do is to try to make vocabularies we don't like 'look bad' (1989: 44). If Vico and Grassi are right, this is nonsense, the presentation of a new metaphor *is* an argument.

18. Grassi notes that the term 'metaphor' is itself a metaphor, as it is derived from the verb *metapherein* ('to transfer') which originally described a concrete activity.

19. As Mills (1940: 439) said now more than 50 years ago, "the differing reasons men give for their actions are not themselves without reasons . . . What we want is analysis of the integrating, controlling, and specifying functions a certain type of speech fulfills in socially situated actions."

20. " . . . it has roots, not a single root" (Wittgenstein, 1981: no. 656).

21. Rorty (1982: xiv) quotes Sellars as claiming that philosophy is the "attempt to see how things, in the broadest possible sense of the term, hang together, in the broadest possible sense of the term."

22. See Edwards (1982), who provides an important account of how images are revealing in a way that 'grammatical pictures' are not, and why it was that Wittgenstein thus railed against them. Although I have not drawn many particular resources from it as such, I have benefited tremendously from the spirit, so to speak, of this book. To my own recollection, I first came to my views about prostheses through Bohm (1965).

23. Edwards (1982) also discusses the forming of a 'grammatical picture' in terms of the 'literalizing' of a metaphor. Those who know this excellent book will recognize how much I have benefited from it.

24. "The basic evil of Russell's logic, as of mine in the *Tractatus*, is that what a proposition is is illustrated by a few commonplace examples, and then pre-supposed as understood in full generality" (Wittgenstein, 1980: I, no. 38).

25. Often, of course, it is said that the task is one of "conceptual analysis," and that it is the philosopher's job, as an 'underlabourer' for science, to complete this task *before* scientists can claim to know properly what their subject matter 'is' – at least, this is what I used to believe (Shotter, 1975; Gauld and Shotter, 1977).

26. See note 5, Chapter 7.

Chapter 8

1. I am surprised at the use of the words 'behind' and 'analysis' here, given Vygotsky's explicit aversion to analysis as such.

2. Recall here Garfinkel's (1967: 22) claims mentioned earlier concerning coders in an outpatient clinic selecting applicants for treatment, in which he remarked that *"ad hoc*-considerations are consulted by coders and *ad hocing* practices are *used in order to recognize what the instructions are definitely talking about"* (emphasis in original).

3. While evidence and coherence may be sufficient for the truth of such theories, if the theories are of entities of our own making, it is not difficult, of course, to say true things about them. Proof of their truth is not proof of their adequacy.

4. In this chapter, I speak as a professional academic psychologist myself.

5. Although I have been, in general, critical of the resources provided by poststructuralism, when used to make claims about the fundamental nature of the human condition. When it comes to an investigation of the workings of texts, then they cannot be ignored, for that is where they are most 'at home', so to speak.

6. A slightly unfortunate metaphor, as it was finally discovered that dragons could not, of course, *conceivably* exist.

7. In fact they draw back from this proposal to an extent, remarking that although it would be "an admirable ideal" it is impractical, as it would require "a massive program embodying a large number of *ad hoc* assumptions . . . A preferable approach rests on the distinction between a *theory* and a *model*. Scientists and engineers are familiar with building models to represent only certain aspects of their theories. However, the practice is rare in psychology" (Johnson-Laird and Wason, 1977: 10).

8. The idea of an effective procedure plays a central role in computational approaches, in that it is assumed that every psychological phenomenon can be described in terms of a succession of mental states "within the mind" (says Johnson-Laird), which, to the extent that it can be described by an effective procedure, can be described independently of human intuitions, "or any other 'magical' ingredient" (Johnson-Laird, 1983: 6) – like, say, Bakhtin's responsivity. In other words, they can be carried out by a machine, and require no qualitative (that is, human) judgements for their implementation – a one-sided image in which, as Billing (1987: 129) remarks, "thinking has become reduced to the unthinking operations of a filing clerk."

9. Elsewhere also, for instance, she says "McCulloch and Pitts did not simply argue the general materialist position . . . they *proved* that certain . . . neural nets could in principle compute certain sorts of logical function" (Boden, 1990: 3; emphasis in original), and this is repeated again a few lines below.

10. Whorf (1956: 153), in discussing the claim that relativity theory had shown how mathematics could *prove* people's *intuitions* of space and time wrong, suggested the claim that people had 'intuitions' as such of space and time was wrong. "Newtonian space, time, and matter are no intuitions. They are recepts from culture and language. That is where Newton got them."

11. The whole issue is clearly much more complicated than is stated. The discrepancies between who one presents oneself as being, and who are feels one ought to be, etc., are investigated by Goffman (1959), among others, of course.

Chapter 9

1. The term is Mink's (1978), whose influence in this chapter is pervasive.
2. As Mink points out, the idea of history as the as-yet-untold story, of Universal History, in which the unfolding of a single great theme discovered by the historian is represented, is at least as old as Augustine's *City of God*, and was introduced into modern thought in Vico's *New Science* – in which, of course, "divine providence" is the hero. Equivalent to the doctrine of the uniformity of nature in physics and the uniformity of human nature on anthropology, it began to lose its appeal, Mink suggests, with the emergence of cultural pluralism in modern common sense.
3. The requirements of the great narrative Other.

Chapter 10

1. Giddens (1991) draws upon *Second Chances* (Wallerstein and Blakeslee, 1989) to argue that it is talk of the "crisis" of divorce as "providing new opportunities" for "finding a new sense of identity" for oneself, that is indicative of basic themes characterizing modernity.
2. But clearly on their way out towards the whole populace at large. Such books these days are not so much 'about' social processes, as materials for use by people in their constitution.
3. See also Meyrowitz's (1985) account of how the 'situational geography' of social life – the communicative activity within which we have our psychological being – has become disconnected from the physical geography in which we live.
4. "All words have the 'taste' of a profession, a genre, a tendency, a party, a particular work, a particular person, a generation, an age group, the day, the hour. Each word tastes of the context and contexts in which it has lived its socially charged life; all words and forms are populated by intentions" (Bakhtin, 1981: 293).
5. Especially with the failure of centralized planning in Socialist and Communist states.
6. Indeed, even as late as 1973, I myself talked of human beings as possessing within them *natural powers* which could, with the appropriate forms of 'instruction', be appropriated by individuals themselves as *personal powers* (Shotter, 1973a).
7. The view I took in Shotter (1973a).
8. As the unnamed (anti-)hero of Joseph Heller's novel, *Something Happened*, says, about his working in an office: "I have a feeling that someone nearby is soon going to find out something about me that will mean the end, although I can't imagine what that something is" (Heller, 1975: 22). Indeed, all the characters in the book are afraid of each other in this way, and, as Heller says, something must have happened for everyone to feel like this – although what it is, no one knows.
9. ". . . And to imagine a language is to imagine a form of life . . ." (Wittgenstein, 1953: no. 19).
10. First, we can note that in one interpretation, the dimension of real numbers can be identified with actuality, and the imaginary dimension with possibility. It is the realm of the imaginary that makes 'movement' between actualities possible.

    Perhaps some of the best examples of imaginary objects, which can none the less generate in one a sense of their 'reality', are currently to be found 'in' one's keyboard-mediated interactions with computer-generated displays. Davis and Hersh (1983: 400–5) discuss interacting with a computer display generated by the equations for a four-dimensional hypercube. They describe how, by interacting with the display long enough, by turning "it" that is, the set of projections of the 4D cube on the 2D screen, around and so on, they gained a *feel* for it as a unity. However, this is not only an imaginary object, it is *impossible* one, too — in the sense that no reality yet known to us will *permit*, *allow*, or *afford* it; no reality we know of is open, as yet, to being interpreted within the scheme of possibilities it allows. Yet, the gaining of an intuitive grasp of its nature is clearly perfectly possible. And as Davis and Hersh say: "These imaginary objects have definite properties. There *are* true facts about imaginary objects." But in what sense are they true? It cannot be a matter of correspondence with reality, as in the testing of physical or empirical truths. It can only be a matter of achieving *reproducible results* by the use of socially sharable (mathematical) procedures.

But as Davis and Hersh point out, this means giving up the idea that mathematics is *about* objects, existing in an ideal realm in the same way as in physical reality. It means that, even in mathematics, not only is there no undisputable concept of "proof," but also *convincing* proofs do not just consist in the application of a procedure, but also in *persuasive testimony* (sometimes implicit) that the procedure was correctly applied. Without at least the possibility of such testimony, the "proof" is incapable of commanding universal asset. And my point here is the same: that our ordinary, everyday talk abounds with references to such imaginary things — many of them also impossible in the sense mentioned above. Like Escher drawings, they have the property of being *incomplete* in any one perspective; and while they may seem open to further specification (of an already specified kind), other perspectives present in the 'object' prevent it. Their nature is such that, as Wittgenstein (1980: no. 257) says: "Here *is* the whole. (If you complete it, you falsify it.)"

11. Of course, I would rather he had called it "Imaginary Communities."

Epilogue

1. My actual friends, Ken and Mary Gergen, wondered once why what I write is so littered with quotes from others, often the same 'others' continually. "When are you going to write in your own words?" they said. "It's because I'm having a conversation with them", I said. Hence, *they* called them my 'textual friends'. It was not until writing this book, however, that I realized why I rely so much upon their actual words. For me, it's not their 'ideas' and what they represent that count, but how they say what they say; I need to sense their words.

2. I pointed out earlier, for instance, that while Vico saw fear as the initial cause for the formation of a sensory topic, and Gadamer saw play, Volosinov saw merely the shared contemplation of a snowy day in May sufficient. In each case, to imagine a language is to imagine a form of life.

Index